SHAKESPEARE'S WOODEN O

A GAME AT CHESS

Title-page of Quartos I and II(*a*)

SHAKESPEARE'S WOODEN O

LESLIE HOTSON

London
RUPERT HART-DAVIS
1960

First published 1959
Second impression 1960

Printed in Great Britain by
Latimer, Trend & Co., Ltd., Plymouth

TO
THE PROVOST AND FELLOWS
OF KING'S COLLEGE
CAMBRIDGE

CONTENTS

7

ILLUSTRATIONS

All the illustrations in the text except the map on page 311
have been drawn by Nicholas Wood

9

ACKNOWLEDGEMENTS

FOR the rich materials on which this study is based I must first thank the glorious company of late Renaissance authors, both English and Spanish, who wrote their unequalled plays for the living stage. And next, the great band of devoted students past as well as present of the European theatre. Among the many to whom my text betrays my debt, I should mention especially Edmond Malone, William Poel, Gustave Cohen, W. J. Lawrence, Sir E. K. Chambers, Percy Simpson, T. S. Graves, G. F. Reynolds, Robert Stumpfl, H. A. Rennert, and N. D. Shergold. The understanding and the distinguished graphic skill of Mr Nicholas Wood have illuminated the text with illustrations. The Staffs of the British Museum and Bodleian Libraries, and those of the Yale and Cambridge University Libraries, to whom I have more often turned, have always been ready with help. I am deeply grateful to the Provost and Fellows of King's College, Cambridge, for electing me to a Fellowship. Generous in its term and in its concentration on research, this has made the opportunity for uninterrupted study in the best surroundings. And throughout, my friend Mrs Winifred Bryher and my wife have given me steadfast encouragement.

PROLOGUE

EVER since the publication of *The First Night of 'Twelfth Night'*, which revealed that that play's performance at Court was 'in the round', arena-fashion, I have followed the trail of Shakespeare's theatre and of his stage-practice in it—a trail which has baffled us all for close on two centuries—step by step not only recovering lost features of that Elizabethan staging in detail, but also tracing them to their sources. Now for the first time we can understand and visualize the stage of the Globe. But on coming to give an account of it, why not begin at the end, with the game already bagged? In emulation of the old tracker, why not make the sight of the captured quarry bring forth the story of the chase? In a murder mystery, we do not object to being offered an *end* at the very beginning. On the contrary, the detective in each of us finds that preposterous method agreeably stirring.

At the very outset, then, we shall go to the Globe—to witness in imagination an actual performance, as it was produced on those historic boards. In violent contrast with *Twelfth Night*, whose less-than-least sinister usage of an ambassador provoked no international incident, the play we are going to see offered a foreign power the most offensively bellicose insult ever known in England. Needless to say it was not written by Shakespeare. The reason for choosing it is however irresistible: we have more lively contemporary reports and more illuminating evidence about this particular production than about any other known performance at the Globe.

I

SCANDAL PACKS THE GLOBE

WE are sitting in the crowded bar of the Boar's Head Tavern, Great Eastcheap, on a summer morning in 1624. It is so loud with excited talk that the pot-boys' refrain of 'Anon, anon, sir!' is hardly distinguishable.

What we hear on every hand is that at the Globe since Friday of last week those abstracts and brief chronicles have been acting the play of the century, with a daring unheard of. Scandalizing princes. A red-hot political satire. Everyone says it must be seen to be believed. Pouring contempt on 'high-seated greatness'. Aristophanes? Aristophanes was child's play to this. All agog, if not rabid, the citizens, both the baser troops and the more eminent rank, nobility too, are streaming to Bankside. You would take your corporal oath every Londoner able to set one foot before the other has sworn to get to see it if it's his last act. A fantastic success. The Globe began by trebling its usual prices, and is still turning swarms away. But if the play is so scandalous, why has not the King put a swift stop to it? How can he—off on a progress in the north, and just now a hundred and sixty road-miles away in Sherwood Forest? Trust those sly dogs the players to watch their time, till Authority is long gone and they will have a good run, with good money for it, before they can be silenced.

What is the situation? Today is Saturday, 14 August 1624. For a generation past, James the Appeaser, bent on his feckless policy of trying to reconcile the irreconcilable, has been sinking his Protestant kingdom to the level of a satellite of her great enemy, Catholic Spain. The self-styled *Rex Pacificus* has suffered 'a peace more damaging than a war'. And this despite the fact that for more than six years now the sound instinct of his people has been to shock the advancing Catholic armies with guns in the 'old Elizabeth way'. Floods of surreptitious pamphlets, such as the famous *Vox Populi*, voice the nation's hostility.

But that brilliant and cunning plotter, King Philip's ambassador Gondomar, anticipated every countermove, flattered King James, wound him round his finger, notoriously cajoled him to a point where he actually took Spain's game to be England's. Not only the King, but that all-swaying peer Buckingham as well. And how many of the Court have been hispaniolized with gold? Small wonder that every one of our parrots and starlings learns first and foremost to utter 'A curse o' Gondomar!' For under his baleful influence James obediently beheaded Ralegh, imprisoned Lord Southampton for attempting to aid the Protestants on the Continent, and was even ready to destroy the Virginia Colony.

Apprehension reached fever-pitch on Gondomar's determined attempt to marry Prince Charles to the Spanish king's sister:

> Our Prince went to Spayne
> Her love to obteyne,
> But—God be thankëd!—he mist her.

The breaking of the match broke the nightmare-spell. Last October, when Charles came home a bachelor and Buckingham with him, both now at length aroused and turned hostile to Spain, you never saw such universal joy.

Bonfires everywhere, jubilation unparalleled. At long last the King has been brought to allow the raising of at least a token force to oppose the Catholic powers which seized his son-in-law Frederick's kingdom of Bohemia. Since June the nation has been levying troops, fitting out ships, buying guns and powder for battle on the Continent. With Lord Southampton as one of its commanders, the expeditionary force is on the point of sailing. Diplomatic relations with Spain, however acrimonious, are not yet broken off: the present ambassador, Don Carlos Coloma, is still sitting surrounded by a highly hostile London.

Such then is the charged atmosphere in which the Globe last week touched off its bombshell: Middleton's infuriating portrayal of Gondomar and the King of Spain —*A Game at Chess*. The very title declares war; for 'he that invented chess-play made a model and brief map of the art of war':

> Ye Papists that can play at Chesse,
> and guide your men in battell ray . . .

> Our King and realmes good Lord defend
> against all those that would us check.[1]

Eight days ago, Friday, 6 August, saw the first performance rousing London like a stick thrust into a nest of hornets. As John Woolley wrote that same evening:

All the news I have heard since my coming to town is of a new play acted by his Majesty's servants. It is called *A Game at Chess*; but it may be a *Vox Populi*, for by report it is six times worse against the Spaniard. In it Gondomar's devilish

---

[1] J. R[hodes], *The Country mans comfort* (1588), 1637.

plots and devices are displayed, and many other things too long to recite.

The conclusion expresseth his Highness [Prince Charles's] return, and a mastery over the King of Spain, who being overcome is put into a great Sack with [the Infanta] Doña María, Count of Olivares, Gondomar, and the Bishop of Spalat[r]o, and there tied up together and by his Highness trod upon.

Such a thing was never before invented; and assuredly had so much been done the last year, they had every man been hanged for it.[1]

Coloma the ambassador waited only one day, found that there was no chance of the Privy Council in London moving to suppress the damnable thing, and at once sent his secretary riding post-haste the hundred and sixty miles up to Derbyshire to deliver to the King his outraged protest and demand:

The Players called the King's have yesterday and today presented a comedy so scandalous, impious, barbarous, and so offensive to the King my master—if the greatness and inestimable worth of his royal person could receive offence from anyone, least of all from men so base as the authors and actors of suchlike fooleries commonly are—that it has obliged me to take pen in hand and to beg (in few words and with the humility which I owe your Majesty) for one of two things: that you will be pleased to give order that the said authors and players be publicly and exemplarily chastised, whereby your Majesty will vindicate your honour and the reputation and civility of the English nation, or that you will command that I be given a ship to cross into Flanders, with the requisite safe-conducts which you give to the ambassadors of other Kings.

May it be your Majesty's good pleasure to give me leave that this be done at the earliest, the one or the other.[2]

---

[1] Trumbull MSS., Alphabetical Corresp. 48/134, with spelling modernized. Berks Record Office, Reading, by the kindness of Mr Peter Walne, County Archivist.

[2] Original in French. P.R.O., S.P. 94/31, pt. 1, f. 132.

That letter started north last Saturday. The players took the Sunday off, but both Monday and Tuesday again saw the Globe stuffed to suffocation, as Coloma wrote home on Tuesday to Philip's ruling minister, Olivares:

The actors whom they call here 'the King's men' have recently acted, and are still acting in London a play which so many people come to see that more than three thousand were there on the day the audience was smallest. There was such merriment, hubbub, and applause, that even had I been many leagues away I could not but have taken notice of it. . . .

The subject of the play is a game of chess, with white house and black house, their kings and other pieces acted by the players; and the king of the blacks has easily been taken for our lord the King, because of his youth, dress, and other particulars.

The first act, or rather game, was played by their ministers, impersonated by the white pieces, and the Jesuits, by the black ones. . . .

The second act was directed against the Archbishop of Spalat[r]o, at that time a white piece, but afterwards won over to the black side by the Count of Gondomar, who, brought on to the stage in his litter almost to the life, and seated on his chair with a hole in it (they said), confessed all the treacherous actions with which he had deceived and soothed the king of the whites. . . .

The last act ended with a long, obstinate struggle between all the whites and the blacks, and in it he who acted the Prince of Wales heartily beat and kicked the 'Count of Gondomar' into Hell, which consisted of a great hole and hideous figures; and the white king [drove] the black king and even his queen [into Hell] almost as offensively.

All this has been so much applauded and enjoyed by the mob that here, where no play has been acted for more than one day [at a time], this one has already been acted on four, and each day the crowd is greater. . . .

I do not expect a reply [to my letter of protest] until the

[13th or 14th] of this month, as the King of England is some distance away. . . . It cannot be pleaded that those who repeat and hear these insults are but a handful of rogues, because during these last four days more than twelve thousand persons have all heard the play of *A Game at Chess* (for so they call it), including all the nobility still here in London.

All these people come out of the theatre so inflamed against Spain that, as a few Catholics have told me who went secretly to see the play, my person would not be safe in the streets. Others have advised me to keep to my house with a good guard, and this is being done.[1]

On Wednesday Woolley wrote again with the latest news:

The play of Gondomar is not yet suppressed, but it is feared it will be ere long, for the Spanish Ambassador hath sent post after post with letters to complain to the King of it, and takes it very heinously that such a thing should be played against his master.

But the players loseth no time, nor forbeareth to make hay while the sun shineth, acting it every day without any intermission; and it is thought they have already got near a thousand pounds by it.[2]

Since English post-horses were no pamper'd jades of Asia, Coloma's messenger, after racing up to Court at Rufford Abbey in Sherwood, must have been kept waiting a couple of days for the King's reply: for Secretary Conway dated it only the day before yesterday, Thursday the 12th. But he is riding hell-for-leather the hundred and sixty miles back, and will deliver it to Coloma today, Saturday. On the other hand, the English courier bearing the King's instructions to the lords of the Council will

---

[1] Tr. Edward M. Wilson and Olga Turner from Madrid Archives, in 'The Spanish Protest against *A Game at Chess*', *Modern Language Review*, 44 (1949), 476–482.

[2] *Loc. cit.*, No. 135.

make no more than reasonable speed: it may be Tuesday or even Wednesday before their inhibition will be imposed. Meanwhile the play goes on, Coloma gnaws his nails, and money rolls in. If however we are to make sure of seeing what we came to see before it is suppressed, we had better get someone to take us across the Thames without delay.

Any sneaking hope of securing William Shakespeare as our guide to the Globe is long out of date. He has been dead these eight years past. In this emergency mine host Richard Austen [1] of the Boar's Head shows himself a young man of resource. He can supply an able cicerone. Not indeed a leader, like the regretted poet, drawn from the head and front of the King's Men—far too prosperous and busy this week to be bothered. No, if the truth be told, a man rather from the company's extreme tail, to which till of late he was attached. Yet this humble colleague of Shakespeare's has his points. He boasts the magic initials 'W.S.', and is but two years the late dramatist's junior. More than that, he began in trade as a glover, like Shakespeare's own father. What would you have? In short, he is an active old stager hailing from Ralegh's corner of Devon, by name William Strange, described in his time as one who 'attendeth the King's players at their

---

[1] '1623. "John Rhodoway, vintner att the Bores head was buried"
1624. "Richard Austen and Dorothie Rhodoway [John's daughter and co-heir] both of this parish, were married the 24 August by licence"
Richard Austen now takes John Rodoway's place [in the churchwardens' accounts], paying the 4s. rent for ground and lights each year.' Quoted from the record of St Michael Crooked Lane by Dr Kenneth Rogers, *The Boar's Head Tavern in Eastcheap* (1928), 28, 33.

plays, and goeth abroad of arrants'.[1] As a former stage-attendant, possibly a curtain-drawer or stagekeeper, old Will Strange knows the workings of the playhouse inside out. This veteran 'W. S.' from the Globe and Blackfriars is clearly the very man for us, and mine host sends out to fetch him.

Meantime we are warned to fortify ourselves against an extended afternoon of sitting in the theatre. Such is the incredible vogue of *A Game at Chess* that if we would be sure of excellent seats—though the trumpets will not sound till three—we must be on the spot well before one. It is already getting on for eleven. Mine host Austen serves us up a substantial dinner. Under his urging we do it justice: rather summary, to be sure, for a good half-hour before noon our guide Strange turns up with the signal to start. We pay our reckoning, thank mine host in farewell, and hasten out after old Will down the cobbles of St Michael's Lane to the broad Thames Street and Fish-mongers' Hall. A few yards to the right among the coaches, the carts, the fish-porters, and the smells of Stockfishmongers' Row, and we turn south again, in a growing stream of well-dressed foot-passengers bound for the Thames. Down through the narrow Ebgate Lane, shaded with houses almost meeting overhead, to Old Swan Stairs, and the river glistening in the sun.

Ordinarily in vacation-time, it seems, these stairs are thronged with the blue-coated watermen wrangling bitterly over the rare passenger, besieging him with cries of 'I'm your first man!' But the case is altered; with the return of the wars and especially with this play at the Globe,

[1] *Overen v. Paine*, Lib. Test. Exam. Cur. Cons. Lond. 1609–11, f. 340.

business is booming. It is now the thronging passengers' turn to shout 'I'm your first fare!' Threading the traffic under sail, wherries are crossing to Bankside and return-ing in steady lines. Luckily for us, old Strange knows just where and how to catch the calculating eye of the stroke of this big two-oar just coming in. And on the promise of double fares he has us promptly embarked, not without indignation from the less lavish.

Shoving off, we may be thankful for a tide just at the full. The flood not only covers the slimy foreshores from which this high August sun would otherwise be drawing a mighty stench, but also gives us almost slack water for a quick passage. We look across eagerly as our guide points out a white spot to the left of the Hope or Bear Garden—the Globe's flag, flapping in lazy triumph from its staff high above the chimney-tops and greenery. Sail-ing-barges move sluggishly in the slight air from the southwest. It is close, and Strange thinks we may be in for an afternoon shower. Our two 'oars' give way with a will, the sooner to be back for another fare. Paralleling the Bridge covered mostly with tall houses except at the draw, we catch now and again a glimpse through its arches beneath of the shipping crowded at Billingsgate and beyond.

As we approach the Surrey side and the grisly show of traitors' skulls bleaching on poles at Bridgefoot, we are making for the stairs lying between my Lord Bishop of Winchester's handsome palace and the Clink Prison. But boats from other quarters are converging on the same point. Closing in, fierce contention for the landing grows so threatening that when at last we have thrust in along-side, paid double, and scrambled out, we find even the lively shouldering crowd a relief. Gathered into it, we push along with growing excitement past the walls of the Clink, south to Globe Alley, then westward between its mean cottages, beckoned on by the flag floating high in the sun over the great ring of tiled roof surmounted by the twin pointed gables of the 'hut'.

Most of these single-minded pilgrims have trudged over the Bridge, through its filthy crowded traffic-tunnels. Now they are heading for the amphitheatre's main door, somewhat to the right, facing northeast towards the river. But here our leader draws us out of the throng—'best places this way'—to a path on the left, which the well-to-do and 'persons of quality' are taking. It leads round past a tall square turret pierced with windows, jutting forward from the wall. That, as we learn in passing, is one of the two external staircases serving the galleries of lower price. To get to them, you first pass through the main door of the house into the ring of open-air yard, then by an under-passage at the side, through to one of these staircases climbing outside the wall to the two upper stories.

We continue round, passing the alehouse belonging to the theatre, to the other door. Lying on the southwest side opposite the main gate, it serves the best galleries and the stage. A couple of feet below ground level, at the end of a sloping trench which channels the crowd, stands the large double door, with one leaf open. Edging down the ramp and closer to the door as the queue ahead is steadily admitted, we catch sight of a stout turnstile planted just within. A business-like woman 'gatherer' is taking money, under the sharp eyes of two others, a man and a woman—'appointed by the housekeepers', Strange tells

23

us—checking the exact number of admissions, while a brawny attendant manipulating a bar stops and releases the turnstile-arms on her signals. Though the fee at this door like all the rest has been trebled, it is eagerly offered.

Once inside, amongst trees, gates, arches, green banks, and stone-grey battlements of canvas-and-frame, we are evidently in a lower property storeroom. As we are swept along to the stair-foot, there is scarce time for Strange to do more than point across at the players' entrances to the 'cellarage' under the stage, near companion-ladders leading to openings overhead. For we are already climbing to the main floor, and emerge at the top into the ample property-dock, lined with capacious presses, adjoining the stage. With this it communicates by two great folding doors left and right. Pointing to a stately sedan chair —a litter with shafts fore and aft for two horses—standing splendid in black and gold near the closed doors at the left, old Will observes, 'That's Gondomar's. And they've got two mules to carry it.'

At the right, one leaf of the other folding door stands open, guarded by another money-taker—a man—and his overseers. Past them we have just a glimpse of stage-floor stretching out to the heads of the crowd in the sun-lit yard beyond. Some extravagantly-dressed gentlemen are leaving us and making for this door, but first for a heap of low three-footed stools beside it. These are for hire at a stiff figure; and each gallant after tucking a stool under his arm pays the last and highest price and disappears through the door on to the stage. Others of our crowd are hastening off left and right to barriers leading to segments of gallery at stage-level.

But most of us are going higher. And when we have

gained the next floor—'the upper wardrobe' as Strange
calls it—he beckons us away. We leave some again seek-
ing the gallery-entrances left and right, and the majority
mounting aloft to the top gallery. It is now in the company of bright silks, jewels, and feathered beaver hats
that we make for the backs of the spacious central boxes,
the 'lords' room' directly over the stage. Barely in time,
too, for those in the middle are full, and one of the others
is taken up while we wait. But by getting the ear of the
box-opener—and perforce that of her assiduous male
'shadow' as well—as they are proceeding to unlock a door
remaining at the right-hand end, Strange contrives with
eloquent bribery, beyond the ruinous treble price, to get
us in; and he stands now at our elbow, flattened against
the partition. So many have pressed into the box that we
sit crowded. For all that, our bench is padded with rush
matting. Better still, it has a back. Best of all, it is the
lowest bench in front. Uncertainty is past, we can draw a
long breath, rest our elbows on the broad rail, and look
about.

One's first and overwhelming impression is of a coliseum, a circus: the effect not dissipated by Roman vast-
ness, but concentrated by intimacy. Three circling popu-
lous galleries swing away right and left, curving round
without a break. Overhead we hear the gallery-gods,
while below girdling the sunny and swarming yard we
see the lowest gallery, all fenced in front with iron bars to
discourage climbers-in. Conspicuous in our commanding position, we are sitting like one of the 'potent Caesars'
in his podium. For the sky-blue underside of the 'shadow'
or stage-cover high overhead stretches forward beyond
its two supporting pillars, an imperial canopy against the

25

sun's heat and glare, while action presented before us on the open stage below will develop close at hand. The oblong platform's whole centre is covered with a stage cloth painted in sixty-four great squares of black and white: a human chessboard some twenty foot square, a battlefield for the royal war-game.

Tobacco-smoke drifts to our noses from the pipes of those ultra-fashionable stool-holders just beneath us. Chatting, reading, playing cards, they sit, a many-hued insolent phalanx of several dozen, backed by the property-dock wall—the 'ground front' between the folding dock-doors right and left—and forward to the very edge of the chessboard. Thus the central glistening show of their expensive silks and feathers confronts that formidable field of upturned faces beyond the stage's railed outside edge: the Cockney groundlings, the stinkards standing below in the open yard. And these stage-sitting exquisites have all acted upon Dekker's advice to the feathered gallant—to plant himself like a cannon on

the Throne of the Stage . . . on the very Rushes where the Commedy is to daunce, yea and under the state of *Cambises* himself, . . . beating down the mews and hisses of the opposed rascality.

As we survey them, old Strange shows unusual interest. He leans over, and points out a blue-coated attendant circulating among the gallants, selling them tobacco—a small boy at his heels with a smouldering slow-match, giving lights to pipes. 'See him?' says Strange. 'That's Precious John. He's got my old job. Stagekeeper, with tobacco on the side.' 'What is that black affair pushed back on his head?' we want to know. 'Vizard,' is the answer. 'Wear that over your face in the play, while you

FROM THE LORDS' ROOM—THE 'WRONG BEDROOMS' SCENE IN *A GAME AT CHESS*

walk about opening and shutting curtains. Two stagekeepers always on deck.' 'But where did he get a name
like Precious John?' 'Oh, they all call him that. He's
John Precious by rights.'

Our amphitheatre, already compact with company and
loud with undulating multitudinous hubbub, presents
an eye-filling spectacle. Painted in stately colours—the
carved wooden pillars on the stage and the 'principals' of
the house-frame so much like marble pilasters as to deceive an expert—small wonder that this playhouse, rebuilt after the fire a decade ago, was held to be 'the fairest
that ever was in England'. To sit a spectator in 'the
Globe's fair ring' is to understand the aptness of its name;
for

> The world's a theatre, the earth a stage
> Plac'd in the midst.

As in the centre of Shakespeare's 'huge rondure',

> The earth's a stage to heav'n's surrounding eye,
> For men to act their parts.

Here for the audience will be no cool objectivity as before
a peep-show, but concentration: a drawing-in to one
magnetic experience.

> Nay, when you look into my galleries
>   . . . a thousand heads are laid
> So close, that all of heads the room seems made . .
> Throng'd heaps do listen.

And the play will arise in the bosom of the gathering:

>   below,
> The very floor, as 't were, waves to and fro—
> And, like a floating island, seems to move
> Upon a sea bound in with shores above.

Its contrast with our familiar objective stage-at-the-end is profound. How to express it? There, we wait casually for something to be *exhibited*. Here, we expect—roused by the certainty that something powerful is going to *happen*, and that we shall be in it.

Already when we reached our seats, in the galleries ringing the round,

all the rooms
Did swarm with gentles mix'd with grooms,

but more and still more have been relentlessly thrusting in, and a heightened buzz of expectation fills the air. Listening critically to the sound, old Will says, 'Never heard 'em more stirred up.' All but the three front rows— who got in first to sit on the steps—are standing, and packed into what looks like a solid mass. Yet vendors of fruit and bottle-ale are still miraculously squirming through 'where a weasel scarce could pass', or clambering over, performing marvels of merchandising. One would certainly have expected more fighting than we have seen, but most of the contentious are too intent on what is coming to indulge in fisticuffs. For that matter, what room is left to swing an arm? The crush in the yard below threatens to crack the walls.

It is now getting on for two o'clock. And as we have sat watching, the sun has moved farther behind us to the southwest, and is now striking full into the fronts of the far galleries facing the stage, right in the eyes of their occupants. Looking at it, one can only wonder how we ever could have imagined the Globe presenting its plays in depth, against a 'scenic wall', with an 'inner stage' below, and a 'balcony stage' above—just where we are now

sitting: preposterously giving the best view of the production to the 'penny stinkards' in the yard. For in fact
the Globe is obviously oriented so as to make all that
quite impossible. Our protected southwest side adjoining the stage is clearly the only really good spectator-
side; and those gallery-patrons viewing the stage from the
far side of the yard enjoy some of the worst seats in the
house. Not only remote from the stage, but also squint-
ing squarely into the afternoon sun.

But should not that same westering sun, now dazzling
them, also deepen the shadow here within on the stage?
Yet it does not seem to do so, and we turn to old Strange
for the explanation. He points directly up, to the underside of the 'hut'—which is continued forward as the blue
stage-cover, high overhead. On the hither side of the
hut's square scuttle—through which the 'throne' for descending gods is lowered to the stage—all the joists stand
open, uncovered—no flooring at all. What is more, those
open joists are all whitewashed and gleaming with sunlight—a bright grid of indirect lighting for the stage below. Strange says the source is large windows in the hut's
twin gable-ends, which rise well above the main roof-
level, and face right into the southwest sun.

It is impossible not to observe how the Globe's orientation serves the seating—gives the high-paying customers
the shaded southwest or good side,[1] as well as the best
and closest view of the production on the open stage.
But it does more. We shall soon discover that at the same
time it also serves the age-old spiritual symbolism of the
drama.

---

[1] Like the pavilion at Lord's or the boxes at the Yankee Stadium.

For what now absorbs all our attention is the traditional arrangement of the stage-scenes, as adapted for this *Game at Chess*. Out towards the stage's edge along our end of the great oblong, to the right of the central chessboard, extends a stately loggia: a double row of white pillars more than six foot high, joined at the top by strong rails, making a gallery or walk more than five foot wide by some twenty foot long. This inner end of it is roofed; and set on top is a booth or 'room', which is draped round breast-high with a blue cloth adorned with golden sun, and moon and stars of silver. We can see that it is reached from the loggia below by a stepladder to a hole in the roof. Across the chessboard and facing in opposition from Stage Left stands a similar loggia, but with all its pillars and top-framing painted a gleaming jet-black. Opposite the 'upper room' of the white loggia, the inner end of the black also has a room 'above', but its posts are full six foot high, and it is completely hung round with black curtains. It is similarly reached by an inside stepladder.

Before we have time for questions about these opposed fronts of White and Black, a small party of blue-coated attendants sallies out from the dock-doors below us at the left, past the crowded 'front' of stage-sitters, bearing loads of cloth, some black and some white. Their entrance is welcomed with a round of applause. A wag among them, acknowledging with an elaborate leg, draws a laugh. Putting down their armfuls, they select the black cloths, and set about hooking them up like curtains with open rings on slender metal rods running round the top rails of the black loggia. The mob takes offence at this activity, and vents its feelings in groans, catcalls, and hoots, with a few well-aimed pieces of fruit thrown in. These curtains—by the shimmer as they are handled, and the slimness of their folds when drawn back with cords to a pillar—are evidently of silk. The hangers have borne all this disapproval patiently, and they have their reward when they come across to dress the White House in its shining robes. For now it is nothing but applause, waving of caps, and bursts of enthusiastic cheers from the long-suffering, steaming audience. And hundreds of eyes, as though spellbound, follow every deft motion. Now, leaving both houses shrouded in contrasted silk, the hangers have finished and gone.

We turn to old Will, questions crowding the tip of the tongue, but he forestalls us. 'Hell,' he says, with a knowing lift of the head. 'They can't wait to see Gondomar put in it. Hell and the tormentors—a rare good sight, too.' Well, we think, why not? Let him begin with Hell, and work away from it.

Hell, he now reminds us, has from time immemorial stood over there at Stage Left, and he points to the far end of the Black House. And he adds something fresh and fascinating. The oversized trap in that corner, he says, has always served not merely as the gullet for Hell Mouth, but also as a box for the prompter or bookholder—'suggestions of the fiend', 'promptings of the Devil'. Ruminating this revelation, we begin to realize the incredible conservatism of the theatre. For on our West End and Broadway stages, that same medieval Hell Corner remains Prompt Corner to this day. What is more, the narrow red curtain or 'flat' called 'the tormentor' is still there beside it to mask the prompter—though all memory of the fiendish source of the name is long lost. And the devils and imps in the Christmas pantomimes still appear today from the Hell side, Stage Left, just as their predecessors did when Chaucer was a child.

But Strange has more to tell. To match the Prompt Trap at Hell Corner, he says, there are three more traps near the other corners of the stage: that is, one under each end of the two opposing houses—and the inevitable fifth one at centre-stage, the large Grave trap. All the traps, as we know, open down into the cellarage. Yes, but here Strange makes a further disclosure. Cellarage and tiring-house, he points out, 'is all one'. The traps are the entrances to the stage. Up through the traps from underneath, he tells us, come not only ghosts and devils, but the human characters as well. These latter however usually mount up unseen at the corners into 'houses', round which the stagekeepers have just closed the curtains. There they can be 'discovered' for 'interior' scenes by a reopening of the curtains round about, or else they can make their entrances from them on to the stage; and at once the curtains are again all drawn back, so as not to obstruct anybody's view.

But, we ask, if the low-pitched cellarage of the stage is the tiring-house, isn't it black as night down there? Strange assures us it is not as bad as all that: glazed windows on three sides let in light, and the interior finished all over with lime whitewash makes the most of every bit that gets in.

This arrangement, when we give it a moment's thought, seems logical, even obligatory. With audience on all four sides, where can the tiring-house stand but underneath? And a most strategic location too, offering advantages both obvious and great. From below, entrances are made with speed and ease at any corner of the stage. As they come and go, the players by using the several traps can keep closely in touch with the action at any point. Most important of all, the prompter must be audible both in the tiring-house and on the stage. Here, in his hole at Hell Corner, head on the stage, body in the tiring-house, he is ideally placed.

Since the Black House at Stage Left harbours Hell, the White House opposed at this end must evidently stand at the post of Heaven. Old Will corroborates this, and adds more. Heaven, he says, used always to be presented here at Stage Right as a city wall or castle. Garrisoned with angels in armour patrolling the battlemented top. Satan's horde, swarming out of Hell Mouth, would advance yelling across the stage with scaling-ladders to the assault. Fighting on the walls, very hot and obstinate, would hold the auditory enthralled with its varying fortunes until the angels, gaining the upper hand, would sally out in the final charge that drove the black mutineers back, and down into Hell.

Combats so thrilling made 'the walls' prime favourites with the public. Nowadays those gated battlements are often employed for scenes such as Corioli in *Coriolanus*, Flint Castle in *Richard II*, and Harfleur in *Henry V*. Property cannon are mounted on them: the actual roar produced by 'chambers'—small multiple-barrelled mortars set upright on the floor to fire blank charges vertically. That was what burnt down the Globe eleven years ago. During the presentation of Shakespeare's *Henry VIII*, from these walls at the south end of the stage a salute for the King's entry was fired. Flying up, a burning wad caught in the roof-thatch overhead here on the south side,

34

and the fire ran right round the building. In an hour the Globe was gone.

Yet the battlements' origin as the walls of Heaven, we are assured, is far from forgotten. It is because the citadel of Heaven is the seat of harmony and song that the 'music room' has always been located 'above', on top of the house or mansion here at Stage Right. We have already seen it—just below us, a second story to the White House, at this end: the 'room' enclosed by the heavenly cloth of sun, moon, and stars. The trumpets will be there very soon now.

As we consider this arena stage from the commanding position of the 'lords' room', we realize that Stage Right and Stage Left are not so called from the actors' stand-point, but from *ours*. Actors playing in the round can have no fixed or consistent right and left. No, it is for this upper or 'Throne' side of the audience—the 'gentles', originally (and still today in the palaces) the King and his Court—that Heaven stands, as it must, on the Right, and (as Milton has it) 'on the left hand Hell'.

And sitting in this shaded southwest side above the long stage with its end-scenes opposing the Good to the Bad both in their stations and in their colour, we begin to perceive part of its high ancestral symbolism. Not only is the Globe correctly set in regard to the sun for the seating, but its stage is also properly oriented for outward visible accord with the spiritual content of the drama—a drama which took its rise in religion.

For at the Right or Heaven, the corners of the stage stand east and south. At the Left, north and west, with Hell Corner at the north, following both pagan philos-ophy and Christian belief. 'Pythagoras, Plato, and

Aristotle take the East for the right part, and the West for the left.'[1] The blessed abode of Heaven is ever east and south, shown in the orientation of churches. And in Donne's words, 'an Eastern light . . . the light of grace . . . a South light . . . the light of glory'. 'Most other Courts, alas, are like to hell . . . our Court, an everlasting East.' The ground adjoining Chichester Cathedral known as 'Paradise' lies at the south.

As for Hell, on the sinister or left hand, 'all evils rise out of the north'. In Christian churches the north is 'the devil's side', where Satan and his legion lurked to catch the unwary, the side on which most people utterly refused to be buried. Hell can lie nowhere but at 'sharp north' or 'declining west', and Heaven at the orient east: compass-points at which as we know they were severally placed for the great open-air mystery plays of the Middle Ages. For the Whitehall performance of *Twelfth Night* before Queen Elizabeth seated at the south, we saw the traditional orientation unmistakably maintained by Shakespeare's text. At the Queen's right the fair Olivia— 'Now heaven walks on earth'—has her house in the east, opposite the melancholy Orsino's, left, in the dark drooping west.

Rising tumult in the packed yard, and importunate yells of 'Sound!' 'Sound!' call our minds back to the still more absorbing business of the moment. It lacks five minutes of three o'clock. Up through the hatch into the 'music room' just below us on top of the White House come three scarlet-coated trumpeters. They form up in rank to the breast-high blue cloth, raise their bannered trumpets as one, and break into the shrill clangour of a

---

[1] Plutarch's *Morals*, tr. Philemon Holland (1603), 820.

flourish. Pause. Sound it again—and yet again. Then sink down on low stools below the cloth's edge. Great bustle in the galleries of settling down, and a higher hum of expectation. Two stagekeepers, Precious John and his mate, grim black masks now hiding their faces, go to the Black House. Handling the cords, they draw open all its curtains except for a square enclosing the trap at the inner end, directly beneath the small black-hung 'room' on the top. Between the black pillars at the outer end the prompter's head shows through the trap at Hell Corner. Now the stagekeepers come across the chessboard and do the same for the White House.

At the end of three minutes the trumpets rise up, and again sound the flourish, this time twice. Disappearing now for but one minute, they rise to blow the final sound: once only, ending on a high prolonged chord. It is the signal to begin.

Out from the square of closed curtains below the White House's music-room appears a tall figure robed in black and crowned with laurel—the Prologue.[1] Pacing gravely to the centre of the chessboard, he lifts his hand for silence; turns to our 'Throne' side of the house, and sinks in three low obeisances. Then, taking in the whole surrounding audience, and in a voice clear and pitched to reach three thousand pairs of ears, he declares

> What of the game called chess-play can be made
> To make a stage play, shall this day be played.
> First you shall see the men in order set—
> States and their Pawns, when both the sides are met—

---

[1] In the early drama the Prologue was always one of the clergy, admonishing the people to take the scriptural play for their edification. This custom fixed both the Prologue's black robe and his entrance at the Heaven end, Stage Right.

The Houses well distinguish'd. In the game
Some men entrapp'd and taken, to their shame
Rewarded by their play; and in the close
You shall see checkmate giv'n to Virtue's foes.

At this, pointing the accusing finger at the Black House,
he is interrupted by applause thunderous and long. He
steps back towards the White House; then—

But the fair'st jewel that our hopes can deck,
Is so to play our game t'avoid your check.

Again louting low, to take leave of the 'gentles', and he is
gone through the white silk hangings.

From his exit here at Stage Right the general gaze leaps
to the 'above' at Stage Left, for the black curtains atop
the closed inner end of the Black House are all sliding
away to the pillars, and up there we see the spirit of
Ignatius Loyola appearing, Error at his foot as asleep.

Ignatius. Ha? Where? What angle of the world is this?

After venting strong indignation that his Jesuits have not
yet established supreme control everywhere, and that his
own 'sainting' was delayed until a mere five years ago, he
wakes up Error. This 'father of supererogation' reveals
that he has been dreaming of 'a game at chess between our
side and the White House', and Ignatius at once insists on
being shown this game. That is the music's cue. Cornets,
sackbuts, and drums, replacing the trumpets in the music
room, strike up the Spanish march.

Through the black curtains below the watching Ignatius and Error come two black Pawns, preceding two
Rooks or 'Dukes'. One of these 'Dukes', recognized at
sight as King Philip's hated minister Olivares, draws a

broadside of hisses and catcalls. With exaggerated Spanish deliberation, the four pace out along the black pillars of their open loggia, then across the board, in along the White House, across once more past the 'front' of stage-sitters: then they divide to take up their posts at Black's corner-squares, each Rook fenced by his Pawn. Now to the patriotic beat of the English march, this parade is precisely matched from the White House, whose 'Dukes'—one of them obviously Buckingham— are hailed with tumultuous cheers.

But when the Black Knights enter after their Pawns to take their tour about the stage, yells, hoots, and whistles swell to a storm of execration. For the Knight on the right hand is the prime villain of the piece, the old familiar Gondomar to the life—every step, every turn of the head until he comes to his place next to Olivares. Now, ushered forth by their Pawns, the White Knights step out in reply; and the cheering rises delirious, for the White Knight walking on the upper hand is the spit-image of Charles, Prince of Wales. Their triumphant progress to the English march brings all the Knights to their squares by the 'Dukes'—and Prince Charles next to Buckingham.

Then follow the Bishops of the Black—one of them the Jesuits' Father General, led by his Jesuit Pawn. But the answering White Bishops' welcome is discordant: applause for Archbishop Abbot, walking on the right, is overwhelmed in the wave of jeers and derision for his companion—a great fat man. Old Strange shouts in our ear that this is the actor-playwright Will Rowley, playing the fat Archbishop of Spalatro, the ambitious turncoat from Rome who turned his coat back again. As he waddles in episcopal pomp, to the delight of the mob his white robe falls a bit open, revealing a black one underneath. Last of all comes the climax with contrasted royalty—howling-down for Spanish Philip and the Infanta as the Black, and an ovation for the widower King James and the 'Church of England' as King and Queen of the White. The Queens and their two Pawns, all played by boy-actresses, are the only female characters in the cast.

Now all eight alternate entries are completed. Thirty-two 'men' fill the sides confronted on the board, ready for the game. Ranged on the Hell side stand the enemies of England and her religion—

> this is the Black House; look
> Now t' th' White, Virtues' pure sacred rest:
> Our Majesties', like Heav'n's, are best express'd
> In duteous silence.[1]

Surveying the ranked forces from their corner above the Black House, Error tells Ignatius,

> You have your wish.
> Behold, there's the full number of the game.

Like twin *tableaux vivants* the two sides stand on show while Ignatius further exposes his unscrupulous ambition. Then music sounds, and both sides execute a quarter-turn towards the yard. The two files of Pawns set forward in symmetry. Turning inwards, they double back towards us along their own third rows of squares to the 'front' of stage-sitters, followed in file by the Pieces. At the board's edge, leading away to their respective

---

[1] See G. Bullough, 'How *A Game at Chesse* Struck a Contemporary', *Modern Language Review*, April 1954.

Houses, each file of Pawns divides and halts to form the hedge of honour before the door. Without a pause in their measured gait, the Pieces pass out in state between them, and the Pawns, last going first, follow two by two.

Error. Observe, as in a dance, they glide away.

Opening with the Queens' Pawns—the ladies—the game unfolds an underplot of melodrama: showing the Black Bishop's Jesuit Pawn's vile and relentless efforts to seduce the virtuous Pawn of the White Queen, not sticking even at attempted rape. Lurid matter, but it has its amusing side. For while his dark design is ostensibly helped by that 'bouncing Jesuitess' the Black Queen's Pawn, she secretly foils his repeated attempts on the White Pawn in order in the end to get him for herself. This continued intrigue provides the thread of story whereon to string the great glowing beads of hot political interest. Spanish and Jesuit plots undermining England, in the upshot uncovered and thwarted. The Fat Bishop's ambition—to fill with his Falstaff-flesh 'the biggest chair ecclesiastical'—played upon by Gondomar to lure him into deserting to the Black House. The White Knight Prince Charles's simulated sympathy with the Blacks, which draws them on to reveal the boundless appetite of their vast ambition. And best of all, that inimitable Gondomar exposing his own brilliant machinations and duperies with the cynical relish and self-appreciation of another Iago.

The acting is excellent, the impression of an animated three-dimensional merciless political cartoon overwhelming. Bold Middleton shows himself an English Aristophanes in coarse vigour of wit, supreme confidence of attack, and the unerring aim of each deadly hit. Complete topicality gives his play this astounding momentary success. But it is far from deserving any comparison with that earlier topical comedy, *Twelfth Night*. For even when oblivion has stripped away every last delicious bit of topicality from it, Shakespeare's comedy remains instinct with the life of wit, of poetry, of character, by which it triumphs through the ages, over time and translation. This topical *Game at Chess*, on the contrary, presents no dramatic poetry in its satirical–political bludgeoning, no character-development in its portraits, its puppetry, its caricature. Yet who cares? Who in this cheering, laughing, jeering, hissing cauldron of three thousand partisans wants poetic drama? Granted, the play will soon be lying dead as a stick. But now, a nine days' wonder, it roars up a flaming rocket.

Not having suffered the tensions of the first two decades of this seventeenth century, we sit as virtual strangers to its peculiar power. The full force of many a topical stroke misses us—though at times we feel the whiff and wind of it—yet the mere sight of the passions boiling on every side is stirring. In addition, we find our own special excitement in something which all the others take for granted: the method of staging the performance. And this essentially is what we came so far to see.

The unfamiliar characteristic which strikes us at once is the arena stage's necessary sacrifice of 'illusion by concealment'. As old Will told us, these long 'houses' or loggias of pillars opposed at the stage-ends are kept open and transparent except during brief periods. Curtains are momentarily closed round this or that corner, or even the whole, to cover an entrance or an exit, or the placing of a property in preparation for the 'discovery' of an interior scene. But no part is allowed to stand closed, blocking the view of some spectators on that side, for any appreciable time. Obviously, what makes such suppleness possible is the presence of the tiring-house immediately underneath and co-extensive with the stage, and the traps giving prompt access to every corner of it.

As it unfolds, the performance provides characteristic examples of the method. In each of the last three acts, parts of the Black House are appropriately employed. In Act 3 for an 'interior'—a conjuring episode with an apparition seen in a magic mirror; in Act 4 for a dumb show or silent miming of the trick with the 'wrong bedrooms'; and in Act 5 for the revelation of an altar with images which move or dance. Each of these illustrates a different use of the stage's facilities, and may be briefly described.

At the close of the first act, the 'presenters' Ignatius and Error disappear from their post above the inner end of the Black loggia, not to return. Their stools and ladder, together with the planks which made their floor, are taken away to permit even top-gallery sitters to see down into that corner with its trap. In Act 3 the curtains are closed round it, to make a 'room' for the apparition scene. At once the two Queens' Pawns, Black and White, come up from the tiring-house to take their places in it, the Black bearing her magic mirror. Now the curtains are drawn back on all sides, discovering the interior with the ladies. Soft music of recorders from under the stage. The White Pawn is told that if, after the magical invocation, she looks fixedly into the mirror without turning round, she will see her future husband. The Black Queen's Pawn intones the invocation. Then, at a change in the music, like an apparition up through the open trap behind the ladies rises the villainous Jesuit Black Pawn, disguised in rich attire; presents himself so as to be seen in the mirror by his intended victim, and sinks again, disappearing through the trap.

Act 4 presents the dumb show of the 'wrong bedrooms' (see p. 27), with four separate places convincingly represented. The briefly-closed inner corner of the White House will provide an entrance for the White Queen's Pawn. Opposite, the inner corner of the Black is however left open. But the Black House's outer corner containing the Hell trap, and a section next to it, are closed by curtains, making two separate chambers—which we may call respectively H and N—and the scene begins.

Up through the trap in the open inner corner of the Black House the Black Queen's Pawn is seen to enter with a lighted candle in her hand. She crosses to the White, and fetches out the White Pawn in her night attire—whereupon the White curtains are again opened. She takes the White Pawn back across, and introduces her into the Black chamber N. Then returning to her own entrance-trap, she is seen to fetch up the Black Jesuit Pawn in his night dress, and to conduct him past N to the other closed 'bedroom' H at Hell Corner. After putting him into this unoccupied chamber, she waits a moment or two, then blows out the light and follows him in. While this trick of hers is being relished by the audience, all three players have descended by the Hell trap to the tiring-house, and the curtains are all reopened.

The altar with the moving images shown in Act 5 makes an imposing piece of stage-machinery. It is hoisted unseen into the briefly-closed Hell Corner through the large trap, and set down on supports over the hole. Upon the 'discovery' by the reopening of the curtains round about, mechanicians working from below as in a puppet-show can thus manipulate the marvellous 'dancing' statues from inside it—and at the close it can be removed as expeditiously.

On the other hand we are also offered examples of scenes taking up the whole stage. Most striking are the two which present all the Blacks and Whites confronted as though on a royal field of chivalry for the trial of truth: the first for the White Queen's Pawn's accusation of the villain, and the second for proof of his guilt. In these scenes the two stagekeepers are reinforced by two more for simultaneous action with all the curtains.

For the first, in Act 2, both houses are completely shrouded. Under cover the two sides come quickly up, using all four traps, to make their entries. First, at the corners, the White Pawns and Rooks or Dukes step forward through the curtains to their squares, and are answered by the Blacks opposite. In similar alternation follow the Knights, then the Bishops, and last the Kings and Queens. When both sides of the board are full, all the curtains slide away at once.

The second confrontation, in Act 3, is still more impressive. Again both houses are closed. And when the two sides have ranked in their order within, the hangings are all pulled back at once, discovering a grand tableau. For a moment they hold the effect, then front to front set forward to the field. In time and step to music, the troops take up their ground.

Here in Middleton's play exposed to the view stand the

embattled fronts of two mighty monarchies. Before our eyes this oblong displays conflict and contrast with every resource of colour, position, and movement. Can there be proof more conclusive that no stage jutting from a single unified background with doors and an 'alcove' could conceivably mount such a production? And conversely, had the Globe's oblong open stage not offered the traditional Heaven and Hell opposed and confronted as a schematic basis, would any such Game at Chess have ever suggested itself?

What the mob is waiting for, as Will Strange foretold, is the 'mastery' or fight—the medieval violence centred on Hell which will cap the play's climax. But in the course of the fourth act comes an unlucky contretemps. Storm-clouds have rolled in over us from the rainy southwest. And although their gloom lends some verisimilitude to the Black Pawn's officious candle in the night-scene of the 'wrong bedrooms', the wind rises with them, and they plainly mean business. Not waiting for the end of the act, the first great drops splash upon the 'understanders' jammed in the open yard, then grow to a downpour—which the wind drives slanting in to the fronts of the far galleries facing the stage. The soaking which those front rows now share with the mass of groundlings reminds us again that that unenviable side, which gazes dazzled into the afternoon sun, also faces into the teeth of the prevailing wind. By contrast, on our stage-side protected by the great 'cover' we sit not only dry, but in windy weather under the house's sheltering lee.

In time for the opening of the long-awaited final act, rain-clouds give place once more to the warm and drying sun. The stage has been fitted to show the White Knight

Charles's visit to Madrid, ending in checkmate to the Spaniard. Over the Black House's inner corner roof-planks and ladder have been put back to restore the 'above'—this time for a speaker's curtained rostrum—and all stands ready.

To the sound of cornets and sackbuts from the music-room now enters the prize show-piece of the whole production. Out from the great property-dock doors below us to the left, and past the crowded tribunal of stool-holders, comes the elegant black litter borne before and behind by two white mules; and in it, nodding through the window, rides the Black Knight, Gondomar, just as he used to ride through London streets. While the walking lackey guides the lead-mule in a ceremonial tour of the chessboard, this perfect mimicry of the hateful, well-remembered equipage stirs a tumult of laughter, cheers, and hoots. The circuit completed, Gondomar puts out his head and calls, 'Hold! Hold! Is the Black Bishop's Pawn, the Jesuit, planted above for his concise oration?' The curtains above slide away, and the Pawn replies in orotund Latin, 'Behold me set on Caesar's triumphal arch!' So imminent is the Blacks' defeat that the dramatic irony of this vaunt is apparent to the weakest intellect. Then Gondomar alights, and the litter is carried off.

Now hautboys strike up royal music for two entries: from our side the White Knight and Duke, and from the other the Black King, Queen, and Duke. The two Whites cross the intervening 'sea' to be royally received 'in Spain', while the Black Pawn from his high rostrum delivers in Latin the concise oration of greeting. Now 'in Madrid', all the Black hosts conduct their guests along out through the Black loggia, and at Hell Corner follows the exhibition of the altar with the dancing images already described. We are fast approaching the climax.

After cunningly luring his Black hosts on to betray in detail the secrets of their vice and their insatiate ambitions of conquest, by pretending to share them, the White Knight springs the trap. He throws off his cloak of simulation with the shout, 'The Game's ours! We give thee checkmate *by discovery*, King, the noblest mate of all!' Consternation among the Blacks, and the King cries, 'I'm lost! I'm taken!' A great shout and flourish of trumpets greet the triumph, and the audience roars it to the echo. Now the curtains at Hell Corner—closed for a couple of minutes to cover some fresh activity there—are again drawn open. We see that a voluminous black canvas affair resembling the front of a tent has been dragged up through the great Hell trap, its lower end still in the hole. This is obviously the Bag, into which captured chessmen are put. But though its front lies collapsed on the stage, we can discern the internal framework of bows which will set it up to gape open, as well as some painted features added in lurid reds and livid blues.

Now enter the White King and Queen, leading their side across to the enemy's camp. On the White Knight's report of the checkmate—'a game won with much hazard'—the White King condemns the vanquished to oblivion. At this cue the bows of the Bag rear up; it takes shape as a horrible Head, with a monstrous crowded vermilion Mouth gaping to swallow more.

White King. And there behold the Bag's Mouth, like Hell
    opens
    To take her due, and the lost sons appear.

48

Packed in the gullet writhe captured Blacks, along with the 'lost sons': the Fat Bishop and a traitor White Pawn. The wretches are being fiendishly driven down at the fork's end by very brisk 'tormentors'—devils in flame-coloured skincoats—egged on by savage yells from the yard.

The infernal disclosure sets off a Donnybrook Fair of fighting—the buffets interspersed with buffoonery from the Fat Bishop. The White pieces—royalty included—fall upon their opposite numbers, the White Knight Charles on Gondomar, and with blows and kicks sharpened with opprobrium hurl them one after another into Hell Mouth. When all are in, the jaws of that Bag are hauled together and made fast. The White Knight springs up on top of the squirming mass and prances about, subduing it with his heels. From this exuberance loud music calls him away to the stately exit of the panting but triumphant Whites. Amid frantic and fierce acclaim from every side of the theatre they recross the board in procession, turning in to thread the white colonnades, and disappear beneath us into the white curtains under the music-room.

Before the hurricane of applause has begun to die, out comes the White Queen's Pawn—the boy-actress with deep curtsies as graceful as any Maid of Honour's—to give the brief and moral Epilogue. But along with her final vanishing our vision is coming to an end. The multitude is on the move, stagekeepers are taking down the hangings, the chequered stage grows dim, and the great Globe itself is ready to dissolve, an 'insubstantial pageant faded'.

II

IN PURSUIT OF A STAGE

PROFESSIONAL or amateur, modern striving on both sides of the Atlantic for excellence in the staging and acting of Shakespeare's plays is a growing fascination of the theatre. And yet more and more, while savouring such a production set before us, or re-reading a favourite comedy or tragedy, we find ourselves inescapably wondering—if indeed it were not first produced at Court, like *Twelfth Night*—what it looked like on its original first afternoon on the open-air public stage which has vanished away. For we realize that it was that lost performance of long ago, at the Curtain or the Globe, which to Shakespeare *was* the play. As an experienced actor, he was steeped in the traditional traffic of the boards—which he called the 'scaffoldage'. Even more than most skilled playwrights, the greatest of all actor-poets must as he wrote have conceived the proper staging of his scenes in full detail.

Shakespeare invented his dramatic construction to suit his own particular stage.

The plays were shaped to suit the theatre of the day and no other.

These were the insights of William Poel. Startling, even revolutionary, when he first offered them, by now they strike us as self-evident. Poel 'believed and proclaimed that Shakespeare knew his job . . . and that we had only to find out what he did, and follow it, to realise what he meant and to make it manifest'.[1]

Certainly no thinking person will be dissuaded from demanding to see Shakespeare's plays produced on Shakespeare's stage by the owlish objection that this would be 'archaism for archaism's sake'. For he knows that no play comes into its own, finds its real being, its true life of action, until it is presented on the kind of stage for which it was conceived, in the shape, the manner planned by its author. In comparison with this essential 'bodying forth', the style of costume employed is relatively unimportant. Yet we do not hear doublet and hose for Prince Hamlet carped at as 'archaism for archaism's sake'. But more often than not this querulousness about 'archaism' is no doubt a healthy reaction to efforts misconceived or abortive, where the attempt and not the deed confounds us.

An objection equally quaint is occasionally raised against 'going back to primitive or outgrown methods' of staging. Curiously enough, the objector is not found refusing to go back to a play so primitive and outgrown as *Hamlet*. How can anyone prove our methods of staging to be in any respect better than Shakespeare's before we have learned what Shakespeare's methods were? Everybody recognizes our drama to be inferior to his. And since no comparison has ever been made, for all we know our methods of staging may be inferior likewise.

The unprejudiced mind indeed would expect to find Shakespeare's staging definitely the superior; since his native stage had been developed through centuries as a

---

[1] Sir Lewis Casson, 'William Poel and the Modern Theatre', *The Listener*, 10 January 1952, p. 56.

stage for action, a stage for drama. Our modern Italianate stage can make no such claim, invented as it was by architects for the purposes of picture, of spectacle, of the 'sung story in scenes' known as *opera*. How alien it is to the European stages which gave birth to great drama is recognized by the Italians themselves. Venice in 1951 offered an impressive show of seventeenth-century theatrical drawings by the Italian masters of scene-design —*Il Secolo dell' Invenzione Teatrale*; and Gerardo Guerrieri prefaces its Catalogue with the following statement:

One of the paradoxes of the history of the theatre is that the nation most unprovided—in the seventeenth century, at least—with dramatic literature, imposed in that century its own concept of spectacle on Europe.

The modern theatre-building, perspective illusion, the picture-frame [proscenium arch] and the stage-machinery, the auditorium with boxes, and everything which still today makes up the 'theatre', do not come from the England of Shakespeare, nor from the Spain of Calderón, nor from the France of Molière, of Corneille, of Racine. They are inventions worked out in Italy through nearly two centuries of experiments and of provisional projects and schemes: and produced (what is stranger still) out of an environment of architects and decorators rather than of men of the theatre.[1]

---

[1] 'Uno dei paradossi della storia del teatro è che la nazione più sprovveduta, nel Seicento almeno, di letteratura drammatica, abbia imposto in quel secolo la propria concezione di spettacolo all' Europa.

'L'edificio teatrale moderno, l'illusionismo prospettico, il quadro el il macchinismo scenico, la sala a palchi, e tutto quello che costituisce ancora oggi il "teatro", non vengono dall' Inghilterra di Shakespeare, nè dalla Spagna di Calderón, nè dalla Francia di Molière, di Corneille, di Racine. Sono invenzioni elaborate in Italia attraverso quasi due secoli di tentativi e di progetti e schemi provvisori: e prodotte, il che è anche più curioso, da un ambiente di architetti e di decoratori prima che di uomini di teatro.'

Mr Richard Southern is to be thanked for calling attention to this work.

The essential incapacity of such a spectacle-stage to present the works of Shakespeare is the discovery of our own century.

Yet in our own struggles to get free of it, one cannot say that the men of the theatre have yet shaken off the stranglehold of their Old Man of the Sea, the architect and decorator. On our so-called 'modern-Elizabethan' stages, the able player still looks in vain for his birthright, a free field for quick-changing action and reaction upon which to rivet his audience's attention. All too often he is confronted with an eye-filling, 'interesting' monumental edifice, twin-brother to a war-memorial, complete with that damnable nuisance to the actor, decorative flights of steps. What have such architects' appeals to the sight-seer to do with the *stage*? 'It is not so, nor it was not so, but indeed God forbid that it should be so.' Sir Balthazar Gerbier, though himself of the tribe of architect-and-scene-designer, has a salty bit of common sense on the point:

ill Builders . . . hearken to the diversity of opinions, which have been and are the causes of many Deformities and Extravagancies in Buildings; and especially those who seem to have had for Models Bird-Cages, to jump from one Roome into the other by Steps and Tressels, to cause Men and Women to stumble.[1]

Tyrone Guthrie rightly holds that

Shakespeare will always have to be butchered so long as his work has to be produced in a sort of theatre for which the plays were not written, to which they are positively ill-adapted; a sort of theatre designed for effects which are

---

[1] *Of Magnificent Building* (1662), 17.

irrelevant to Shakespeare's purpose, and inimical to the kind of effects which he sought.[1]

Useless to offer us ingenious substitutes. As with the Italians, the product of modern scenic art and applied science is magnificent, but no one can pretend that it is Shakespeare. 'It is to the Elizabethan theatre,' wrote G. M. Trevelyan, 'that we owe Shakespeare and all that he created.' Only recover even the form of his stage, to enable us to guess how his scenes were enacted upon it, and we shall come closer to understanding his work. To that end of increased knowledge and delight, we must (as Quiller-Couch well said) 'keep asking ourselves *how the thing was done*'. In imagination, join the Elizabethans in their living theatre. For we are convinced, as Granville-Barker was convinced, that 'unless that life can be re-created imaginatively, the plays, even the greatest of them, will be but half alive'.

There is no denying the need. And if we have not yet succeeded in imagining Elizabethan productions in their habit as they lived, it is not for want of trying. Generations of students of the stage have devoted their best thought to the problem of recovery. Pertinent records of every kind have been eagerly sought and repeatedly canvassed, and the plays combed for illuminating stage-directions. Numerous conjectural reconstructions of Elizabethan 'public' or open-air theatres have been offered, both in drawings and in small models.

After witnessing efforts so intense and unremitting, might one not suppose that—while details no doubt remain to be supplied—we now command a 'working knowledge' of Shakespeare's theatre and of his stage?

---

[1] *The Listener*, 10 April 1958.

Unhappily that supposition still reflects rather a wish than a reality. For if such a 'working knowledge' were actually available, would not the keen interest in Shakespeare-production have put it to work? Would not someone, somewhere, have offered us the plays in a 'wooden O'—a daylight Elizabethan theatre 'partly open to the weather'—faithfully reconstructed according to ascertained historical facts?

The truth is that although there is sound evidence enough for us to achieve a passable replica of the general form and dimensions of the *house*, it is quite another story with the *physical arrangements of the stage*. Of these not enough fact has as yet been ascertained to enable anyone to set about building it.

'It may not be wholly unamusing to examine the inside of [*the Globe* Play-house], and to exhibit as accurate a delineation of the internal form and œconomy of our ancient theatres, as the distance at which we stand and the obscurity of the subject will permit.'

'There is nothing more difficult than to form a vivid and satisfying picture of the material conditions under which Shakespeare worked: and there is nothing more fascinating than the attempt to do so.'

The first voice is Edmond Malone's [1] from the eighteenth century; the second, William Archer's from the twentieth. That most elusive and longed-for thing, a convincing image of Shakespeare's stage: small wonder that search for it has been prosecuted now for close on two hundred years.

For to begin with it is not really palatable to be told by an Elizabethan that 'they are always children which

[1] Supplement (1780) to the Johnson-Steevens *Shakespeare*, xi. 1.

know not that which was done before their time'. And what is more, many are beginning to suspect that a stage which could bring unequalled drama to life must have been a stage qualified for its task. Dramatic subtlety does not suggest theatrical crudity. We smile at the little Restoration and Queen Anne critics looking down their complacent noses at Shakespeare's dramatic construction; and yet are we much cleverer today if in ignorance we glibly disparage his stage, or 'make allowances for it'? Without a doubt, that stage when found will prove itself a powerful instrument of great artistic resource shaped to its purpose. No question but that it must be found.

In our own time such a host of hunters has joined the pursuit that the quarry has been held to be at least in view, if not positively run to earth. Already by writers of school-books and popular manuals, indeed, theory has long been presented as dogma. Pupil and public are given a definite picture of a 'typical' Elizabethan public stage, as if the thing were common and familiar knowledge.

The thoughtful observer cannot however fail to note three points about this 'typical' stage, each of them sufficiently disturbing. For all three bear on the very existence of the feature so long and so dogmatically held to be the essential characteristic of the Elizabethan stage: namely, *an 'inner stage' centrally recessed in a 'scenic wall' at the back of the open platform*. Here are these three points:

(*a*) Such an inner stage's sole reason for existing would be a manifest effectiveness in practice. But experience has shown that it has less than none—as indeed might have been foreseen. For what producer in his senses would stage his important *intimate* scenes *more remotely* from his audience than his street scenes? Bernard Miles, upon giving it the fairest of trials in the professional theatre, found the 'inner stage' impossible. And the amateur producer Ronald Watkins, once its enthusiastic advocate, has in practice abandoned it.

(*b*) That distinguished and cautious investigator Professor George F. Reynolds has serious doubts about its use. Reynolds was the first to suggest the medieval 'simultaneous' settings—separate 'places' to which the actors moved to show change of locality—as the principle of the Elizabethan public stage.[1] And although he clings to the theory that the Elizabethan stage (like the modern) used its long side opposite the yard for a 'background' with a balcony or 'upper stage', close study has convinced him that all action presumed to require an 'alcove stage' in that background could well have been presented out on the platform, in curtainable spaces or in large properties, where it would be at once more visible and more audible.

(*c*) A central 'inner stage in a scenic wall' is after all sheer assumption. What is worse, it is an assumption drawn not from any Elizabethan evidence, but directly from latter-day Italianate picture-stage ideas. No one has been able to show that there ever was such a thing as an 'alcove' or 'inner stage'. In the only known contemporary drawing of the inside of an Elizabethen theatre, there is no 'inner stage' at the back at all.

---

[1] And this view, as Mr Walter Hodges has recently remarked, 'has such a large and persuasive body of evidence to support it, that it looks as if it cannot much longer be resisted'.

Very well (I hear it replied), in view of these objections the case for that hypothetical 'inner stage' could hardly be weaker. Shakespeare may not have had anything of the sort. But the fact remains that he *did* have some kind of excellent stage on which to present action 'within' and 'above': a stage of remarkable versatility, too. If you reject the suggested 'inner stage', you must offer us something not merely more credible historically, but better in practice. This alternative no one has been able to provide.

Fair enough. 'Put up or shut up' is a good rule. But just as I am about to take up the challenge and join in the hunt for Shakespeare's stage, experience puts in this warning, which it will be important to heed: 'Never forget the instinctive and ingrained conservatism of the stage. Every man of the theatre knows that beneath all specious appearance of variety, no institution clings more tenaciously to well-tried and traditional ways. If you really want to learn what the Elizabethans' stage was like, don't begin by inventing things, or be decoyed by cleverness into looking for novel influences from abroad. Remember that the Elizabethans' poetry was still essentially medieval. What is more, theirs was a *popular* theatre: national drama is notoriously conservative. Look *back*. Consult their fathers and their grandfathers.'

Most of this advice, however often it has been disregarded, is both well-founded and obvious. And the handbooks do attempt to account historically for that famous phenomenon, the Elizabethan theatre—'this unique conception', as Pierre Sonrel[1] calls it, which

---

[1] *Traité de Scénographie*, 1946.

'attained one of the summits of our civilization' and 'at one time might have become the prototype of all European theatres'. They surmise that it was directly developed from 'temporary or removable inn-yard stages', made of barrels or trestles covered with planks. But since no picture or description of any such improvised Elizabethan stage has been found, every element of its scenic arrangement and method of production is still left to speculation.

Yet one thing is certain. No primitive makeshift or barrels and planks could suffice to produce anything like the scenic effects and the 'mighty state' to which the acted Mysteries had for centuries accustomed the Englishman: Mysteries which the guilds were still presenting on their pageant-stages long after public playhouses had been built in London. The Bakers of York performed their Corpus Christi play on their pageant in 1584; the Newcastle plays survived into 1589; *The Destruction of Jerusalem* was acted at Coventry in 1591; the Beverley Corpus Christi plays lasted till 1604; and those of Preston, Lancaster, and Kendal were seen in the reign of James I.[1]

In the face of such comparison, it would be no surprise if the inn-yard stages, which led up to the theatres of the metropolis and co-existed with them, should turn out to have been highly efficient affairs, gorgeously painted, complete with stately scenic 'houses' and properties, and equipped with trap-doors. When Queen Elizabeth observed that the tragedy of *Richard II*—in the emphasis on which she detected the seditious intent of Essex's

---

[1] L. Toulmin Smith, *York Plays* (1885), xxxv, lxvii, lxvi; A. W. Pollard, *English Miracle Plays* (1890), lix; H. C. Gardiner, *Mysteries' End* (1946), 85.

faction—had been 'played forty times in open streets and houses', she was not complaining of trumpery or beggarly buskers. Evidently something noticeably better than a Just So Story of barrels and planks is called for to explain How Shakespeare Got His Stage.

III

THE PAGEANT

PAGEANT, removable medieval stage on wheels, play-wagon. The Elizabethans had it, like their fathers and their grandfathers before them. Not only is this fact thoroughly familiar, but its significance has frequently been pointed out:

The 'body' of pageantry is represented by the car, the introduction of which, in *disguisings* at the court of Henry VII, prepared the way for modern theatrical scenery.[1]

The old platform stage might as readily be styled the pageant stage.[2]

The hint could hardly be made broader: to wit, seek the direct source or prototype of the Elizabethan public stage *in the pageant surviving from the Middle Ages*. When you come to think about it, it seems natural enough, even obvious. Where else would the Elizabethan stage have come from? And yet has anyone, from the days of Capell and Malone to the present moment, in fact followed this conspicuous pointer so far as to scrutinize the theatrical economy of the pageant, and then to compare it with that of the Elizabethan stage? And if not, why not? Have all our minds, in subjection to the tidy pigeon-holers of Hist. and Eng. Lit., filed *Pageant* away under 'Medieval', and left it there?

It may be no accident that it has taken the unacademic imagination of an experienced professional producer of

---

[1] Robert Withington, *English Pageantry* (1918), I. 85.
[2] W. J. Lawrence, *Pre-Restoration Stage Studies* (1927), 251.

Shakespeare to recall us to the right direction. For while some scholars strangely enough would have us trace England's traditional theatre in Baroque pictures from abroad, and others hopefully ask us to father the resourceful Elizabethan stage on a putative makeshift of trestles and planks, Mr W. Bridges-Adams rightly declines to join them in disregarding both tradition and England's long-developed skill in pageant-production. On the contrary, after reminding us that 'every pageant was a little travelling stage bearing its . . . properties, setting . . . and . . . all apparatus necessary', he goes on to give us this sound tip straight from the stable:

if . . . the pageant-cart . . . were stationed at the side or end of an inn-yard that was surrounded by one or more galleries, . . . we have at once the rudiments of the Globe.[1]

Now although the unpredictable Mr Bridges-Adams leaves it at that, fails to follow his own lead, this remains easily the most acute observation in all his very discursive book: and one stirring enough to awaken the dormouse in any mind. But before setting forward along the clear trail he has pointed out, it will be politic first to brush up our small stock of notions about the pageant.

The classic brief *locus*, often quoted, is David Rogers's description in Shakespeare's time of the 'pagiante' or 'cariage' of the Chester Whitsun Plays, thus:

a highe place made like a howse with ij rowmes beinge open on the tope, [in] the lower rowme they apparrelled &

---

[1] *The Irresistible Theatre* (1957), 146. The convincing practicality of this view is missing from Professor F. M. Salter's notion (*Medieval Drama in Chester*, 1955, p. 13) that the pageant-cart blocked the inn-yard's main gate: an excessively unlikely stage-location first imagined by Malone.

dressed them selues, and in the higher rowme they played, and they stoode vpon 6 wheeles.[1]

And we know further that in 1565 the Grocers of Norwich provided for their play a similar 'Howse of Waynskott paynted & buylded on a Carte w^t fowre whelys'.[2] Obviously the stage—the 'higher rowme' for acting—must have stood fairly high to accommodate beneath it the enclosed tiring-house and trap-cellar below deck on the underslung wagon chassis. Further, although often equipped with a high rain-cover-and-sounding-board,[3] the production was medieval, arena-fashion, surrounded by the audience; for Rogers adds, 'beinge all open on the tope, that all behoulders might heare and see them'.

Englishmen likened their method of pageant-production to the ancient one of the Greeks, which George Puttenham describes about 1575 as follows:

The old comedies were plaid in the broad streets vpon wagons or carts vncovered, which carts were floored with bords & made for remouable stages to passe from one streete of their townes to another, where all the people might stand at their ease to gaze vpon the sights.[4]

From Cromwell's time, Sir William Dugdale recalls the stages of the famous Coventry plays:

which pageants, being acted with mighty state and reverence ... had theatres for the several scenes very large and high, placed upon wheels, and drawn to all the eminent parts of the city for the advantage of the spectators.[5]

---

[1] B.M. MS. Harley 1944, f. 22.
[2] R. Fitch, *The Grocers' Play of Norwich*, 1856.
[3] Suggested by Professor Salter, *op. cit.*, 69.
[4] *The Arte of English Poesie* (pr. 1589), Bk. 1, ch. 17.
[5] *The Antiquities of Warwickshire* (1656), 116

And James Wright, quoting the foregoing from Dugdale in his *Historia Histrionica* of 1699, adds the observation that

> plays in England had a beginning much like those of Greece; the Monologues and Pageants, drawn from place to place on wheels, answer exactly to the cart of Thespis.

But nowhere except in Rogers's few phrases and in some doubtful stage-directions in the plays is any light thrown upon the pageants' theatrical economy or technique. We shall have to go farther for our information.

Meanwhile, as we look at it, we realize that plays had not only a beginning, but a continuation on pageant-stages throughout Elizabeth's reign—the open-air wagon-play co-existing with the performance indoors, and commonly presented by the same actors: 'the plaiers with the waggon' (Exeter, 1576–77); 'the Queenes players which played in the colledge churche yarde'; 'a wagon in the pageant' (Gloucester, 1589, 1594); 'a wagon or coache of the Lo: Bartlettes [Berkeley's] players' (Faversham, 1596–97).[1] Dekker's *Satiromastix* reminds 'Horace' (*i.e.*, Ben Jonson), 'Thou hast forgot how thou ambledst . . . by a play-wagon in the high way, and took'st mad Ieronimoes part.' And Middleton's Sir Bounteous Progress, asking the strollers 'Where be your boys?', is assured that 'They come along with the waggon, sir.'[2]

So far indeed from dissolving with the monasteries, the medieval pageants or play-wagons of the better travelling companies evidently rolled on undisturbed through

---

[1] J. T. Murray, *English Dramatic Companies* (1910), 2. 270, 274, 284, 285.
[2] *A Mad World, my Masters*, 5.1.

seventeenth-century England, normal, contemporary, familiar; and, like the London stages, abominated by the Puritan: 'these lewd pagenteeres'.[1]

'Pageants, Theaters, Sceans, and Player-like representations'.[2]

And they likewise rolled into inn-yard playing-places in London. For although some of these inn-yards certainly had permanent scaffolds built against the walls for specta-tor-accommodation, permanent *stages* in *all* of them would doubtless have so encumbered the yards as to make them unusable by the regular carriers. Here re-movable pageant-stages would provide the solution: rolled in only on playing-days.

At the Restoration the Englishman's foible for novelty far-fetched and dear-bought had finally choked his tradi-tional open stage with costly Italianate 'perspectives' detrimental to the drama and ruinous to the management. Fashion, however, in its curious way believed this scene-painter's attempt at optical illusion to be an advance in theatrical art; and we consequently find the stylish Queen Anne wits as contemptuous of the seedy but obstinate survivor of the proud old-time pageant-play as they were of everything 'Gothic' in the arts:

Epping, April 18, 1711. We have now at this Place a Com-pany of Strolers . . . the Stage is here in its Original Situation of a Cart. *Alexander* the Great was acted by a Fellow in a Paper Cravat.[3]

---

[1] John Gee, *New Shreds of the Old Snare* (1624), 16.
[2] William Prynne, *The Antipathie of the English lordly prelacie* (1641), 123.
[3] Richard Steele, *The Spectator*, No. 48.

Ubiquitarians an't please your Honour, the only Performers in *England*, who keep up the original Rules of the
Drama, as 'twas instituted by the mighty *Thespis* our Foun-
der.—Our Heros, Sir, travel in Carts, eat in Carts, sleep in
Carts, and sometimes make their Exit [*sc.* at the Gallows] out
of Carts.[1]

From the flat unraisëd spirits of the coffee-houses we
turn back in relief to Shakespeare's England. Here in his
London the power of dramatic poetry was 'so liuely ex-
pressed and represented vpon the publike stages &
Theaters of this citty, as *Rome* in the *Auge* of her pompe
& glorie, neuer saw it better performed'.[2] And here often
enough it was not only the second-rate troupes which
toured the countryside—the humblest of them upon the
hard hoof, 'glorious vagabonds . . . their fardels on their
backs'—but also the best tragedians of the city. 'How
chances it they travel?' inquires Prince Hamlet. Under
the 'inhibition' imposed after Essex's rebellious 'innovation', Shakespeare's own company had to take the road.
When *Hamlet* was acted 'in the two Vniuersities of Cambridge and Oxford' it was most probably on this tour.
Can one imagine that in such an emergency, or whenever
the all-too-frequent rise of the plague deaths above the
danger-point[3] inexorably closed their theatres, these

---

[1] Captain John Durant de Breval, *The Play is the Plot*, Drury
Lane, 19 February 1717/18.

[2] Sir George Buc, Master of the Revels, *The Third Universitie
of England*, 1615.

[3] Set at thirty a week in 1603; altered to forty about 1607. See
Chambers, *Eliz. Stage*, I. 330–331; and compare

> . . . I dwindle at a Sargent in buffe,
> Almost as much as a new Player does
> At a plague bill certefied forty.
>> Lording Barry, *Ram-Alley* (1611), sig. F4.

leading metropolitan companies were caught unprovided with play-wagons to present at least a part of their repertory in the provinces? Certainly, when fair-crowds or market throngs offered a rich harvest, town halls were not always so readily available as inn-yards.

Like the circus still parading in triumph today, the prime tragedians' four- or six-horse pageants, splendid in crimson and gold, martial with trumpets and drums, came sounding into town—manned by players from 'the stately and our more than Romaine Cittie Stages': 'with banners spred . . . thy souldiers marcht like players, With garish robes'.[1]

Gorgeous, gaudy, gilded, painted, pompous, glorious, triumphant: thus the English poets portrayed the Pageant.[2] The three rolling pageants, each drawn by four horses, which Dekker designed for the Lord Mayor's Show in 1612, he calls 'triumphs'. For the Italians, Florio echoes with '*Arcotriomphante*, a pageant or triumphant charriot', and Torriano with '*Carro-triomphale*, a pageant'; for the Dutch with their *wagenspel* or pageant-play, Sewel offers 'Pageant, *een triomfwagen*'; and finally, the City Council of Madrid describes the theatrical pageants for presenting the *autos sacramentales* as '*los carros triunfales*'.[3]

Triumph, carro-triomphale, triomfwagen, carro triunfale: these significant appellations at long last reveal the meaning of Captain Tucca's threats of the havoc he will

---

[1] Marlowe, *Edward II*, 984–986.

[2] Joshua Poole, *England's Parnassus* (1657), 141.

[3] See N. D. Shergold and J. E. Varey, ' "Autos Sacramentales" in Madrid, 1644', *Hispanic Review* XXVI (1958), 52. Dr Varey tells me that the pageants trace their name to Petrarch's *Trionfi*.

make of the players' property, if they dare to satirize him on their Bankside stage:

an you stage me, stinkard, your mansions shall sweat for 't, your tabernacles, varlets, your *Globes*, and your *Triumphs*.[1]

For we realize only now that it is not merely the stage of 'the *Globe*, the Glory of the *Banke*', with its rich hangings making *mansions* and *tabernacles* which the raging Tucca will wreck, but their pageants, their Triumphs, their lofty rolling 'ships' for the road as well:

> argosies with portly sail—
> ... the pageants of the sea—
> Do overpeer the petty traffickers.

Let the strutting insolent stiff-toe beware, or he will leave him ne'er a hollow stage whereon to stalk and

> To hear the wooden dialogue and sound
> 'Twixt his stretch'd footing and the scaffoldage.

Plainly, it is time we made an effort to visualize Shakespeare's play-wagons, and in as much detail as we can. To come closer to understanding how he employed these medieval theatres of his—which in one fabric combined dressing-room, trap-cellar, and open stage with built-up multiple scenes for action 'within' and 'above'—this means getting down to practicalities.

First of all, size. Although—as we shall see—the great contemporary play-wagons of Spain measured more than 23 English feet long, these were eight-wheeled constructions designed to be moved only on streets within the city. It is to be doubted that ponderous wagons of such a length would stand up to prolonged rough travel over

---

[1] Jonson, *The Poetaster* (1601), 3.4.193.

English roads. We cannot assume that the tourers' pageants, the Thespian 'triumphs' of England, reached proportions so majestic. Yet the perennial problem was to provide a stage ample enough to accommodate two-storied 'houses', castles, or scenes for entrance and exit at its two ends, and also open platform between sufficient for an army to 'march about the stage', fight, lay siege to battlemented walls. For that, even a length of 23 foot is too little.

A practical solution which does not demand a wagon as long as the Spanish *carros* obviously remains. Build *a pair* of wagons more wieldy—say 15 or at most 16 foot long—each with a curtainable openwork 'house' or castle *at one end*, and the rest clear deck: the whole covering the understage tiring-house or trap-cellar. Roll the two together with the square deck-ends meeting flush, and you have it: your two scenes for entrance or for action 'within', fronting each other from the ends left and right as backgrounds, and your stage lying open for manoeuvre between them. In a word, each of your wagons is a demi-pageant or half-stage for production in the amphi-theatrical or circus manner of tradition.

I say 'practical' advisedly, because we shall see that this very method was what the Spaniards expertly employed with the *medios carros*. And had not the same been in use also in England from medieval days? As Pollard noted,

in some cases, e.g. in that of the *Trial of Christ*, for the proper performance of a play two scaffolds would be required, and the actors would go from one to another, as between the judgment halls of Pilate and Herod.[1]

---

[1] *Op. cit.*, xxvi.

Among others, the familiar Towneley *Second Shepherds'*
Play presents a similar case, its characters moving from
the action in Mak's house, at one end of the conjoined
stage, to that in the Bethlehem stable standing in opposition at the other.

It would be naive to suppose the better Elizabethan
touring companies unable to afford more than a single
play-wagon. The players of Lord Eure,[1] for example,
were certainly not a company at all comparable either in
rank or means with the King's men or the Admiral's men.
But even this minor troupe, when I find them at Stourbridge in Worcestershire early in 1610, had 'cartes &
waggens' which are not mentioned as anything excep-
tional:

the plaiers with theire apparell drumm & trumpettes cartes &
waggens being then at theire said Inne [viz[t] the Crowne].[2]

Here we have the actors with their play-wagons or removable stages—*not* 'boards and barrel-heads'—and not
presumed but actually reported in the inn-yard of the
Crown at Stourbridge. The discerning suggestion
thrown out by Mr Bridges-Adams begins to look more
and more like a perception of historical fact.

Rogers's all too brief and summary sketch of the
English pageants' theatrical economy finds illuminating
definition in neglected reports of the contemporary *carros
de representación*, the unsurpassed pageant-stages of
Spain: Spain, the other country of Europe which fostered

---

[1] 'the servantes & plaiers of the right honourable the Lord
Euery'—*i.e.*, Ralph third Lord Eure, of New Malton, Yorkshire,
Lord President of Wales and the Marches.
[2] P.R.O., Sta. Cha. 8/307/14.

a popular theatre, alive with a national drama in literary stature second only to England's, and very similar to it; Spain, whose stage like England's was still medieval, traditional, unaffected by either humanistic or perspective notions out of Italy. Seduced or bemused by these later scenic impositions, most historians of the English stage have to their loss overlooked the one important contemporary theatre closely related to Shakespeare's: namely, Lope de Vega's.

Our first account in Elizabethan times of a contemporary Spanish pageant comes from Alcalá, 1568. Francisco de las Cuebas describes the staging of his *Representación de los martires Justo y Pastor*. This they were able to present on a single play-wagon with portals or scenes at its two ends:

a pageant or mobile castle was made . . . it measured in width ten feet [9 ft. 2 in. English] and more, and in length seventeen feet [15 ft. 7 in. English] . . .

To come up on this floor [*i.e.*, the open stage for acting] were two portals with stairs descending into the same pageant (and since it was enclosed on all sides, from no point could be seen where the players went down into and entered from a room made inside the pageant): all built upon the same two axles whereon turned the four wheels by which the whole pageant moved.[1]

---

[1] 'se hizo un carro o castello movedizo . . . tenia de ancho diez pies y mas y de largo diez y siete . . .

'para subir en este suelo auia dos puertas y escaleras que cayan en el mesmo carro que por estar zerrado por todas partes y por ninguna parte se beian por donde baxaban y salian los representantes de un aposento que dentro del carro se hazia, fundado todo sobre los mismos dos exes donde iban las quatro ruedas con que todo el carro mouia.' Quoted from an MS. in the Bibl. Nac. Madrid by Erich Schmidt, *Die Darstellung des spanischen Dramas vor Lope de Rueda* (Berlin 1935), 43–44.

The Spaniard has here made specific what Rogers left us to infer: namely, the two scenic portals for entrance facing each other from the ends of the stage. These concealed the openings of the trap-stairs leading up from the understage *vestuario*—Rogers's 'lower rowme' in which 'they apparrelled & dressed them selues'.

For a season each year Spain's leading companies closed their *corrales*, their open-air patio amphitheatres, to produce their magnificent Corpus Christi *comedias* on pageants in the city streets. And by the beginning of the seventeenth century their *medios carros* had grown to such a size that two of them joined end to end provided a stage even longer than the 43-foot one of London's new Fortune Theatre.

As so often happens, for really informative descriptions we must thank not the natives but foreign visitors: in this instance a Portuguese and an Englishman. In June of 1605, a few months before England's Gunpowder Treason, these two were present in crowded Valladolid. The great occasion was His Most Catholic Majesty's entertainment of England's ambassador Lord Nottingham, sent by James to restore relations after hostilities a generation long.

Both these visitors witnessed, among other grand festivities, the skilful pageant-production of the Corpus Christi *autos sacramentales*; and here is what the Portuguese gentleman reported:

This evening (and all this octave) there are public plays; and they give the comedians a thousand ducats to go presenting them in the streets before all those of the King's Council, the Municipal Government, and other dignitaries, in front of their windows; and for this they have their great pageants, each of 34 *palmos* [23 ft. 4 in. English] long; and putting two together, they perform very conveniently [*i.e.*, with plenty of room]; and at their ends they have houses and towers excellently painted and in part gilded, and rooms from which they enter [on the stage]; and thus they go through the whole city.[1]

This important account finds its corroboration, with fascinating structural detail, in the companion-piece by the anonymous English follower of Lord Nottingham. So far as I am aware, this second description is unknown to historians of the Spanish theatre. I find it preserved only in a Dutch version published in Antwerp, of which I attempt a re-translation, as follows:

Their Pageant-stages (*or* Theatres) are very strongly made. There was built of wood all together (*or* in one fabric) one half of a pageant: at the one end an enclosed room, like a house with a room above it, and a stair to go up into it. The lowest room [*i.e.*, *the cellar or tiring-house*] had a door for entrances, opening in a rather broad gallery. For support underneath they had iron tie-bars with wheels; they draw them along the streets with men. So that two of these, being brought together, made a complete Pageant-stage (Theatre) with a four-sided house at each end; and there the Players made themselves ready, and [had] handsome room to come forth to act.

---

[1] 'Esta tarde e todo este oitavario ha comedias publicas, e dão aos comediantes mil ducados pelas andar reprezentando por las calles a todos os do Conselho real, Regimento e outras pessoas, diante das suas janellas; e para isso têm seus carros grandes, que cada hum tem 34 palmos, e ajuntando dous reprezentam muy dezembaraçadamente, e nas cabeças têm casas e torres muy bem pintadas e douradas em partes e apozentos de que sahem, e assim correm toda a cidade.' Thomé Pinheiro da Veiga, *Fastiginia* (see B.M. MS. Addl. 20812), pr. Oporto, Bibl. Publ. Municipal, *Collecção de manuscriptos inéditos agora dados á estampa* III (1911), 117.

There were five or six of these, and every pageant 4 pair of wheels to roll it away.[1]

Later, as Drs N. D. Shergold and J. E. Varey have authoritatively shown, the two lengthy *medios carros* gave way to shorter ones supplemented by a third, an open stage on wheels (*carrillo*), set between them: 'When the *auto* was performed the two *medios carros* were placed facing each other, with a *carrillo* set between them; the three carts were in line.'[2]

For vividness nothing can equal the eye-witness report. And here the age-old twin-pageant production is brought before us in its living technique. What strikes us at once—upsetting our modern fixed Italianate idea of a theatre—is that this is a production 'in the round'. This stately stage has not been rolled together against any *background*, but in front of wealthy *spectators* filling the 'stage boxes' and 'lords' rooms' of a Councillor's or a President's house. The performance is given specifically

---

[1] 'Haer Speelhuysen zijn seer sterck gemaect. Daer waren [*sic*] gebouwt van hout een heelft van een huys heel te gader, aen deen eynde een gesloten ruymte, gelijck een huys met een ruymte daer over, ende eenen steeger om daer op te gaen. De leechste ruymte hadde een deur om wt te gaen welcke quam in een galderie wat breet[.] om haer te dragen hadden sy onder yseren banden ende wielen welcke sy dragen lancx de straeten by mannen. So dat twee van dese tsamen ghebrocht zijnde maeckten een heel Speelhuys met een viercant huys aen elck eynde, ende daer de Speelders haer selve gereedt maecten ende schone ruymte om voort te comen om te speelen. Daer waren van dese vijf of ses, ende een yeder speelhuys .4. paer wielen om haer wech te voeren.'
Waerachtich verhael Van de Reyse van den Ambassadeur van Engelant naer Spaignen . . . Ghemaect by een Engelsman die mede geweest is, in Engelsch, ende uyt het Engelsch overgheset in Duyts. Tot Antwerpen . . . 1605. Sig. A3ᵛ.
[2] For this and a wealth of new material with contemporary graphic illustration, see their important paper cited above.

for him, his family, relations, and friends, on show in their richest dresses from his great balcony-windows, facing the stage's near or front side. Seated in state, flanked by his 'court', the dignitary symbolizes the King or Judge, hearing the dramatic conflict between Heaven on his right and Hell on his left:

right and wrong—
Between whose endless jar justice resides.

Thronging both the street behind the pageants and the windows and roofs opposite, the people can behold the glittering 'court' of *gente principal* across the open stage. That is one feast for their privileged eyes. The other is their excellent view from the back of the play's action, the actors playing mainly to the 'best seats'.[1]

The high-standing stage formed by the twin wagons is more than 46 foot long, supported on 16 wheels, and set at its ends with richly-painted *décor simultané* presenting at least two distinct localities for action: towers or two-storied houses, fronting the open stage between. Estimate the width of the stage at 14 foot, allow the opposed scenic houses a good 8 foot of depth each, and you have the neutral area left clear between them measuring 30 by 14 foot, on which one may certainly act *muy edʒembaraçadamente*.

The crush of populace in the street below makes it not merely convenient but obligatory for the actors to have

---

[1] 'Les deux bandes de Comediens, qui sont à Madrid, ferment . . . leurs Theatres, & passent un Mois à representer de ces pieces saintes. Ils le font en Public . . . devant la Maison du President de quelque Conseil. . . . les Acteurs joüent le dos tourné à l'Assemblée, qui est dans la Place.' [Frans van Aerssen], *Voyage d'Espagne* (1666), 142–143, 'De la representation des Autos, ou Comedies spirituelles.'

their tiring-house *in the pageant*—that is, under the stage.[1] To enter on the stage, they come up inside one of their opposed houses, which are built in the Spanish fashion. Its ground-front is a broad open pillared gallery, familiar in Lope de Vega's stage-directions as *el corredor*. This can be hung round about with retractable curtains and furnished to present action as passing 'within'. Above, supported by the *balahustes* or turned posts of the *corredor*, opens the great window or balcony of the house, reached by the stair mentioned in the Englishman's report. This upper story is the *alto*, the upper stage for action 'above', 'at the window', or 'on the walls'— sometimes at one end of the stage only, sometimes at both.

Utterly unlike the 'scenic wall' of the classical stage, or the broad back-drop of our picture-stage (which today closes off what in Elizabethan times was the main 'front' of spectator-boxes), the pageant-setting is plastic, the performance amphitheatrical, in the round. Since the audience encloses both its long sides, this open stage evidently presents no pictorial *fondo*, no flat unifying scenic wall containing doors, for two-dimensional acting, no upstage, no downstage. What it affords instead is the perfect symbolic arena for dramatic conflict. High opposing 'houses' seen in profile, facing each other from Stage Left and Stage Right: glorified corner-stools for protagonists meeting in the theatrical prize-ring. It is in short a stage for drama, a stage for actors. It is not a painter's

---

[1] The *carros* designed for Seville in 1594 by the city architect Juan del Río de Zelaya were each fitted with an understage dressing-room. See B. W. Wardropper, *Introducción al Teatro Religioso del Siglo de Oro* (1953), 56.

framed picture, a unified *tableau* with lay-figures prettily grouped.

Striking illustration of the kind of houses built for the conflict of Good and Evil on these *medios carros*—some of them 'discoverable' for action 'within'—comes from Seville in Shakespeare's time:

In a half-pageant is to be a great house—into which all the company of this *auto* go—with its turrets, spires, and pinnacles, in the which are to be painted attributes of grace and virtues . . . also this house is to have four-square hangings [*i.e.*, a traverse, curtains hung round about for 'discovery'] of suitable height and breadth. (*El Mesón del Alma,* presented by Alonso Riquelme, 1607.) [1]

In the other half-pageant, there is to be another castle, infernal, painted with devils and horrid monsters, and in the midst a frightful Hell-Mouth: and at the sides two doors, the World painted on the one, the Flesh on the other. (*La Nave mercenaria,* presented by Nicolás de los Ríos, 1609.) [2]

And Calderón later prescribes 'discovery' similarly for the demi-pageants presenting his *El Diablo Mudo*:

when the verses are spoken, a celestial globe opens, which shall be one of the pageants . . . The other pageant opens, which shall be a terrestrial globe.[3]

---

[1] 'En un medio carro a de aver una casa grande, donde van toda la compañía deste auto, con sus torres, chapiteles, y remates en la quala de yr pintada atributos de la gracia y virtudes . . . item esta casa a de tener lienzos en quadrado con la largura y anchura que le convenga.' Qu. José Sánchez Arjona, *El Teatro en Sevilla* (1887), 302.

[2] 'En el otro medio carro, A de aver otro castillo, infernal, pintado de dimonios y bestiglos y en medio una boca de infierno espantable y á los lados dos puertas, en la una pintado el mundo, en la otra la carne.' *Ibid.,* 304.

[3] 'cuando lo dicen los versos se abre un globo celeste, que será uno de los carros . . . Ábrese el otro, que será un globo terrestre.' Qu. A. A. Parker, *Allegorical Drama of Calderón* (1943), 99.

Now, with the clear features of the Spanish contemporary pageant-production fresh in mind, let us shift the scene to England: to a spacious carriers' inn-yard lined with galleries—say the Crown at Stourbridge. Though the scale here is less magnificent than it is in the streets of Valladolid, every principle, every element of theatrical arrangement remains the same.

Before the performance the players rolled their ship-like wagons, their two lofty demi-pageants, together to make one continuous stage, with companion-ways rising from the tiring-house hold below into the opposed end-castles. They have placed them close to the 'front' of choice galleries: those at the southwest, shaded from the afternoon sun and therefore reserved with seats for the gentry and other high-paying patrons. The less important elements of the audience also are placed where their counterparts are found in Spain. The Valladolid street-crowds behind the *carros*' outer side are matched here by the press of 'understanders' or penny stinkards choking the yard behind the wagons; and the thronged windows and roofs across the Spanish street, by the Crown's opposite galleries, all packed full of people, even though the sun is right in their eyes.

Naturally, here too the actors are playing primarily to the best seats, the 'front' of galleries alongside their high stage, which are in effect stage-boxes below and a 'lords room' above. The yard behind, and the cheaper distant galleries, must get what they can. Fair is fair; those who pay highest should receive most. But the skill of the players appears in the uncanny way in which they manage to provide enough all round to keep every part of the house satisfied.

AN INN-YARD PAGEANT PERFORMANCE

Ask the business manager of these actors playing for their bread, and he will tell you that this arrangement, which provides an advantageous sector of seats 'in the stage's front' fetching top prices, is imperative. Chewing upon that, we shall not unconsciously pull their stage about to suit our Italianate prejudice, and ignorantly imagine those actors taking one of the gallery-lined walls to form a 'scenic wall' for their stage, thereby precluding their best profit. (As readily picture a hard-pressed theatre today turning the highest-paying section of orchestra stalls into an enlarged acting-area.) For to deny that 'front' to spectators is to lose money which cannot be made up. There are no other excellent seats near the stage to sell. Those in the galleries opposite are second-rate—farther from the performance than the 'understanders' in the yard. And anyhow, why take a wall? What conceivable need could the players have for a wall? Everything they require—dressing-room, scenes, doors, stage—is built into the pageants.

If we were to follow these players further on their tour we should learn that the play-wagons were not confined to performances in inn-yards open to the sky. Great stone tithe-barns also offered amphitheatres for their pageant-productions. In bad weather or for a performance at night they afforded welcome shelter. Several of these ancient barns survive today. One example is the Tithe Barn of Buckland Abbey, the Devon home of Sir Francis Drake. In this barn (which measures 120 by 30 foot) the Friends of Buckland Abbey have made a practice of presenting plays.

The form of these barns is a spacious oblong hall. In the middles of the two long sides, great wagon-doors

open opposite each other. Roll the pageant-stages together in this central cross-alley, admit the public into the
two ends of the barn, and your amphitheatre is complete.
Apropos such wagon-plays in barns, we find Tom Dekker chaffing poets and players for

making fooles of the poore country people, in driuing them
. . . to sit cackling in an old barne . . . vpon this ancient
Theater you present your Tragicall Sceines, for here you shall
be sure to be clapt . . . you make but a hungry liuing of it by
strowting [strutting] vp and downe after the *Waggon*.[1]

And Middleton's *Mayor of Quinborough* (5.1.77–78):

I wold faine see yᵉ proudest hee lend a Barne to em: now
sirs are you Comedians?

More than a hundred years later, when (as we have seen)
Dick Steele reported of the poor company of strollers at
Epping that 'the Stage is here in its Original Situation of
a Cart', he added that 'they have had a full Barn for many
Days together'—showing where the wagon-play was still
finding its amphitheatre in the days of Queen Anne.

What has our search yielded us so far? It has given us
our first comprehensive view of the pageant method of
production, as it was perfected through centuries of practice. We now see that for wagon-plays in streets, barns,
and inn-yards, the audience was divided by the stage into
two confronted auditories. Spectators enclosed the open
oblong stage on both sides; and the front of seats close
to the pageant was manifestly the best and most expensive
side. By its very nature, this open-stage or amphitheatrical arrangement made any unified background impossible.

---

[1] *Iests to make you merrie*, 1607.

There could be no 'scenic wall'. Instead, *multiple backgrounds* were provided by the scenic 'houses' facing each other from the ends of the stage. From these the players, having come up from the tiring-house under the stage, made their entrances.

IV

THE PUBLIC STAGE

UNFAMILIAR as most features of this pageant-technique seem to us today, we must remember that it was all second nature to the Elizabethans, as it had been to the generations which had gone before. Remember, too, that theirs was the English stage; and that the un-dramatic alien picture-stage which we have adopted would strike them as both limited and remote—as indeed the bitter objections to its first introduction (at Oxford in 1605) show. Bringing their pageant-technique to light once again in the twentieth century is in fact no more than a 'restitution of decayed intelligence'—restoring for-gotten knowledge. But the differences between our modern Italianate stage, born of the alien opera, and the Elizabethan public stage, born of the native pageant, are as striking as they are fundamental. Let us consider what one or two of them imply.

To begin with, we unconsciously think of the actors' dressing-room as located somewhere backstage. This fixed idea, correct enough today, has prevented us from realizing that to the Elizabethan mind it was *not* back-stage. For them, the dressing-room was normally situ-ated where it then was (and had always been) located in the pageant—that is, in the cellar, *under* the stage. We have failed to notice that the Tudor and Stuart poets significantly applied the same epithets to their stage as they did to a ship, a shell, a sepulchre: that they wrote of the '*hollow* stage', the '*vaulty* stage'.[1]

---

[1] Poole, *op. cit.*, s.v. Stage.

This Stage, the Ship, vpon whose Decke
The seas tost *Pericles* appeares to speake.
Enter [from below] *Pericles a Shipboard.*[1]

And for them, to mention 'the grave' or 'the sepulchre'
in a theatrical context infallibly conjures up the hollow,
half-lit tiring-house underfoot:

The *stage* . . .
Prepar'd it selfe thy *Sepulcher* to be.[2]

So play thy part . . .
Then when th' art in the tiring-house of earth . . .[3]

Mutes . . . wear good clothes for attendance, yet all have
exits, and must all be stripped in the tiring-house (viz. the
grave) . . .[4]

T'untire vs then retire we to our tombe
Where all's put of we tooke from mothers wombe.[5]

His play now ended, thinke his graue to be
The retiringe howse of this his tragedye . . .[6]

. . . now that he gone is to the graue
(Deaths publique tyring-house) . . .

Wee wondred (Shake-speare) that thou went'st so soone
From the Worlds-Stage, to the Graues-Tyring-roome.[7]

---

[1] *The Play of Pericles Prince of Tyre* (1609), sig. E^v.
[2] William Habington, 'An Elegy upon the Death of Ben.
Iohnson', *Jonsonus Virbius*, 1638.
[3] John Davies of Hereford on Robert Armin, Shakespeare's
fellow-actor. *The Scourge of Folly*, 1610.
[4] William Rowley, Dedication to *A Fair Quarrel*, 1617.
[5] Anon., expansion of the familiar lines beginning 'What is our
Life?' attributed to Sir Walter Ralegh. B.M. MS. Addl. 10309,
f. 125^v.
[6] 'An Epitaph on Mr Burbige'. Bodl. MS. Rawl. Poet. 117, f. 25.
[7] Hugh Holland and I[ames] M[abbe] on William Shakespeare,
in the First Folio, 1623.

THE GLOBE'S STAGE, SEEN FROM THE NORTHEAST (CHEAPER) GALLERY

If we ask why the dressing-room of the Elizabethan theatre continued under the stage as it was in the pageants, the answer is, because the production was similarly amphitheatrical: the method most *efficient* in bringing the largest number of hearers close to the actors; the method most *economical* in not wasting the best audience-space on 'backstage production areas' which yield not a penny of revenue. Since there was no reason to change, and every reason for not changing, Shakespeare's stage still had the audience reciprocally placed on both its long sides. What we today call the 'back' was in those days 'the stage's front', devoted to the best and most expensive seats.

Their cellar-situated tiring-house makes a difference both radical and revealing in the matter of stage-entrances. For where today an actor thinks of a stage as a three-walled room into which he walks from a level backstage, the Elizabethan actor saw the stage as the flat roof over his dressing-room. To employ Shakespeare's own terms, he was in the *cellarage*, and had to get to the *scaffoldage*. To this deck he climbed, mounted, or ascended to make his entrance, just as he did in the pageant.

> Emperour, king, and kaiser [Time]
> Doth mount vpon the stage.[1]
>
> I that obscur'd haue fled the Sceane of Fame . . .
> Now mount the Theater of this our age.[2]
>
> And now that I haue vaulted vp so hye
> Aboue the Stage-rayles of this earthen Globe,
> I must turne Actor. . . .[3]

---

[1] Richard Robinson, *A Golden Mirrour*, 1589.
[2] Thomas Lodge, Induction to *Phillis*, 1593.
[3] T[homas] M[iddleton], *The Blacke Booke* (1604), sig. Bᵛ.

Our sharpest wittes, that climbe the sceane of fame . . .[1]

Having shewed my selfe once before upon the stage . . . In mounting up thus soon againe . . .[2]

While soc *or* buskin *shall ascend the Stage.*[3]

't is not our business here to mount a Stage . . .[4]

Stage. . . . Others [draw it] from the AS *Stigan*, the Teut. *Steigen*, or the Belg. *Steeghen*, *Stüghen*, to go up.[5]

Mount up upon the stage, climb the scene, mount the theatre, ascend the stage. These common iterations re-build for us the hollow stage which Shakespeare knew. They drive home to our minds something we have never even suspected, namely that before 'going on' the player normally found himself under the boards, below deck. This now at length explains J. Cocke's witty word for 'A common Player'—'he *playes above board*'.[6]

In brief, just as always in the pageant, in the theatre the stage and tiring-house made one fabric. The first was the roof or ceiling of the second. Think of the tiring-house as a box whose flat cover was the stage. Only when we have this picture unmistakably clear in mind are we at length equipped to understand the contract for building the Fortune Theatre. In all its essentials the square Fortune was modelled on the round Globe—recently completed, and built by the same carpenter, Peter Street.

In re-reading the terms of this agreement, only now for

---

[1] Robert Roche, *Eustathia, or the Constancie of Susanna* (1599), sig. A5.

[2] Philemon Holland's *Pliny* (1601), The Preface to the Reader.

[3] James Howell's verses to Ben Jonson. *Letters* (ed. Jacobs), 45–46.

[4] *Divine Poems* (Anon., 17th c.) Bodl. MS. Eng. poet. e. 51, p. 3.

[5] *Gazophylacium Anglicanum*, 1689.

[6] John Stephens, *Essayes and Characters*, 1615.

the first time can we approximately visualize this play-house. The contract clearly stipulates two main constructions—a 'howse' and a 'Stadge'. Specified first is the 'howse': a square frame, 80 foot each way outside and 55 foot each way inside, enclosing a yard. This frame is to 'conteine three Stories in heighth' of specified dimensions, to be divided into galleries, 'gentlemens roomes', and 'Twoe pennie roomes', and fitted with outside 'Stearcases to be covered with Tyle'. Not a word about any tiring-house to be contained anywhere in this fabric.

Then comes the second building—the stage-and-tiring-house, to be erected inside the square yard of the first construction:

a Stadge and Tyreinge howse to be made, erected & settupp within the said Frame, with a shadowe or cover over the saide Stadge.

No question but that 'within the said Frame' means *'in the enclosed yard'*. It *cannot* mean 'inside the house', where we have unwarrantably presumed the tiring-house to be; for to talk of *erecting the platform stage inside the house* would be complete nonsense.

The same two distinct constructions, (*a*) house, and (*b*) tiring-house-and-stage, are specified in the contract for the Hope Theatre, 1613. For this playhouse, since its yard was to be cleared on some days of the week for bull- and bear-baiting, the stage-and-tiring-house had to be made removable. Here it is stipulated that Gilbert Katherens the carpenter shall

newly erect, builde, and sett vpp one . . . Plaiehouse . . . and also a fitt and convenient Tyre house and a stage to be carried or taken awaie, and to stande vppon tressells.[1]

---

[1] *Henslowe Papers* (ed. W. W. Greg), 1907.

Thus both contracts distinguish the two fabrics:

Fortune: (*a*) howse (Frame) (*b*) Stadge and Tyreinge howse
(Stadge . . . with windowes
. . . to the . . . Tyreinge
howse)
Hope: (*a*) Plaiehouse (*b*) a Tyre house and a stage to
be . . . taken awaie

The separation of the second fabric from the 'house' in both contracts in itself lays bare our universal error. In defiance of these explicit terms we managed to suppose that the tiring-house was *not* 'erected & settupp' *together with the stage*, but somehow contrived in the already-built house, 'behind' the stage. Prejudice can play strange tricks with our minds.

The contracts thus demonstrate once again that tiring-house and stage are integral, as they are in the pageant: the stage roofs the tiring-house, and is itself protected against rain by a lofty 'shadow' or 'cover' supported—except at the Hope—on two tall pillars.

Now compare these two distinct fabrics, (*a*) house, and (*b*) stage-cum-tiring-house, respectively with (*a*) a galleried inn enclosing a square yard, and (*b*) a pageant-stage, rolled together at one side of the yard, comprising its own cellar or tiring-house, and covered high overhead with a 'top'. The similarity is complete, the generic and evolutionary connection palpable.

To look south across the sea to Madrid—where in the Corral de la Cruz (built 1579) and the Corral del Príncipe (built 1582) Spaniards were acting the same kind of drama as the English in open-air *coliseos*, amphitheatres closely similar to London's Globe and Fortune—is to find precisely this same arrangement. The tiring-house is under the stage: 'under the stage, which they call the lower tiring-house' (Cruz); 'in the first or chief *corredor* [pillared stage-house or "scene"] over the tiring-house' (Príncipe); 'the beam . . . over the tiring-house which should extend across the stage' (Príncipe). And the two great pillars supporting the 'shadow' or 'cover' (*texado*) go down to the ground through the stage (*tablado*) and tiring-house (*vestuario*).[1]

The reason why in addition to the *vestuario bajo* under the stage the Spanish theatres had another tiring-house above (*vestuario alto*) within the theatre-building, is that unlike the English they had actresses. This additional and removed dressing-room was required to accommodate the women.

Like the English theatres, the *corrales* of necessity had a property-dock within the building alongside the stage, like that shown in the incomplete drawing of the Swan labelled *mimorum aedes*, through whose great folding-doors they brought on large properties such as beds, chariots, or gibbets, and 'entered' crowds or armies on to the stage.

Now to return to the Fortune contract. From the most

---

[1] 'debaxo de la representazion que llaman bistuario baxo' . . . 'En el corredor primero encima del bestuario' . . . 'la viga . . . encima del vestuario que atrauiessa el tablado de la representacion' 'el armadura alta [del texado]' 'los dos pies deuajo del tablado' 'devajo del vestuario los dos pies principales'.

These important entries of repairs to the *corrales* in 1641 and 1642 are among the rich materials from the municipal archives of Madrid, knowledge of which we owe to Dr N. D. Shergold. They are extracted here from pages 23, 28, 35, 46, 30, and 5 of his indispensable work 'Nuevos documentos sobre los corrales de comedias de Madrid en el siglo XVII' published in the *Revista de la Biblioteca, Archivo y Museo* del Ayuntamiento de Madrid, Año XX, Núm. 61–62 (1951).

THE SWAN PLAYHOUSE
From the contemporary sketch after Johannes de Witt.

protected and shaded inner side of the house-frame with its 'gentlemens roomes' and 'Twoe pennie roomes', the stage extends forward 'to the middle of the yarde' (*i.e.*, $27\frac{1}{2}$ foot), and 'shall conteine in length Fortie and Three foote'. That is, it takes up with its long sides 43 of the total 55-foot width of the yard, leaving clear beyond its ends two alleys of six foot in width. Similar alleys at the stage-ends are shown also in the unfinished de Witt sketch of the Swan. One necessary purpose of these alleys now becomes evident: to give light to the end-windows of the understage tiring-house or cellarage. For the stage is to be paled in below with oaken boards, and is to be 'contryved and fashioned like vnto the Stadge of the said Plaie howse called the Globe; *With convenient windowes and lightes glazed to the saide Tyreinge howse*' (italics mine).

Some of these convenient lights must also have been let into the long yard-wall of the tiring-house or cellar. Two such windows—mistaken hitherto for supports—are indicated under the stage in the de Witt sketch.[1] To make the most of the light admitted to the low-pitched cellar by its windows on these three sides, its cover—the stage—was to be ceiled underneath and rendered with lime or whitewash:

the said Peeter Streete shall not be chardged with . . . seeling [with lathe, lyme & haire] anie more or other roomes then the gentlemens roomes, Twoe pennie roomes and Stadge before remembred.

---

[1] The stage-and-tiring-house of the Swan (like those of the Globe and the Fortune) was a fixed construction, as the great pillars supporting the 'cover' show. The only removable stage-and-tiring-house in a regular playhouse of which we know was that of the already-mentioned Hope, taken away on bear-baiting days.

To recapitulate: the new, illuminating, revolutionizing fact which must be rehearsed and dwelt upon until it can be realized is the *pageant-principle* of the Elizabethan stage. To make their entrances from the opposed scenes or houses, the players 'ascended the stage' by trap-stairs near the corners of the oblong cellar or tiring-house beneath. Like the pageant, the stage-cum-tiring-house was a separate construction, self-contained and about five foot high, lighted with windows in three of its walls, its fourth side communicating with the lower property-dock inside the 'frame' or 'house'. Since their tiring-house was underneath, they were not forced to sacrifice the excellent side adjoining the stage to a 'scenic wall' and tiring-room (as we have always mistakenly imagined), but kept it as the best spectator-side: for the crowd of stool-holders in front of the property-dock wall, for stage-boxes alongside, for gentlemen's or lords' rooms and twopenny rooms above,[1] and for the third gallery at the top.

As it was in the descriptions of the Globe–Fortune and of the Swan–Hope just cited, this fact will be driven home to our minds once again when we come to consider the orientation of the Boar's Head, Whitechapel—an important and veteran inn-yard playhouse with spectator-galleries built up against all its four sides. For here we shall find specified 'the stage tireinge howse & galleries on the west side of the great yarde' . . . 'the saide weste galleryes over the said stage'.

For the moment, however, let us pursue a little farther

---

[1] 'come and sit in the two-pennie galleries amongst the gentlemen', Dekker, *Seven Deadly Sins*, 1606; 'where (as if you sat in the moste perspicuous place of the two-pennie gallerie in a Play House) you shall clearly . . . beholde all the partes'. *Ravens Almanacke*, 1609.

our scrutiny of the Elizabethan actors mounting up from below to play 'above board'. Traps, 'cuts', 'risings', or openings in the Elizabethan stage are nothing new. We have always known that players did customarily 'ascend the theatre' from the cellarage when they appeared through traps on the open stage as spirits, devils, or ghosts:

Thus farre the *Prologue*, who leauing the Stage cleare, the feares that are bred in the wombe of this altring kingdome do next step vp, *acting* thus . . .[1]

> Lucifer *ascending, as Prologue to his owne Play.*
> Now is Hell landed here vpon the Earth,
> When *Lucifer*, in limbes of burning gold,
> Ascends this dustie *Theater* of the world.[2]

> . . . where man's breath,
> Desert, and guilty blood ascend the stage.[3]

But what we have not known is that *all* actors in human roles, in order to appear on the stage in or from the localized 'scenes', had to come up from below, as they did in the pageants.

From the tiring-house the 'risings' or trap-steps led up into the 'houses' near the ends of the stage: *e.g.*, in William Percy's *Necromantes* (1602), Gelanthis and Melanthis ascend *to either end of the stage from within.* This facility afforded the characters' entrances a variety of treatments. Since each 'house' was—as we shall see—an open framework of posts and rails hung round about with

---

[1] Dekker, *The Wonderfull Yeare, 1603,* ?1603.
[2] T[homas] M[iddleton], *The Blacke Booke* (1604), sig. B.
[3] John Fletcher, *Four Plays in One* (pr. 1647), Prologue to *The Triumph of Death.*

retractable curtains, it could be variously employed. For example:

Left open, with curtains drawn back, it would repre-

TIRING-HOUSE, 'HOUSE', AND 'ABOVE'

sent an 'interior'. The player would mount through the hatchway or tiring-house door in full view of the surrounding audience—a character coming up into a room from downstairs: *e.g.*, Falstaff, Bardolph, Pistol, into the Boar's Head room (*2 Henry IV*, 2.4).

Briefly closed; the players come up into it unseen, take their places for a scene 'within', to be 'discovered' by the reopening of the curtains: *e.g.*, Ferdinand and Miranda in the 'cell', playing at chess (*The Tempest*, 5.1).

Briefly closed; the players come up unseen, make their entrance from it to the open stage as from a house-door to the street, whereupon all the curtains are again opened, so as not to obstruct the view. Common in most plays.

And similarly in reverse for exits.

It is curious to reflect that though we never think of a dressing-room door as lying flat in the floor, the Elizabethans always did so. When the stage-house's tapestry was pulled back—that is, when it was not 'artificially drawn, and so covertly shrowded that the squint-eyed groundling may not peep in'—that tiring-house door or trap-opening was plainly visible. The gradual emergence through the floor of a surprised head, exhibiting a silent sequence of indescribable expressions, offered the prime comic an opportunity which he did not miss:

> Tarlton, when his head was onely seene,
> The Tire-house doore and Tapistrie betweene,
> Set all the multitude in such a laughter,
> They could not hold for scarse an houre after.[1]

A graphic description, published 1594, of the public stage's scenic arrangement has been available now for more than fifty years.[2] As Chambers truly says, this 'is

---

[1] Henry Peacham, *Thalia's Banquet* (1620), Epigr. 94.
[2] A. E. Richards, *Studies in English Faust Literature: The English Wagner Book of 1594*, 1907.

our nearest approach to a pen picture of an Elizabethan stage'. He also rightly points out that it has been 'a good deal overlooked'.[1] But why has this most valuable testimony continued in neglect even since Chambers's massive work appeared in 1923? One reason at least is obvious enough. The contemporary picture it presents shows a *transverse axis* utterly incompatible with our favourite latter-day notion of a 'scenic wall' or flat background embracing the theoretical 'inner and upper alcove stages'. For this description of 1594 shows no Renaissance 'scenic wall' whatever. On the contrary, what it does present is the traditional open pageant-stage, with its scenes opposed at the ends:

there might you see the ground-worke at the one end of the Stage whereout the personated diuels should enter . . . made like the broad wide mouth of an huge Dragon . . . the teeth of this Hels mouth far out stretching . . .

At the other end in opposition was seene the place wherein the bloudlesse skirmishes are so often perfourmed on the Stage, the Wals . . . with high and stately Turrets of . . . a faire Castle.

Here is ocular evidence of the transverse axis—that the Elizabethan stage maintained the 'places' or *sedes* of the medieval pageants, standing opposed, facing each other as multiple scenes. Already we have seen the seventeenth-century half-pageants of Seville setting the house of 'grace and virtues' over against Hell: just as two hundred years earlier in 1424 two of them had similarly shown 'paradis e infern'.[2] By means of these two mighty opposites, the Elizabethan stages still presented

---

[1] *Eliz. Stage* 3. 71–72.
[2] Qu. W. H. Shoemaker, *The Multiple Stage in Spain during the Fifteenth and Sixteenth Centuries* (1935), 12.

those strange effects
That rise from this hell, or fall from this heaven [1]

—acted to the life by the player

Who hath a heaven and a hell of his own,[2]

Hell being vnder euerie one of their *Stages*.[3]

'Ugly hell, gape not!' Hell Mouth, gaping horribly at one end of the stages both public and at Court, armed the poets' imaginations:

The Devills mouth I run into affright[s] me . . .[4]

This is my playes last scene . . .
I hels wide mouth o'restride.[5]

As for the Walls—the 'faire Castle' standing 'at the other end in opposition'—for centuries before Milton's time they had shown 'Heavens Battlements' or 'the airy Battlements' [6] manned by

Legions of Angels . . .
In cristall armor proofe from death and sinne,[7]

to give Marlowe's Tamburlaine his lyric line

Now walk the angels on the walls of heaven
As sentinels . . .[8]

---

[1] Chapman, Prologue to *All Fools*.
[2] Ben Jonson on the death of Richard Burbage, pr. H. J. C. Grierson, *Poems of John Donne*, 1. 443.
[3] Dekker, *Newes from Hell*, 1606.
[4] Beaumont and Fletcher, *Women Pleas'd*, 1. 2.
[5] Donne, Holy Sonnets VI and VIII.
[6] Poole, *op. cit.*, s.v. Heaven.
[7] W. Rankins, *Seaven Satyres*, 1598.
[8] *2 Tamburlaine*, 2983.

G   97

What this evidence reveals despite all prejudice to the contrary is that the long-fancied usual picture of the Elizabethan stage is not merely slightly distorted, but hopelessly misleading. It is a full ninety degrees out of true: an error which has sufficed to throw all our thinking on the subject into confusion.

Manifestly the stage of the Globe was not oriented like our modern Italianate picture-stage,[1] front-to-back, in depth against entrances in a 'scenic wall' or back-drop. For had that stage's main entrances been at the 'back' as they are today, there would have been no need to keep the tiring-house under the stage, no need to climb up from below to make an entrance. But since *spectators* of the most lucrative sort at the Globe sat 'in the stage's front' (occupying what we now call the 'back'), and the scenes *stood near the ends* right and left of the 43-foot-long open platform, the only possible access to those scenes, for localized entrances, was necessarily from under the stage, just as it was in the pageants. Accordingly, the axis of the Elizabethan stage, like that of the pageants, extended in its long dimension, from right to left. As we have noted, the great double doors to the property-dock shown in the Swan drawing were used for putting out large properties such as gibbets, beds, and chariots, and also for *unlocalized entrances*, especially for crowds and armies.

Here is a good point at which to pause and consider some implications of the fact which emerges unmistak-

---

[1] Compare Gerardo Guerrieri, *op. cit.*: 'The axis of the production, which up to the end of the sixteenth century was transverse, developed into depth, and achieved the miracle of infinite distance.'

'L'asse della rappresentazione, che era fino alla fine del Cinquecento trasversale, si sviluppa in profundità e conquista il miracolo della lontananza infinita.'

able, namely, that Shakespeare's stage, like those of the Middle Ages, lay in the midst of his audience. First, this fundamental feature of 'the round' made it a *plastic* stage, differentiated it utterly from the two-dimensional—from the classical or Renaissance façade-stages, from the Italian 'perspective' stage, and from the usual modern stage: in short, from all 'one-side' or 'objective' stages. It is from this historical basis of *audience divided, confronted, and enclosing the stage* that all study of Shakespeare's stage-technique must begin.

But certainly this completely forgotten fundamental is not easy for us to realize, or we should have realized it long ago. It upsets our conventional prejudices. Long habituation to the alien, Italianate, or 'picture' stage has trained us to allow only for a single audience, limited to one side. Despite much recent and satisfying experience, notably in America,[1] with performances 'in the round', at the word *play* do not most of us still automatically think of a stage, with a front curtain, at one end of a room, faced by a unified auditory? So much so, indeed, that modern attempts to visualize the form of Shakespeare's native English stage find themselves deluded at the outset by the unconscious trick of imposing our own Italianate outlook upon the past.

This unthinking mental habit has obstructed re-discovery of authentic fact from the very beginnings of serious study. For example, even after his years of 'unceasing solicitude', Edmond Malone—the pioneer, and still today the greatest single contributor to the subject—assumed that Shakespeare's stage had a front curtain. As

---

[1] Ever since 1932 Glenn Hughes has employed an arena-stage, the Penthouse Theatre, at the University of Washington, Seattle.

lately as the first decade of the present century, as Professor G. F. Reynolds remarked, 'scholars were mainly anxious to find a place in the Elizabethan theatre for a front curtain'.[1] Some are found still looking for it, even today. And why? Because all the stages they had ever seen were Italianate, with a front curtain. It was *unnatural* to think of a stage without one, almost indecent. In similar fashion it was assumed in the eighteenth century that of course Shakespeare had modern movable scenery. Here, however, Malone knew better. But he was forced to argue hard, and with a wealth of evidence, to dislodge this equally 'natural' and equally mistaken assumption.

As for the third error, which still persists even in the minds of authorities—the assumption of a façade, of staging in depth, with alcoves at the back, 'inner stage', 'balcony', or both—where did it come from? Although none of the authorities names him as the pioneer, Edward Capell was the first so far as I can find to put the notion into print, in 'Part the first' of his *Notes and Various Readings to Shakespeare*.[2] To illustrate a note (pages 51–52) on *Antony and Cleopatra*, Capell wrote:

the platform was double; the hinder or back part of it rising some little matter above that in front; and this serv'd them for chambers or galleries; for Juliet to hold discourse with Romeo and for Cleopatra in this play to draw up Antony dying. . . . That this was their stage's construction . . . is evinc'd beyond doubting, from entries that are found in some plays of rather a later date than the Poet's; in which are seen the terms— *upper*, and *lower*; and dialogues pass between persons, standing some on the one and some on the other stage.

---

[1] *The Staging of Elizabethan Plays at the Red Bull* (1940), 49.
[2] Published without date; but the author's *Advertisement* in the volume is subscribed 'Dec. 20. 1774'.

Malone followed in 1780, in his Supplement to the Johnson and Steevens *Shakespeare* [1] (xi. 15–16) with a similar notion. But where the postulated 'hinder' stage of Capell's imagining, which was to serve either 'for chambers or galleries', was elevated only 'some little matter', Malone's is definitely on an upper story:

> Towards the rear of the stage there appears to have been a balcony, or upper stage; the platform of which was probably eight or nine feet from the ground. I suppose it to have been supported by pillars. [2]

No proof was thought necessary by those who credited Shakespeare's stage with movable scenery or with a front curtain. None was offered by either Capell or Malone for their equally baseless assumption that the Elizabethan acting-place 'above' was at or towards the 'rear' or 'back'. But since by their time the English stage had for more than a century been Italianized, furnished with a unified 'back', as it remains today, the only place for an 'above' which occurred to them—unmindful both of the opposed

---

[1] Chambers seems strangely enough to have missed not merely Capell on the point, but this first publication of Malone's as well—which was however subsequently quoted in Max Herrmann's *Neues Archiv für Theatergeschichte* (1929), 83. In the bibliography to Chambers's monumental *Elizabethan Stage* (1923) the earliest Malone item is dated 1790.

[2] J. J. Eschenburg's notes of 1787 (*Ueber Shakespeares Leben und Schriften*) on the structure of the stage are close translations from this work of Malone's, which indeed (215*n.*) he acknowledges as his source. In 1800 Ludwig Tieck (*Kritische Schriften*, 1. 175–176) also echoed Malone: 'Was man . . . für nothwendig hielt, war eine Art von Balkon, der im Hintergrunde auf Säulen ruhte.' Apparently unaware of all this, however, W. J. Lawrence, in *The Physical Conditions of the Elizabethan Public Playhouse* (1927) 57, imagined that Tieck, in his description of an 'Elizabethan stage' in *Der Junge Tischlermeister* (1836) 264–266, 'was the first to postulate the existence of the [elevated] rear stage'.

ends so often prescribed by Elizabethan stage-directions and of the Restoration use of opposed proscenium doors with window-stages over them, which continued the traditional Elizabethan practice—was in the depth of the imported Italianate 'scene': at the 'back'.

Although now nearly two centuries old, Capell's mistaken assumption is still commonly made today about both the English and the Spanish stages of Shakespeare's time. But Anglo-American and Spanish studies of the earlier theatre are not alone in having been frustrated by the tyranny over the mind's eye of the alien 'one-side' or façade-stage. The German has suffered similarly. Expeditus Schmidt (1903) fancied that under Renaissance influence the early German stage showed 'at the back' a row of booths—the so-called *Badezellen* or 'bath houses' —with *Vorhang* or curtains in front: unaware that stage-houses on the contrary (as we shall see) had *Umhang* or curtains *round about*, necessitated by the encircling audience. Schmidt was followed in the façade-notion of staging-in-depth by the influential book of C. H. Kaulfuss-Diesch (1905), whose bizarre fancy of the English comedians' stage is a monster of Italianate 'one-point perspective'. The consequent reign of error lasted unopposed until the advent a generation later of the clearsighted scholarship and common sense of Robert Stumpfl.[1] For the habitual unthinking assumptions, Stumpfl substituted evidence drawn from stage-directions; and with them he demonstrated that the 'houses' or 'scenes' for entrance were *not* a row or façade at the back, but on the contrary were placed in the customary

---

[1] 'Die Bühnenmöglichkeiten im XVI. Jahrhundert', *Zeitschrift für deutsche Philologie* 54 (1929), 42–80.

medieval manner at the 'sides' (ends) of the open stage; that the Dutch Rederijkers' humanist stage was the first outside Italy to set scenic entrances at the 'back'. But excellent as this is, I cannot find that Stumpfl went on to realize the concomitant to end-scenes: namely that the audience was double—the select part at the head above the stage, the inferior below.

In the enterprise of re-discovering and re-creating the early theatre it is however the French who have shown the way. Under the inspiration of Gustave Cohen and his school, recovery of the common European tradition which preceded the adoption of the Italian picture-frame stage has gone from strength to strength. And not content with fruitful scholarship, they have for a generation been proving the power of the medieval staging in actual practice. Since 1933 the student-company of the Théophiliens have produced the ancient and ever-youthful *jeux, farces, sotties*, mysteries, and miracles, at times in the open air before popular audiences numbering as many as five thousand. Even the earlier efforts of this theatrical *avant-garde* so impressed Gaston Baty that he wrote to Professor Cohen:

What a lesson you give us all on the possibility of going back to the scenic conventions of long ago, and of getting them accepted at one stroke! [1]

Originally stirred by William Poel, many minds in Britain and America are likewise confident that in its turn the Elizabethan drama will realize its true power only when it lives again on its native stage, and under the

---

[1] See Paul-Louis Mignon, 'Une Compagnie d'Avant-Garde', in *Mélanges . . . offerts à Gustave Cohen* (1950), 283–285.

traditional scenic conditions which first bodied it forth. What these were we shall perceive more clearly if we look first at what preceded the advent of the façade or objective stage.

The essence of the early open or arena-stage for acting-in-the-midst is pictured for us in the 'Coliseus sive Theatrum' of the Venice *Terence* of 1499. The theatre is oval; we are the inferior part of the audience, the 'public', viewing the central stage from one side, looking across it to the two tiers of select spectators facing us from the other. Our satisfaction is double: we are close up, like the groundlings at the Globe, and thus see at once both the players and the 'persons of quality', which is more than can be said for the gallery-patrons today, presented with the *backs* of the orchestra-stalls. One player is addressing them, his back to us; another is making his entrance from one of the two scenes or 'houses'—small constructions hung round with curtains—set at the ends left and right. Naturally there is no unified scenic wall, and no place for anything of the kind. The fundamental contrast between this theatre-in-the-round, this *coliseus*, and the pseudo-Globe with a façade-stage foisted upon us as 'Elizabethan' is obvious at a glance.

The picture published in Paris by Jean de Roigny in the 1552 *Terence* shows a similar performance in the round, with balconies for spectators encircling the hall. Here there is no attempt whatever at illusion or concealment; and J. C. Scaliger at the time testified that even when they employed the traditional method of 'simultaneous settings', the French made no use of naturalism:

In France at present they act plays in such a manner that everything may be in view; all the properties set out in

COLISEUS SIVE THEATRUM
From the Venice *Terence* 1499.

elevated places. The characters themselves never go off: those who are silent are considered absent.[1]

Another representative example of the open stage, at Mantua in 1501, before the coming of the 'perspective', was described as follows:

[The theatre's] form was a quadrangle, somewhat extended in length . . . Two sides [*i.e.*, the ends left and right] were 'scenes' given over to actors and players; the other two were for stands appointed [on the one side] for the ladies, and on the other for Germans, trumpeters and musicians.[2]

But the country whose contemporaneous theatre was most like the Elizabethan English was Spain. And Spain's stage like England's remained medieval and traditional, similarly unaffected by humanist and architectural notions out of Italy. Although this obviously close likeness was illustrated in detail as early as 1909 by H. A. Rennert,[3] it has been astonishingly neglected.

We find the bare essential features of Spain's 'modern theatre' (*theatrum odiernum*) thus given in 1581 by the dramatist Rey de Artieda:

ten planks, two tapestries, and a carpet.[4]

---

[1] 'Nunc in Gallia ita agunt fabulas, ut omnia in conspectu sint; universus apparatus dispositus sublimibus sedibus. Personae ipsae nunquam discedunt: qui silent, pro absentibus habentur.' *Poetices* (1561), lib. I. cap. 21, p. 34*a*.

[2] 'Era la sua forma quadrangula, protensa alquanto in longitudine . . . Doj Bande era [*sic*] scena data ad actorj ed recitatorj: le doe altre erano ad Scalini deputati per le donne, et daltro per todeschi Trombecti et musici.' Sigismondo Cantelmo, qu. G. Campori, *Lettere artistiche inedite* (1866), 4.

[3] *The Spanish Stage in the Time of Lope de Vega*. See also John Corbin, 'Shakespeare and the Plastic Stage', *The Atlantic Monthly* 97 (1906), 369–383.

[4]   'diez tablas, dos tapices, y una alhombra, hinchen aquella fabrica tan brava.'
Verses to his tragedy of *Los amantes*.

As Henri Mérimée says of this passage,

with the planks, a platform was made. . . . The tapestries,
hung at the right and left of the trestle, formed two shelters,
which served both as wings [*i.e.*, 'doors'] and as tiring-houses.
Lastly, the carpet hid from spectators' eyes the wretchedness
of this scaffold.[1]

I should agree, except to point out that the 'cellarage'
was probably the tiring-house, and the carpet hung to
conceal it. Note that this is 'theatre-in-the-round' exactly like the pageant-performance of the *autos sacramentales*, with no unified background or scenic wall.
There were two 'houses', and they were *at the ends*.
The audience looked on from both the long sides of the
platform.

Two generations later a contemporary print of one of
the stages erected in Madrid's *Calle Mayor* [2] to entertain
Prince Charles on his Entry in 1623 exhibits the very
same plan. The picture takes in no more than one end of
the stage, with its 'house', and the 'front' side. The
actors are performing to this side, where the royal procession is passing; the crowding populace must be
imagined behind on the other, viewing both the backs of
the performers and the procession.

And the same system was used for performances in-
doors at night. Accompanying Prince Charles in 1623,
Sir Richard Wynn describes such a play put on before
Philip IV in his *Salón de Comedias*. It was 'in the round':

---

[1] *Spectacles et Comédiens à Valencia* (1913), 20.
[2] 'Einzug des Prinzen von Engellandt', attached to the B.M. copy
(G. 6174) of *A True Relation . . . Prince Charles . . . at Madrid*,
1623. Repr. by G. B. Evans, *Mod. Philol.* 9 (1911–12), and by
J. B. Trend, *Revista de la Bibl., Arch., y Mus. de Madrid*, 1926.

royalty occupied the head of the room, just as Queen Elizabeth did at Whitehall for the first night of *Twelfth Night*, and just as at that performance, there was here no built-up stage in the centre—the players acted on the floor.

Within two Dayes after wee saw a Play acted before the King and Queen, in an indifferent fair Roome, where there was hung up a Cloth of State, and under it five Chaires. There was a Square railed in with a Bench, which was all round about covered with Turky Carpets, which to the Stage Side cover'd the Ground two Yardes from the Formes.

The Company that came to see the Comedy were few, besides the English, although there were no difficulty in getting in. But the reason was, as I conceived, because there are none [*of the men*] admitted to sit, no not the Grandees, who may stand covered [*wearing the sombrero*] between the Formes and the Walls.

The Players themselves consists of Men and Women [*the latter still unknown in England*]. The Men are indifferent Actors, but the Women are very good, and become themselves far better then any [*sc. boy-actresses*] that ever I saw act those Parts, and far handsomer then any Women I saw [*in Spain*]. To say the truth they are the onely cause their Playes are so much frequented.

After some time's expectance, enters the Queen's Ladyes by two and two, and set themselves down upon the Carpets, that lay spread upon the Ground [*resting their backs against the bench which surrounded the playing-space*]. There were some sixteen in Number of them. . . . To fill those five Chaires set, there came the King and Queen, the Prince of Wales, Don Carlo, and the young Cardinal, the King's Brothers. First sat the Queen in the midst, the Prince on her right hand, and the King on her left, Don Carlo sitting next the Prince, and the Cardinal next the King. . . . The Play being ended, the Ladyes by two and two, hand in hand, go within three Paces of the Queen, and there make low Courchees, and so sally out all afore her.[1]

From this we shall find it amusing as well as instructive to look back a few years, to the reign of Philip III. That monarch (by contrast with his sombre father, who under theologians' advice in 1598 had forbidden stage plays in Madrid) shared his subjects' passionate affection for the theatre. But such intimate indoor performances as the one just described had their drawbacks for Philip III. For his criterion of royal dignity constrained him when in public to keep his face ever fixed in an unmoving gravity.[2] At the head of the *Salón de Comedias*, facing both players and audience, he was in plain view, and could not both maintain his regally wooden countenance and enjoy the play. And if he was not at ease, neither was the audience. The players too, standing so close to their royal sphinx, could not but find its rigidity dampening to the spirits. Like the English, the Spanish drama was essentially national, popular—the public ruled the theatre.

'T is a full house that makes a *Play* well play'd:
A numerous presence doth at once inspire
Actor and Auditor with mutual fire.[3]

---

[1] Pr. Thomas Hearne, from a transcript of the original manuscript, in his *Historia Vitae Ricardi II* (1729), 330–331. It was on this same canopied royal dais 'at the upper end' of this 'great room in his palace, at Madrid where he died; in which room they used to act plays', that the body of Philip IV was to lie in state in 1665. *Memoirs of Lady Fanshawe* (1829), 259.

[2] A French visitor of 1603, Barthélemy Joly, comments: 'We left the room without the King's having changed or abated a whit of this rigid countenance, of which I took careful note.' 'Sortismes sans que le Roy branslast ni diminuast rien de ceste rigide contenance, à quoy je prins curieuse garde.' Pr. R. Foulché-Delbosc, *Revue Hispanique* 20 (1909), 510.

[3] Thomas Jordan, *A Nursery of Novelties* (?1612), 24.

Without the infused and passionate participation of its massed audience of high and low, it was less than half alive, and Philip knew it.

By a stroke both masterly and significant, the play-loving monarch solved the problem. At Madrid in 1607 he built a theatre, reproducing the city *corral* conditions and admitting the public, in a *patio* of his palace. Here he and his royal family would as always occupy *el lado principal*—the advantageous head of the room, above the stage—like the lords' room in the southwest galleries of the London playhouses. But sitting private and unseen *behind lattice-work*, the King could now enjoy the performance to the full. By the same token he freed the players, now unconstrained by his visible presence and spurred by the popular enthusiasm, to throw themselves into their work as they did in the *corrales*:

'In the second court of the Treasury buildings he had a theatre constructed where their Majesties can see comedies acted just as they are before the populace in the *corrales* appointed for it, so that they may enjoy them more than when presented in their Hall; and so they had galleries and windows made all round about, wherein the courtiers are, and their Majesties will go thither from their Chamber by the passage-way prepared, and will see them from certain latticed windows.' [1]

In the same way Philip and his Queen had been 'present and not present' two years earlier in Valladolid at a play for the English Ambassador. For entertaining Lord Nottingham (King James's envoy, and for many years patron of the London company rivalling Shakespeare's)

---

[1] Translated from Luis de Cabrera de Córdoba, *Relaciones* . . . *desde 1599 hasta 1614* (ed. P. de Gayangos, 1857), 298.

and his suite of more than two hundred, the temporary arrangement made by the Duke of Lerma at his own house in Valladolid in 1605 was precisely the same. The Portuguese guest, Pinheiro da Veiga, describes it:

There was a play in a garden [square court or *patio*] of the Duke's: all hanged over above with awnings, also the openings of the arches round about with glass windows. The stage was prepared below at the head; and in front [*i.e.*, conspicuous, facing the stage and *patio*] in two chairs were seated the Admiral [Lord Nottingham] and the Duke. On the other part [*i.e.*, facing, like the *bancos* below the stage in the *patio* of a *corral*] the rest of the English lords, in twenty-four backed benches quilted with crimson velvet.

In the windows or arches above, on the left hand were the Queen's ladies, who all viewed the comedy from within, and the Duke's kinswomen and daughter-in-law; on the right were some nobles and lords, but few, and in one arch of the latter the Duke's page placed me; and so I suspected that the Queen was [above] in the front gallery, because, although it was the *principal*, the windows were drawn back, and the Duke of Cea's wife and the other ladies were to be seen. . . .[1]

We break into da Veiga's admirably detailed account to quote an English spectator's report of the arrangement:

_____

[1] 'Houve comedia em hum jardim do Duque, todo entoldado por sima com vellas; e assim as janellas, que vão ao redor dos arcos com vidraças: no topo se fês o theatro em baixo, e defronte se assentaram em duas cadeyras o Almirante e o Duque: no outro campo os mais Senhores Inglezes, em 24 bancos de encosto de velludo carmezi acolchoados.

' Nas janellas, ou arcos por sima da mão esquerda ficaram as Damas da Raynha, que vieram por dentro todas á Comedia, e as parentas e Nora do Duque: á mão direita ficaram alguns titulares e Senhores mas poucos e em hum arco d'estes me foy assentar o page do Duque e assim suspeitei que a Raynha estava na varanda de fronte, porque com ser a principal, estavam as vidraças corridas e a Mulher do Duque de Cea e mais Senhoras estavam em publica.

that of Mr Robert Treswell, Somerset Herald. After the Duke's great dinner, says Treswell,

his Lordship and the rest . . . were carried downe into a faire court, paved with square stone, in the middest whereof was a fountaine of cleare water. The whole Court covered with canvas to defend and keepe off the heat of the sunne, which at that time shone extreamely. In this Court was of purpose a stage erected, with all things fitting for a play, which his Lordship and the rest were invited to behold. The King and Queen being in private likewise Spectators of that Interlude.[1]

Treswell shows no more surprise at amphitheatrical arrangement round a built-up stage in the open air in 1605 than Wynn does at the same on the floor indoors in 1623. He finds it natural to have the Duke and the Ambassador at the head, with royalty concealed in the window above them, facing across the stage to the rest of the house: a position which our Italianate prejudice today would misdescribe as 'behind' the stage. In sharp contrast is the reaction to the London amphitheatres of the Dutchman de Witt in 1596. Trained to the one-side or façade-stage of the Rederijkers, de Witt is struck by the Roman form of the English *amphiteatra*, and, neglecting the rest of the house, comments pointedly and graphically by showing the audience in the lords' room on the other side of the Swan's stage.[2] The Englishman Treswell

---

[1] *A Relation of . . . the Journey of . . . Nottingham* (1605), 41–42. And the chief Spanish relation is in agreement: 'los Reyes la vieron desde una gelosía'—'the King and Queen saw it from a lattice'.

[2] More than once the desperate suggestion has been advanced that the de Witt sketch might represent a dress rehearsal: that the persons of both sexes shown above in the lords' room might be actors awaiting their cues. The notion smacks rather of study than of stage. No one familiar with rehearsals can imagine such waiting players herded into audience-boxes upstairs, away from the stage.

however takes central staging, or theatre in the round, as normal: 'a stage erected', he says, 'with all things fitting for a play'.

By great good fortune, we know that the play chosen for this important occasion was the lively and semi-picaresque *El Caballero de Illescas*, written but three years earlier by Spain's greatest playwright Lope de Vega. As Pinheiro da Veiga continues,

El Caballero de Illescas was the play acted, with three *entremeses* [interludes or farces between the acts], the which were greatly applauded by the English, and much more the dances, which they understood better than the language. The Duke and the Admiral were chatting together, the latter very splendid, and his people the same.

Highly commended was a sally of the player [Nicolás de los] Ríos,[1] who, the Duke summoning him and telling him that arguments of love and war were to be presented, and sacred subjects[2] or miracles not to be meddled with, out of regard for the Englishmen; and demanding of him 'Understandst me?' replied, 'I shall comply so [entirely] that even if I sneeze, I will not cross myself'—the which the lords who were there often repeated.[3]

---

[1] *Autor* of *La Nave mercenaria*, the 1609 Seville *auto* cited above.

[2] As Joly remarks (*op. cit.*, 483), 'Their comedies are of two sorts: the pious, which they call *á lo divino*, and those *á lo humano*, of an ordinary subject, composed by a poet much esteemed among them, called Lope de Vega Carpio, who (reduced to the antique penury of poets) sells them comedies at a hundred ducats each; the ordinary subject is drawn from the valiant deeds of Spain *(les vaillances des Espagnes).*' Joly seems to have been misinformed about the poet's remuneration. A hundred ducats (1100 *reales*) is more than twice the 500 *reales* which both Lope de Vega and Pérez de Montalbán report as the usual reward. See H. A. Rennert, *Life of Lope de Vega* (1904), 137n., 146.

[3] 'Representou-se a comedia "Del Cavallero de Illescas", com 3 entremezes, que foram muy festejados dos Inglezes e muyto mais

In his quality as *primer actor*, Ríos must have played the hero, Juan Tomás. And after his celebrated reply to the Duke, the following exchange, with appropriate 'business', in the course of the first act, could not have failed of a laugh:

Captain. God help thee!
Juan Tomás. Did I sneeze?[1]

The 'stage erected'—some five foot high—'with all things fitting' must have been set with the usual 'hangings': that is, two double rows of slim pillars (the *corredores*), hung as required to make 'scenes' near the ends of the stage Left and Right, with entrances through traps from the *vestuario* beneath. The *corredor* at Stage Right (Heaven) had a gallery overhead or second story 'above', known as '*lo alto*'. It is up here, into the 'church tower', that Juan Tomás climbs by its internal stair after killing a man in a fight; and it is from this *alto* that he drops stones to discourage the constabulary below:

> *Let* Clenardo *fall dead within* [the hangings, Stage Left].
> *Clenardo.* Ah! I am slain!

os bailles que entendiam melhor que a lingua: estiveram fallando o Duque e o Almirante, muy lustrozo e o mesmo os seus.
   'Foy muy celebrado um dito do comediante Rios, que, chamando-o o Duque e dizendo-lhe que reprezentasse couzas de amores ou guerras, e se não metesse em couzas ao divino, nem milagres, por amor dos Inglezes, e dizendo-lhe: entendeis-me? Respondeo: "yò lo cumplirè de suerte que, aun que lo estornude, no me tenga de persignar"; que os senhores que alli estavam repetiram muyto.' *Op. cit.*, 111–112.
   [1] *Capitán.* ¡Dios te ayude!
   Juan Tomás. ¿Estornudé?
   It is hard to say whether Ríos gagged this in, or whether it was already miraculously present in Lope's text.

Juan Tomás.	I'd better fly.

Juan Tomás.   I'd better fly.
I shift me to the tower. . . .
       Exit Juan [crossing into the *corredor*, Stage
       Right, and climbing within to the
       alto]. . . .
       Enter the Corregidor, *two* Constables, *and*
       Felino.
Felino.   He is just gone into the church, sir. . . .
       Above [appears] Juan Tomás, *with two*
       cobblestones. . . .
Corregidor.   Come down, villain! Down at once!
       [Juan] *drops a stone from above.*
Juan.   Take this discharge in full.[1]

To recall once more the 'faire court' with audience in all its four sides, as in a public *coliseo*, is to realize this theatre in the round. The 'scenes' stand opposed at the ends of the oblong stage, as they do on the pageants for the *autos*: so that the Duke and the Admiral, presiding conspicuous at the head, as well as the King and Queen above them behind a lattice, have the best view both of Clenardo falling dead into the hangings at Stage Left and of the hero 'above' at Stage Right, dropping the stone uncomfortably close to the police.

[1]   (*Caiga* Clenardo *muerto dentro.*)
Clenardo.   ¡Ay! ¡Muerto soy!
Juan.   Huír conviene.
     A la torre me deslizo. . . .
                   (*Vase* Juan.) . . .
       (*Salen el* Corregidor, *dos* Alguaciles, *y* Felino.)
Felino.   Ya entró en la iglesia, señor. . . .
       (*En lo alto*, Juan Tomás *con dos cantos.*) . . .
Corregidor. ¡Baja, infame! ¡Baja luego!
       (*Deja caer un canto de arriba.*)
Juan.   Toma esa carta de pago.
El Caballero de Illescas, Act I. *Obras de Lope de Vega*, pub. Real Academia Española, new ed. Dramatic Works, Vol. IV (1917).

Watching the brilliant Ríos on the stage in Valladolid would remind the Admiral of his own London company, with Alleyn at their head, on the stage of the Fortune. Illuminating and fascinating as they are, we however do not really need foreign examples of amphitheatrical productions to enable us to picture the true form of Shakespeare's stage. For the Elizabethans themselves pour out graphic verbal evidence and illustration without stint. When they tell us what their stage looked like, they are never even remotely reminded of a *tableau vivant*, a framed 'inner stage', a classical façade, or a row of houses at the 'back', no one of which presents that fundamental of the drama, *opposition*.

On the contrary, what they say it really resembles is a *tennis court*:[1] a playing field, an oblong arena for the direct action and reaction of players, for the bandying to and fro between the service end and the returning or 'hazard' end. The 'service end' of the stage is bounded by a roofed openwork house, as it were the roofed *dedans*; the directly-opposed 'hazard end' by a similar roofed house, as it might be the hazard's *end gallery*. The stage's long property-dock side with its stage-sitters and 'gentlemen's rooms' is like the tennis court's single long *side gallery* containing onlookers. The stage thus vividly recalls a tennis court with its blank fourth wall removed: for that second long side of the stage stands open to the yard below.

---

[1] That is, a court for the royal or real tennis, still very much alive today, played inside a peculiar roofed and walled court specially built for that ancient game: a game very different from its late offshoot, lawn tennis. See Julian Marshall, *Annals of Tennis*, 1878; *Tennis, Rackets, and Fives*, 1891; and J. M. Heathcote, *Tennis, Lawn Tennis, Rackets, Fives*, 1903.

With this striking likeness in all minds, it is natural for Dekker to write for the Fortune (probably indeed its opening or 'christening' piece) a play called *Fortunes Tennis*. It is natural for Mundy to follow with another for the Fortune called *The Set at Tennis*; natural too for Thomas Tomkis on a college-hall stage at Cambridge to show his *Tactus* bandied back and forth between the opposing ends of the transverse platform:

> *He offers to go out at the doore, but returnes in hast.*
> O Diabolo, *Gustus* comes here to vexe me.
> So that I poore wretch, am like a Shittle-cock
>   betwixt two Battledores.
> If I runne there, *Visus* beates me to *Scilla,*
> If here, then *Gustus* blowes me to *Carybdis*.[1]

Natural for the student-characters in *2 Return from Parnassus*, acting on another Cambridge college stage, to see themselves as 'mortall tennis balls': 'Where euer we tosse vpon this troubled stage' of the world; natural for the ghost of Lucrece to present the theatrical scene whereon

> Lust and Desire banded their balles of bloud,
> Chasing my spirit with fiery misteries,
> Vnto the hazard where destruction stoode,
> Ready to strike my soule into a clowde: [2]

natural for the satirist to say of blind Dame Fortune that

> She makes the world her stage, or Tennis-court:
> Where men like bals are banded to and fro:
> Or Player-like, come forth, to acte their parts;[3]

natural for the audience at a performance of *Lust's Dominion, or The Lascivious Queen* to see the prison

---

[1] *Lingua* (1607), 1.7.

[2] Middleton, *The Ghost of Lucrece* (1600), sig. A8. *Chase, hazard,* and *strike into,* are all technical terms of tennis.

[3] Dabridgcourt Belchier, *Hans Beer-pot* (1618), sig. H3ᵛ.

standing at the Hell end of the stage as it might be the end
gallery with its hazard or winning opening:

> *Eleaẓer.* Me thinks this stage shews like a Tennis Court;
> Do's it not, *Isabell?* I'le shew thee how.
> Suppose that Iron chain to be the line,
> The prison doors the hazard, and their heads
> Scarce peeping ore the line suppose the bals;
> Had I a racket now of burnish'd steel,
> How smoothly could I bandy every ball
> Over this Globe of earth, win sett and all.

And again like the 'set of wit well play'd' on the surrounded arena-stage, the tennis-play had always its
intimate company of judicial onlookers:

> *Iohn.* Thirtie all.
> *Nich.* Aske standers by, I touched it not.[1]

> Iudgement gentlemen, iudgement. Wast not aboue line? [2]

> Let us doe as Players at Tennis, be judged by all the lookers
> on.[3]

In sum, the images of 'stage' and of 'tennis court' are
seen as virtually interchangeable:

> [Fortune] makes the world her stage, or Tennis-court:
> Where men like bals are banded to and fro:
> Or Player-like, come forth, to acte their parts.[4]

---

[1] *The Parlement of Pratlers* (ed. J. Lindsay, 1928) from John
Eliot, *Ortho-epia Gallica*, 1593.

[2] Marston, *Antonio and Mellida*, Act 5.

[3] R. Johnson's tr. of Botero's *Relations* (1630), 180; qu. *O.E.D.*

[4]   Whilst we are the blind idoll Fortune's sport . . .
    The world so hazzardfull's her tennis-court.
        Robert Baron, 'Fortunes Tennis-Ball' in *Pocula
        Castalia* (1650), 73.

The *world*, the 'troubled stage' where 'mortall tennis balls' are
tossed, where 'I bandy every ball Over this *Globe of earth*', had

The action upon both these oblong arenas is the human conflict or interplay between the houses opposed at the ends. And the Elizabethans' equating of 'tennis court' and 'stage' is sufficient in itself to explode the misconceived latter-day theory of unified façade, inner-stage, without 'opposition'. For the opposition-in-length, the Left-against-Right, which as we have seen was the traditional transverse axis of the pageants—and indeed of the sixteenth-century European stages generally— is here once again unmistakably shown retained as the universal method of the amphitheatrical Elizabethan stage.

---

already been aptly symbolized in the sign of the Globe Playhouse. We can now see that it was again this unavoidable connotation of stage, tennis court, and Fortune which led Alleyn to give his Globe-imitated theatre the sign of blind Dame Fortune, and probably also to open it with *Fortunes Tennis*:

> Euen as the racket takes the balls rebound,
> So doth Good-fortune catch Ill-fortunes proof.
> Gervase Markham, Grinvile, 1595.

> Arundell . . . that tennis ball whom fortune after tossing and banding brikwald into the hazard.
> Donne, to Sir H. Wotton, ca. 1600.

> Fortune makes all—
> We are her Tennis-balls.
> Massinger, The Bashful Lover, 4.1.

> Whilst we, like various Fortunes Tennis ball
> At every stroake, were in the Hazard all.
> John Taylor, Works (1630), 24.

> Poor mortalls are so many balls,
> Toss'd som o'r line, som under fortun's walls.
> James Howell, Letters (ed. 1753), 127.

V

HOUSES TRANSPARENT

'Houses—Two low Rooms upon a Floor—
through-lights—transparent'

WHEN my short paper 'Shakespeare's Arena' appeared in the summer of 1953,[1] pointing out that
Elizabethan productions with stage 'houses' at Court and
at the Universities were amphitheatrical, 'in the round',
that revolutionary but demonstrated fact was accepted by
the majority. It was accepted partly because the new evidence was various, documentary, and conclusive, and
partly because no firm antecedent theory about the
method of 'private' production held the field. Thought
on the matter had been vague and tentative to a degree.

But when later in that paper I went on to hold that the
same medieval amphitheatrical method was also employed in the public amphitheatres such as the Globe,
some critics demurred. And although former faith in the
theoretical 'inner stage' had been so severely shaken that
no voice was raised in its defence, the majority hesitated
to accept that second thesis: partly because the evidence
I then submitted did not seem sufficiently overwhelming,
but chiefly because the time-hallowed habit of thinking
of Elizabethan production as against a unified 'scenic
wall' had become inveterate, even with professed
sceptics.

Naturally I had myself shared the habit until irrefut-
able evidence forced me to give it up. At length free of

[1] *The Sewanee Review*, July 1953.

it, I find amusement in looking back and uncovering proof of my own former blindness. The most glaring example of this is my reprinting, thirty years ago, of some verses by Sir William Davenant, in complete ignorance of their plain meaning: a meaning which, if only understood, would at once have pointed a clear path out of the swamp of error in which students of the English stage have floundered for close on two centuries.

In retrospect such blindness seems incredible. For everyone knows that the enterprising Davenant, beginning before the Restoration with scenic opera, was the man who first regularly adopted the Italianate masque's unified movable scenery for comedies and tragedies on the English public stage: scenery fronted with a curtain suddenly to unveil its 'realistic' perspectives. Davenant, in short, was the man who introduced the exotic principle of *scenic unity* to the English stage. Sir William Davenant 'first brought scenes in fashion in England,' says John Aubrey; 'before, at plays was only an hanging'; and his epoch-making act marks the turning-point in the history of the English stage.[1]

True, as late as January 1650 we find Davenant disparaging the 'communication' of mere scenic tableaux as markedly inferior to that accomplished by stage action:

And those moral Visions are just of so much use to humane application, as painted History, when with the cousenage of lights it is represented in Scenes, by which we are much less inform'd then by actions on the Stage.[2]

Yet only six years later he was employing this very thing on his stage to lure Londoners: the instantaneously-

[1] See my *Commonwealth and Restoration Stage*, 1928.
[2] Preface to *Gondibert*.

changing scenery of his novel *Siege of Rhodes*. This was opera, 'sung story' illustrated by painted history represented in scenes: '*afar off, the true prospect of the City of* Rhodes, *with a Turkish fleet making towards a promontory*' ... '*The Scene is chang'd into a representation of a general assault given to the town*' ... 'Rhodes *beleaguered*' and the like. In brief, a maximum of picture and music, and a minimum of the life-blood of drama: action and poetry.

This elementary appeal to the eye rather than to the mind was an obvious turn for the worse, a confession of literary debility. We need not pause upon that topic here, beyond observing with Schack that 'almost everywhere the decay of the drama has gone hand in hand with increased scenic splendour'. But we do not therefore forget that this same Davenant—already ten years old when Shakespeare died—had as early as 1630 become a leading playwright; that like Shakespeare he long supplied the Globe and the Blackfriars stages with comedies and tragedies put on in the traditional Elizabethan manner.

Here then is the man who looks both forward and back: the expert who, trained up in the old method, pioneers the new. If there is one man likely to point out to us what that Elizabethan, that Shakespearean stage-technique consisted of, and how to his converted and impresario-mind the revolutionary new one from the Continent surpassed it—the invariable habit of the innovator-promoter—that man is Davenant.

But how many of the innumerable students of the Elizabethan stage seized the opportunity of consulting him on their *desideratum*? Not one. No more did I, although I *can* sheepishly boast that I made his testimony readily available to students of the stage thirty years ago. And if I did not understand it then, neither has any other member of our enormous and earnest flock understood it in the three decades of intense study since 1928. So thick is the mental fog induced by a Belief—false, but universal.

Once more, then, let us hear Davenant, in the course of a poem [1] of congratulation and flattery published in 1663, ostensibly addressing to Charles II an *aperçu* of theatrical art. His Majesty (here smoothly credited with creating the new 'Art' himself) will within two years' time follow Davenant in abandoning the traditional stage-technique by building a new Italianate-perspective stage at one end of his Great Hall at Whitehall, to supplant the Elizabethan stage which extended across the middle of the room.

By way of introduction we need hardly point out that this publication of Davenant's, pretending a learned excursus into theatrical archaeology, is in fact an adroit advertisement, complete with snob appeal, of his own Lincoln's Inn Fields playhouse.[2] Here since June of 1661 he has been enticing theatre-goers with the new eye-deceiving marvels of the 'various', the changeable 'Scene'. Not all men of judgment have however shown alacrity to discard the methods of Shakespeare; and in reviving his own old comedy of *The Witts*, now adapted for the

---

[1] POEM, / TO THE / KING'S / MOST / Sacred Majesty. / BY / Sᵣ WILLIAM D'AVENANT. / *LONDON*, / Printed for *Henry Herringman*, at the *Anchor* in the Lower / Walk of the *New Exchange*, 1663. (Repr. in part by Hotson, *op. cit.*, 218–219.)

[2] For Hollar's contemporary view and my sketch-plan of this first modern English theatre, see Hotson, *op. cit.*, 122, 124.

elegant foreign scenery, Davenant has had to recognize shrewd opposition:

> So divers, who outlive the former age,
> Allow the coarseness of the plain old stage,
> And think rich vests and scenes are only fit
> Disguises for the want of art and wit.[1]

Which, to be sure, they often are. In this subsequent poem to the King he therefore presses the attack:

> The *Theatre* . . .
> Is in the *Scene* so various now become,
> That the *Dramatick* Plots of *Greece*, and *Rome*,
> Compar'd to ours, do from their height decline,
> And shrink in all the compass of design.

Palpable disparagement of his backward competitors— under Killigrew at Gibbons's Tennis Court still employing until May 1663 the traditional pageant- or Elizabethan-technique of staging [2]—he thinly cloaks under pitying contempt of the 'antient' and primitive stage-devices of '*Greece*, and *Rome*'. And with his subsequent assertion that 'at the plain contrivance all did grieve' even that pretence falls away. Naturally no one ever heard the Greeks and the Romans with one accord bewail the shortcomings of their own stage-illusion. For they never felt the need of any.

---

[1] Prologue to the revival, 15 August 1661. Cf. Pepys: 'To the Opera, which begins again to-day with "The Witts", never acted yet with scenes; and the King and Duke and Duchess were there . . . and indeed it is a most excellent play, and admirable scenes.'
[2] Cf. W. J. Lawrence, *The Elizabethan Playhouse* II (1913), 139– 140; and M. Summers, *The Playhouse of Pepys* (1935), 83, 137.

Like Milton in *Il Penseroso*, what Davenant *is* talking about is modern productions passing across the transverse 'buskin'd stage' of the English amphitheatres:

> Sometime let gorgeous Tragedy
> In sceptred pall come sweeping by,
> Presenting Thebes, or Pelops' line,
> Or the tale of Troy divine . . .

Davenant's 'great Monarchs' are no disinterred ancient Athenian or Roman actors, but the century-old attractions of London's tragic stages, celebrated by Tom Nashe:

our Sceane is more statelye furnisht than ever it was in the time of *Roscius*, our representations honourable, and full of gallant resolution . . . consisting . . . of Emperours, Kings, and Princes; whose true Tragedies (Sophocleo cothurno) they do vaunt.[1]

Also by Prince Ludwig of Anhalt-Cöthen:

> Hier [in London, 1596] besieht man vier spielhäuser
> Darinnen man fürstelt die Fürsten, Könge, Keyser,
>   In rechter lebens gröss', in schöner Kleiderpracht.

> (Here one beholds playhouses four, wherein
> Princes, Kings, Emperors they represent
>   Great as in life, splendid in robes of state.)[2]

And complained of by Jonson's Onion:

I was at one last Tearme . . . nothing but kings & princes in it.[3]

---

[1] *Nashe* (ed. McKerrow), I. 215.
[2] *Itinerarium*, Stiel 112, pr. J. C. Beckmann, *Accessiones Historiae Anhaltinae* (1716), 165.
[3] *The Case is Altered*, I.2.67.

In the late 'troubles' Thomas Peyton invoked the shade
of Fletcher to commiserate the war-scattered tragedians—
those wandring things
Thy Stage once rais'd to Emperors and Kings.[1]

In a word, like Timon's subject (in that much-neglected
play *Lady Alimony*, 1.2), Davenant's theme is what de
Witt called London's *amphiteatra*. An amphitheatre is as
it were two semicircular theatres brought together, with
the stage standing between:

Timon. One thing I must tell you, and you will attest it upon
our presentment, that never was any stage, since the first
erection of our ancient Roman amphitheatres, with suitable properties more accurately furnished . . .

And in *The Black Rod* (1630) Dekker speaks of

Arras and Tapestrie, (which commonly doe nowe, and
euer haue adorned, the old Amphitheaters) . . .

The first erection of our ancient Roman amphitheatres was
The Theatre, built by James Burbage in Shoreditch, 1576,
whose timbers at the end of the century were used to
build 'the GLOBES faire Ring'.

Johannes de Witt was not the only stranger to be
struck by the 'circus', 'coliseum', or Roman form of
London's *amphiteatra*. In the summer of 1600 the Bo-
hemian Freiherr von Waldstein heard an English comedy
on Bankside, and reported

the theatre built of wood after the fashion of the ancient
Romans: so shaped that from every side the spectators may
most conveniently see everything.[2]

---

[1] Beaumont and Fletcher Folio (1647), sig. a2^v.
[2] 'theatrum ad morum antiquorum Romanorum constructum ex
lignis, ita formatum ut omnibus ex partibus spectatores commoda-
tissime singula videre possint'. Discovered by Dr J. A. F. Orbaan;
cf. C. A. Mills in *The Times*, 11 April 1914.

With minds somewhat better prepared we may now look again at Davenant's whole revealing discourse on the scenic staging of tragedy:

> The *Theatre* (the Poets Magick-Glass
> In which the Dead in vision by us pass;
> Where what the *Great* have done we do again,
> But with less loss of time and lesser pain)
> Is in the *Scene* so various now become,
> That the *Dramatick* Plots of *Greece*, and *Rome*,
> Compar'd to ours, do from their height decline,
> And shrink in all the compass of design.
> Where Poets did large Palaces intend,
> The spacious purpose narrowly did end
> In Houses, where great Monarchs had no more
> Removes [1] then Two low Rooms upon a Floor:
> Whose *thorow lights* were so transparent made,
> That Expectation (which should be delai'd
> And kept a while from being satisfi'd)
> Saw, on a sodain, all that *Art* should hide;
> Whilst at the plain contrivance all did grieve;
> For it was there no *trespass* to *deceive*.
>   If we the antient *Drama* have refin'd . . .

In its minor way, this passage might claim to rank as the Rosetta Stone of the hieroglyphs of the Elizabethan stage-technique. Davenant would persuade his readers that hitherto the tragic stage has suffered from a weakness inherent and deplorable: poverty of illusion and scenic change. Specifically, on that stage *it has been impossible to*

---

[1] *I.e.*, changes of quarters or residence. 'The Removes of Henry VIII in his progress northwards anno 32. July 1 To Enfeild July 5 St. Albans' etc. H.M.C. *Third Rep.* App. 149*b*. '*Upon the Queenes last Remove*, being dead' Dekker, *The Wonderfull Yeare, 1603*. Also possibly present is a mental play on the game of chess: 'The King removeth but one house [*i.e.*, square] at a time' Beale, *Chess* (1656) 8, qu. *O.E.D.*

keep hidden an interior later to be revealed: 'Rooms . . .
so transparent made, That Expectation . . . Saw, on a
sodain, all that *Art* should hide.' *Now*, however, refining
the 'ancient drama' with the new deceptive and changing
'perspectives', his theatre provides the requisite 'large
Palaces' for the great monarchs: formerly limited in their
changes of quarters to 'Houses', described as 'Two low
Rooms upon a Floor', with *'thorow lights'* transparent.

No single piece of evidence ever discovered on the
nature of Elizabethan staging can compare with this in
significance.

For Davenant is here obviously not excavating from
Pollux and Vitruvius the classical *hospitalia*—the little
houses right and left of the great palace door, assigned to
guests and strangers arriving on the ancient tragic stage.[1]
The 'great Monarchs' of the Athenian theatre naturally
did not move into their own guest-rooms. The King
there appeared out of his hall, and retired into it, through
the magnificent *porta regia*, in the centre of the *scena* or
scenic wall at the back. *Mediae valvae ornatus habeant
aulae regiae*.[2] Were he recalling the historical theatre of

---

[1] *'Hospitale* dicebatur in tragoedia domuncula *hospitibus*, & pere-
grinis advenientibus in scenam destinata. Vitruv. V. 7 *Mediae
valvae ornatus habeant aulae regiae, dextra ac sinistra hospitalia.* In
scenis enim tres de more aperturae, in media nobiliori & principe
erant, praecipue in tragicis, aulae regiae, utrimque vero *hospitalia*.
Pollux IV. 19 de partibus theatri.' Sam. Pitiscus, *Lexicon Anti-
quitatum Romanarum* (1713), I. 917.

[2] Vitruvius, *De Re Architectura* v. 7. Nor can Davenant be
citing J. C. Boulenger's reference to Pollux: 'In regiis erant
διστεγίαι, & διῆρες δωμάτιον, ait Pollux lib. 4. cap. 19. [*i.e.*,
129] *domicilium duobus tectis, & diuisae aedes.*' (*De Theatro*, cap.
xx.) Sir Arthur Pickard-Cambridge's conclusion on the *distegia* is
'The house itself, in tragedy as in comedy, seems to have consisted of
a lower story, with a flat roof, upon which there was set a slightly
smaller upper story.' (*The Theatre of Dionysus at Athens*, 1946,

the Greeks and Romans, Davenant could not ignore its central, dominant, and indispensable feature, the *porta regia*. Nor is he thinking of Palladio's Teatro Olimpico built at Vicenza according to Vitruvius and used for tragedy since 1584, 'with its *porta regia* in the middle of the *scena*, its *portae minores* to right and left, its proscenium doors . . .'[1] For the Teatro Olimpico had no stage 'houses' at all.

In fine, what Davenant *is* describing is what his readers all were familiar with: the immemorial English stage for which the tragic poets of 'our ancient Roman amphitheatres' of London[2] had always prepared their 'dramatic plots of Greece and Rome'—the amphitheatrical or pageant-stage of 'houses' facing each other from the ends left and right. And here, since spectators were on both sides, the 'Monarchs' could have no stately palace-entrance beneath the lords' room and in the middle of the stool-holding critics crowding the 'front' or upper side of the stage. They *were* limited for change of quarters to the 'houses' facing each other from the ends.

If any further proof were needed to show that Davenant does not mean the Graeco-Roman scenic wall and

54.) Two stories, one above the other, are clearly not 'two low rooms upon a floor'. For the Roman treatment of doors in the *scena*, see Professor W. Beare, *The Roman Stage* (1954), 168–170. At p. 283 he points out that 'everything on the inner side of the doors was invisible to the spectators'.

[1] Chambers, *Eliz. Stage*, 3. 11. Inigo Jones closely imitated this classical Palladian stage in his Whitehall Cockpit-in-Court of about 1630. It notoriously failed to satisfy the spirit and the needs of English drama.

[2] Paris, the best of actors in his age,

Acts yet, and speaks upon our Roman stage [*i.e.*, Blackfriars].
Thomas May, verses to Massinger's *The Roman Actor*,
1619.

its doors [1]—the objective, one-side stage which never showed interiors—Davenant provides it in the term *thorow lights*. These are 'Windows on opposite sides of a room, so that the light passes right through'. 'Rooms windowed on both ends, which we call through-lighted' (Wotton, 1624). 'Thorow-lights are best for rooms of entertainment' (Fuller, 1642).[2]

Openings on *opposite* sides of a stage-house or room— through-lights—have but one purpose: to make the interiors of these set scenes visible to an amphitheatrical audience divided by the stage—the medieval-Elizabethan audience, still so seated to see 'interiors' at plays in Whitehall's Great Hall and in Gibbons's Tennis Court when Davenant was writing early in 1663. How much better off were this benefactor's more up-to-date patrons, all now gathered on *one* side, to be happily deceived by his costly, quick-changing Italian perspectives!

It will be recalled that in my 'Shakespeare's Arena' view of the Elizabethan stage, set with what Jonson's Tucca called the public theatre's *mansions* or *tabernacles*, I described these as 'curtained', 'pillared', 'openwork', 'transpicuous'. Several of my critics were unable to imagine how stage-houses could be 'transpicuous'. I still think 'transpicuous' is the right word, but if this term has something unacceptable about it, I am not wedded to it. I am quite willing to change it for Davenant's 'transparent'.

What Davenant here reveals is the Elizabethans' native stage-convention, together with their amphitheatrical

---

[1] The 'prothyra' imagined by some scholars are thoroughly examined and rejected by Pickard-Cambridge, *op. cit.*, 75–99, 266.
[2] Definition and examples from the *O.E.D.*

technique of the hangings or curtains round about the framework houses. So as not to cut off the view of spectators seated behind them, the curtains were *kept open*, except when briefly closed to cover an entrance, an exit, or a 'discovery', for players mounting from or descending to the tiring-house below. 'Expectation (which should be delai'd ...) Saw ... all that *Art* should hide.' Thus the houses *were* transparent—and disregarded—while action occupied the open stage. They took shape (by means of drawn curtains) as doors, rooms, or houses, only during short periods. This type of convention, somewhat reminiscent of the Chinese theatre, is the 'plain contrivance' which the clever Davenant claims inspired such universal grief. He is saying in effect, 'Of course, this simple convention didn't *deceive* anybody. Just fancy, they all had to "make believe". Now if you want to see Art, come to my Italian theatre in Lincoln's Inn Fields. It's the latest thing—very expensive—very exclusive—what they have at Court in the masques. With my front curtain and my *trompe l'œil* perspective shutters and back-scenes you'll be *really* fooled.'

It was believing this kind of talk which lost England her unequalled stage and hastened the decay of the drama. It was this naive concept of Art which subjected the actor to the dictates of the interloping scene-painter; which set him away from his audience, made him dwindle into two-dimensional acting in the picture-frame from which he is only now beginning to emerge.

To illustrate Davenant's 'Two low Rooms upon a Floor' so familiar to his readers—the pillared, 'through-lighted' framework left and right, standing naked and transparent when not enclosed with drawn curtains or hangings—we need go no farther than Act 2 of his own play *The Witts*, as it was produced in 1633-34 on the Elizabethan stage of the Blackfriars:

> *Enter* Elder Pallatine, Meager, Pert, *with a Light.*
> *Pert.* [*to* Elder Pall.] Sir, you shall see the inner Room is
>   hung. . . .
> *Meager.* This Chamber will refresh your eyes, when you
>   Are more prepar'd to enter it.
>   *Leads him to the Hangings.*
> *Eld. Pall.* A sudden change indeed.
>   I see some shew of entertainment there. . . .
>   But Gentlemen why are
>   These other Rooms so naked and deform'd?

Here the rooms upon the stage floor, both furnished and unfurnished, are so patently presented that the only wonder is how any eye could miss them. For if authorities insisted in chorus (as they did) that the *inner Room*, the *Hangings*, meant only 'an alcove at the back', where in the name of common sense were *these other Rooms*, whose obvious and through-lighted nakedness so shocked this Elder Pallatine?

Nothing but the universal blindness imposed by the illusion of a façade, or a readiness to 'shunt the disagreeables', could have concealed from us all the presence out on the Elizabethan stage of the two pergolas, loggias, or double colonnades facing each other from the stage-ends —handed down without a break from the traditional English stage of the pageants. These 'scenes' or 'rooms', like the *corredores*[1] of the Spanish *corrales*, could be covered with ceiling or roof upon which to erect an

---

[1] *'Corredor de casa*, a gallery of a house standing on pillars or turned posts.' *'Balahustes, barahustes*, turned posts like pillars to support galleries or suchlike.' Percivale-Minsheu.

'above' (*alto*), and furnished as required with sliding hangings (*lienços*) to represent 'through-lighted' chambers; or, for a tragedy of revenge, hung with black. It is this handsome opposed double forefront of columns—the wood cunningly painted to simulate marble—which gave *Julius Caesar* both houses and Senate, and made the stage 'stately and more than Roman' when *Sejanus* at the Globe was 'set with that rich foil'.

Posts on the Elizabethan stages both 'public' and 'private'—quite aside from the public stages' twin great supports of the 'shadow' or cover—have long been known to the historians. Their purpose has hitherto remained a baffling puzzle; but their presence should in itself have been a warning against assuming a modern façade-stage.

The Fortune's 'maine postes' of the 'Stadge forwarde' for the houses' corners no doubt went down through the tiring-house or cellar to the ground. Certainly one such must have done so in Madrid's Corral del Príncipe: 'a post in the corner of the right-hand "house", of 25½ foot high'—that is, 23 ft. 5 in. English.[1] Others must have been firmly set in prepared sockets in the stage floor: both for stability, and to make some or all of them removable. Some plays would require more, some less. At the performance of *The Birth of Merlin* quite a number were evidently standing for Joan to wander among 'in these woods', and for her brother to pun upon with 'post'. Tragedies would call for stately 'marble' columns; comedies, for the carved timbers, the 'comical window' above, and the 'upstairs' of taverns and domestic build-

---

[1] 'vn pie en la esquina del corredor de mano derecha de veinte y cinco pies y medio de alto' (Shergold, *op. cit.*, 50).

ings, such as Ricott's house in Heywood's *English Traveller*:

See what a Goodly gate . . . What braue caru'd poasts . . . What a Gallerie, How costly seeled . . . Tarrast aboue, and how below supported.

The 'turned cullumes uppon and over the stage'—to provide the 'within' and the 'above' at the stage-ends—specified in the contract for the Hope Theatre were necessarily all removable, since the stage-and-tiring-house itself was removable. On the Red Bull stage for the 1620 *Virgin Martyr*, 'Enter Dorothea led Prisoner, . . . a hangman . . . sets up a Pillar in the middle of the stage'; and for Heywood's *The Brazen Age* (1613) on the same stage, Hercules brings in two brazen pillars. Here prepared sockets certainly seem indicated.

During Act V of Brome's *The Queen's Exchange*, a windlass is attached to a post close to a trap-door. The post had to be set firmly enough to stand the strain of hauling up two men at once:

> *Enter Carpenter, Mason, Smith, in Divels habits . . .*
> *with an Engine fastned to a Post . . .*
> Carp. Here is the Trap-door, the mouth of the rich mine, which
> We'l make bold to open . . . [*opens*] So, I'le go down;
> And when I shake the rope, then crane me up again.
> [*Goes down.*] . . .
> Carp. [*below*] O pull, pull away . . .
> *Pull up Carp., an Outl[aw] hanging on him.*

In retrospect one wonders how the undeniable presence of columns on the Hope's removable stage and on those of the indoor theatres failed to suggest something to the minds of stage historians. Chambers muses, 'Oddly enough, both *Gammer Gurton's Needle* and *Jack Juggler* contain indications of the presence of a post.'[1] What *would* have been odd would have been the absence of a post. Obsession with an imaginary 'façade', however, precluded the obvious and simple explanation; and Lawrence spoke for them all in abandoning the stage-posts as not only a 'highly perplexing theme' but an obstinate mystery.

So far from being mysterious, posts-and-rails or stanchions-and-ledgers are the evident and indispensable implements for rigging the 'hangings' which appear everywhere in Elizabethan drama. At the Palace of Richmond, Christmas 1588, the Office of Works charged for 'Framing postes and Railes for plaies'; at King James's Coronation in the Abbey, again 'for settinge upp poles in two places for hanginges'; and at Theobalds, 1605–1606, 'setting up firr poles to devide roomes with hangings'.[2] When the touring actors visited the town of Stafford in 1616, bringing along their furniture of hangings, the town set up the posts from which to suspend them: 'Payments for setting up Stoopes for players'—that is, posts, pillars.[3] The churchwardens of Chelmsford in 1563 paid 'for ij loodes of pooles for the stages'.[4]

---

[1] *Eliz. Stage*, 3. 27; further on posts, 3. 38, 57n., 64n., 68n., 75–76, 108, 141n.; and W. J. Lawrence, *Physical Conditions . . .*, 123–129.

[2] P.R.O., E 351/3223; A.O. 1/2417/35, and 2418/38.

[3] H. M. C. *Fourth Rep.*, App., 327a. Compare 'the two stoupes as ye goe to Ludgate' 1576, qu. *Miscellanea Antiq. Anglic.* (1815), 13; 'the stoopes at Powles gate' Malone Soc. *Coll.* III (1954), 67. And cf. *O.E.D.*: 'Stoop. A post, a pillar; a1439 *Rec. Carpenters' Co.* (1914) II. 4. Paide for ij Stulpes and ye settinge up. 1555 Phaer *Æneid . . .* stulps of scaffolds hie. 1593 *Wills & Inv. N. C.* Surtees Soc. (1860) 228 One stoupe bedstead, teaster, valens and curtaines.'

[4] Qu. K. Pearson, *The Chances of Death* (1897), 2. 417.

In George Wilde's *Love's Hospital*—acted before the King and Queen at St John's College, Oxford, in August 1636—'Columella retyres to yᵉ hanging, stands upright against one of yᵉ pillars of yᵉ stage'.[1] Since the royal pair sat on the specially-elevated dais at the head of the college hall, beyond a stage-and-tiring-house built up some five foot high, facing the general audience below on the other side, the pillared hangings—Davenant's transparent *houses*, or *two low rooms upon a floor*—stood, as they had stood for centuries, at the ends of the stage, right and left.

Posts were therefore essential to all these open Elizabethan stages: the bones of the hangings. Accordingly, in describing 'everything which in the like [play]houses either use or necessity makes common', the author of the English Wagner Book of 1594 cannot omit them: 'There might you see . . . the Posts'. For the removable stage of the round Hope Theatre, as we have seen, they were cylindrical: 'turned cullumes uppon and over the saide stage'; for the stage of the square Fortune, square: 'all the . . . postes of the . . . Stadge forwarde shalbe square and wroughte palasterwise, with carved proporcions called Satiers to be placed & sett on the topp of every of the same postes'. And with this fresh light one can at length see the true meaning of William Beeston's specification of 'the timber belonging to the Cellars [2] . . . and *over the stage*': that is, the posts, rails, terrace-boards, etc., of the 'houses' and the 'above' at the Salisbury Court Playhouse.[3]

---

[1] Act 2, Sc. 5. B.M. MS. Addl. 14047, f. 19ᵛ.

[2] *I.e.*, the trap-stairs, platforms, 'machines', in the understage tiring-house.

[3] See my *Commonwealth and Restoration Stage*, 109.

Since they were viewed from every side, the 'houses' or scenes of the Elizabethan players had to be houses: three-dimensional, and with curtains all round. Compare Rowley's 'wise critic' at the theatre who 'with sunne-like eyes Shootes through each Sceane'.[1] For them, *scene* had not yet come to mean a unified façade fronted by tableaux-curtains. Elizabethan references to 'scene' are never to a structural head-wall bounding the stage. Florio, in defining *scena* as 'a pavillion . . . trimmed with hangings', is far from describing a wall. What he *is* describing is a three-dimensional booth, or frame hung with arras. In *The Englysshe Mancyne* (1520), a 'secret corner callyd a sene' is certainly not a wall; no more are the 'trimmed' and 'set forth' 'scenes' of the Prologue of *Acolastus* (1540): 'that is to say, our places appointed for our players to come forth of'.[2] Nor are the *Zelten*, the tents seen by Thomas Platter on the stage of the Curtain Playhouse, a wall.

To the Elizabethan eye 'hangings' represented rooms far more naturally and realistically than they can to ours:

> First, as you know, my house within the City
> Is richly furnished . . .
> My hangings all of *tirian* tapestry: . . .
> Costly apparell, tents, and Canopies . . .[3]

At the other extreme, people of modest means went in for picturesque 'paynted cloth after six pence a yard'.

---

[1] Prologue to *All's Lost by Lust*.

[2] *Place* here is obviously not *platea* or open stage, but another term for 'house', like the French *lieu*, which Gustave Cohen finds used far more commonly than *mansion*. See his 'Un terme de scénologie médiévale, *Lieu* ou *Mansion*', in *Mélanges Huguet* (1940), 52–58.

[3] *The Taming of the Shrew*, 2.1.

When Mistress Quickly is loth to pawn 'the tapestry of my dining-chambers' at the Boar's Head to pay Falstaff's debts, the rogue persuades her to hang something cheaper:

and for thy walls, a pretty slight drollery, or the story of the Prodigal, or the German hunting in water-work, is worth a thousand of these bed-hangings and these fly-bitten tapestries.

Among those employed November 1617 in 'making Redy att two playes at St James for the princis highnes' were 'two yeomen hangers'.[1] They were there to make the rooms, the pavilions, the *scenes* for the plays:

Levar li panni della scena [To lift the hangings of the pavilion], A Proverbe, that is, to manifest or make apparent the secret of any matter.[2]

> The scene is broken downe
> And all uncovered lies.[3]

Thomas.   Sit thee down, Frank,
And see what I have brought thee. Come, discover;
Open the scene and let the work appear.
                              (*Draws out a bottle.*)[4]

For the familiar 'chamber' in *Psalms* 19. 6, Sidney's translation reads

> Who foorth doth come, like a bridegroome
> From out his vailing places.

---

[1] 'Mensis Novembris anno Regis Jacobi Quintus decimo 1617. Mr Peter Yownde gent vsher daly waiter asketh allowance for himselfe one yeoman vsher two yeomen hangers two gromes of the chamber two gromes of the wardrobe and the grome porter for making Redy att two playes at St James for the princis highnes for the space of 4 days which he prayeth may be Rated . . . and payde . . . iii^l x^s viij^d'. Bodl. MS. Eng. misc. c. 4, f. 1.

[2] Florio, *Queen Annas new world of words*, 1611.

[3] Daniel, *The Tragedy of Cleopatra*, end of Act 1.

[4] Beaumont and Fletcher, *Monsieur Thomas*, 3.1.229–231.

Holyoke defines *velarium* as 'a tent or place covered with cloths: Booths, &c.' And for *velaria* the valuable Calepino-Passerat polyglot of 1609 gives

Gall.   Lieu couvert de voiles ou tapisseries.
Ital.   Luoco coperto de vele.
Germ. Ein orth mit thücheren verhencket.
Hisp.   Lugar coperto de velas.
Angl.   Courtaines.

Thus, when an Elizabethan player (complying with a stage-direction) goes to the 'curtains' or the 'hangings' or the 'arras', he goes to a *scene*, a 'place'; that is, *a room enclosed by curtains*: 'a *Place*, or roome' (Minsheu); '*Choragium:* Stuffe, wherewith the places of disguisings or enterludes is adorned' (Cooper).

The Germans very properly called these scene-curtains not *Vorhang* (*i.e.*, on one side) but *Umhang* (round about); and they defined *stage* as 'the raised platform before the little houses, or before the round-about hangings, where the actors presented their play'.[1] And for the English, curtains drawn round the 'house' to 'shut up the scene' resemble a man's enveloping shroud:

> Our winding sheets that shroud vs from the Sunne,
> Are like drawne curtaines, when the play is done.[2]

No very deep cogitation is required to realize that if there *had* been an audience on one side only, simple hinged screens or 'flats' would have sufficed. But as we know

---

[1] 'Die brüge vor der hütten, oder vor den vmbhengen, da die personen ihr schawspil hielten.' Robert Etienne (Stephanus), *Lexicon Trilingue* (1587), s.v. *Proscenium*.

[2] From the expanded version of 'What is our Life?' B.M. MS. Addl. 10309, f. 125ᵛ–126.

from the Revels Accounts, 'framed houses'—clamped or jointed together—had to be provided *because* the production was amphitheatrical, 'in the round'. Those for Winchester School in 1573 were called *domunculis de novo compositis*—'little houses newly framed'.

What of our anxious concern over the 'blocking of sight-lines' while the curtains were drawn round? At the public playhouse, occupants both of the expensive seats 'in the stage's front'—the stools centrally massed on the stage along the wall of the property-dock, the boxes or 'lords' room' above them, and the topmost gallery over the stage—and of most of the rest of the house as well suffered no visual obstruction whatever by the occasional brief closing of the curtains round a 'house' at an end of the stage. It was only those seated 'obliquely' on that side who were temporarily discommoded. We should therefore expect to find that those lateral seats were cheaper. And Ben Jonson tells us that they *were* the cheap seats:

the Fœces, or grounds of your people, that sit in the oblique caves and wedges of your house, your sinful sixpenny Mechanicks.[1]

Jonson's 'oblique' is the Latin *obliquus*, sidelong, transverse, at the sides, describing the 'concave latitudes' of the globe-like amphitheatre.

Set before us by the writers themselves are descriptions of the traditional English multiple setting:

---

[1] Induction to *The Magnetic Lady*. The Simpsons' note (*Jonson*, 10. 341) on these two Latin borrowings of Ben's runs: 'The *caveae* (spectators' seats or benches) and *cunei* (the wedge-shaped divisions of seats) in the ancient Roman theatre.'

There were v . . . paiantis [five pageants or episodes] [1] in the pley. I wyll haue made v stagz or bouthis [*scenas*, stages or booths wherein to perform the pageants] in this playe. I wolde haue a place in the middyl of the pley [*orchestra*, a seat by or in the acting space] that I myght se euery paiaunt.[2]

Here in 1519 is sketched the true image of the amphi-theatrical English stage, with stool-holders sitting as they sat until 1663 'in the middle of the play': the stage common to the Middle Ages and to Shakespeare, as he describes it in *As You Like It*, 2.4:

> This wide and universall Theater
> Presents more wofull Pageants then the Sceane
> Wherein we play in—

---

[1] As well as 'scenic wagon', *pageant* often meant 'dramatic episode':

'this world . . . an ample and large theatre, whereon all things are appointed to plaie their pageants'
Abraham Fleming, *The Footepath to Felicitie* (1581), 38.

'Corcut, thy pageant next is to be play'd'
Selimus, line 1691.

'I will not be slack To play my part in Fortune's pageant'
2 Henry VI, 1.2.66–67.

'How diuersly loue doth his pageants play';
'beholding me that all the pageants play,
disguysing diuersly my troubled wittes'
Spenser, *F. Q.* 3.5.1, and *Amoretti*, 54.

'She [Elizabeth under Queen Mary] that demaunded if the Lady Janes scaffold were taken downe, doubting to play on the same such an other Pageant'
Sir John Harington, *Orlando Furioso* (1591), 393.

'Grief and joy and hope and fear
Play their pageants everywhere'
Philip Rosseter, *Book of Airs*, 1600.

[2] W. Horman, *Vulgaria*, 1519, qu. Chambers, *Medieval Stage*, 2. 137–138*n*.

meaning, *This amphitheatrical stage of the world presents [other and] more woeful episodes than does the open booth, pavilion, or 'house'* (scena) *in which we are acting*, namely, Duke Senior's 'scene'—his shelter, tent, or booth in the wilds of Arden. 'Thus is the stage stakt out, where all these partes be plaide.'¹ These 'scenes' and their like are the normal three-dimensional *curtains* or *hangings* set up on Shakespeare's stage: the 'mansions' or 'tabernacles' which Captain Tucca in Jonson's *Poetaster* threatens to wreck.

Sliding curtains round the 'scene' or 'house' concealed or revealed it on every side. The contemporary German definition of *siparium* (theatrical curtain) again shows that they saw it not as a *Vorhang* or one-side curtain, but encircling, like the hangings of a bed's tester: 'Siparium: *Ein vmbhang oder verhenkdecke der heuslinen in schawspylen*'²—'A curtain round about, or hanging canopy, of the little houses in stage-plays'. To 'draw the curtains' was to draw them back on all sides—as of a pavilion surrounded by spectators. Typical stage-directions read, '*Cleopatra . . . lies in the bed, and the encircling curtains are open*'; '*They draw the curtains round*'; '*Now they open the curtains round about, [and] Antichrist sits like a king on a throne.*'³ In the Valencia *Assumption*, the Virgin mounts the stage and disappears into her 'chamber', which is curtained all round, to kneel at the *setial* and read on a book of hours. Then *let the maidens gather back*

---

¹ Gascoigne, *A Hundreth Sundrie Flowres*, 1573.

² Calepino-Passerat, *Dictionarium Octo-Lingue* (Paris, 1609), 2. 575a.

³ *Cleopatra . . . lydt im bett | vnd sind d[ie] umheng offe . . . Sy ʒient die vmbheng für . . . yetʒ thuonts die vmbheng vff, sitʒt entchris alls ein küng vff eim sässel*. Qu. Stumpfl, *op. cit.*

all the curtains round about so that the people may see Mary.[1]

The *Mystère de la Résurrection* (printed before 1499) provides vivid detail:

And note that Limbo must be . . . in a house which should be in the fashion of a massive square tower enclosed with nets and meshes or other transparent material . . . The said tower of Limbo must be furnished outside all round about with curtains of black canvas, which from without will cover the said nets and meshes (where the souls are confined) and will prevent one from seeing until the entrance of the said soul of Jesus; and then at his coming these curtains shall be subtilely drawn aside so that the audience shall be able to see into the tower.[2]

So much, then, for the 'houses', the transparent, through-lighted rooms forming the 'forefront' at each end of the stage. For great monarchs' tragedies, 'the stage is hung with blacke'—'Black stage for tragedies and murders fell':

A Room in the House of Leonidas hung with black. Tapers on the Walls.[3]

---

[1] 'E les donzelles pleguen tots les vels denturn per tal que lo poble vega la maria.' Qu. José Ruiz de Lihory, Barón de Alcahalí, *La Musica en Valencia* (1903), 84.

[2] 'Et notez que le limbe doit estre . . . en une habitation qui doit estre en la fasson d'une grosse tour quarrée environnée de retz et de filetz ou d'autre chose clere . . . La dicte tour du limbe doit estre garnie tout à l'environ par dehors de rideaux de toile noire qui couvreront par dehors lesdictz retz et filetz (où sont enfermées les âmes) et empescheront que l'on ne voie jusqu'à l'entrée de la dicte âme de Jésus et lors à sa venue seront iceulz rideaux subtilement tirez à costé tellement que les assistens pourront veoir dedans la tour.' Qu. Gustave Cohen, *Histoire de la Mise en Scène* (1951), 94, 145.

[3] Fletcher and Massinger, *The Queen of Corinth*, 3.2.

And in these sable Curtaines shut we up
The Comicke entrance to our direful play.[1]

The houses' hangings constituted the changeable scenery, the 'furniture' of the stage: what Dekker calls the 'Arras and Tapestrie (which commonly doe now, and euer haue adorned, the old Amphitheaters)'. Together with the wardrobe, the library, and the properties, they made up the company's costly stock. And though they did not include fabrics so fantastically precious as the golden 'cloth of tissue' which Heywood's Melpomene says 'Hung round the forefront of my stage', the moveables of the King's men at the Blackfriars in 1635 were very highly valued: 'a stock consisting of apparel, books, hangings, and other goods of the value of 3000^{li} and upwards.' [2]

Before the performance, the hangings (fitted with hooks along their upper edges) are brought out from the store in the property-dock, and set up to run on the metal rods of the wooden rails or ledgers. When the play is done they are at once taken down and carefully stowed away. This is the 'downe' which the ghost of Lucrece describes at the close of her tragedy:

Here stops the streame of tragic bloud and fire
And now *Melpomene* hales my spirit in,
The stage is downe . . .[3]

Taking the hangings down left the 'houses' untrimmed— nothing was left but bare denuded frames:

All . . . our trimme decays . . . like ended playes.[4]

---

[1] *A Warning for Fair Women*, 2.6.
[2] *The Commonwealth and Restoration Stage* (1928), 31.
[3] Thomas Middleton, *The Ghost of Lucrece* (1600), sig. C7.
[4] Donne, *The Calme*.

Now when they part and leaue the naked stage . . .[1]

If such a ones applause thou dost require
That tarries till the hangings be ta'en downe,
And sits, till th'*Epilogue* saies *Clap*, or *Crowne* . . .[2]

It can grow fascinating to note how our stage today despite all modernization still clings to terms centuries old. The hangings of Shakespeare's *scenes* or houses provide an example. We all know the phrase 'set the scene'; and every actor has heard—after the fall of the 'tabs' or curtain—the order to the stage-crew, 'Strike!' meaning 'Take down the "set".' But how many realize that these phrases are identical with the seaman's 'set (sail)' and 'strike (sail)'? That they were born far back in the days of the medieval scene-hangings—*cloths* like a sailing-ship's courses, *set* or hung upon the yards, and *struck* or taken down when no longer needed?

It is one thing to hear Davenant talk about the through-lighted, transparent rooms on the floor of the stage before the Italian picture-scenery swept them away; quite another to see them in action, as they will be seen when the first true Elizabethan stage is reconstructed for us.

Meanwhile we can at least challenge our imaginations with an Elizabethan production of a kind able to put that lost technique through its paces. If we take for example the early passages of Christopher Marlowe's *The Massacre at Paris*, it will appear that these do more than exhibit the extraordinary resources of the Elizabethan 'houses' for swift and vivid vicissitudes of scene. They also expose the utter inadequacy of the theoretical inner-

---

[1] Joseph Hall, *Virgidemiarum* (1598), 1.3.53.
[2] Jonson, Horace's *Art of Poetry*, 220–222.

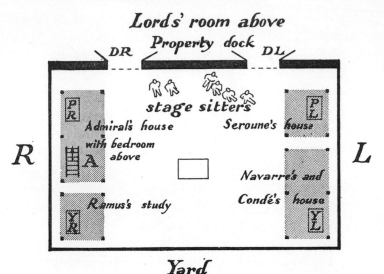

SETTING FOR *THE MASSACRE AT PARIS*

stage-and-balcony for the purpose. What is more, they show that no postulated 'threshold-scenes' can possibly be substituted for the scenes written to be enacted 'within'.

Here, in the brief compass of two hundred lines, Marlowe's play calls for no fewer than *five* distinct localized places. And all but one of these require action to be shown 'within':

Action shown 'within':

    Admiral's house.
    Admiral's bedroom (*above*).
    Ramus's study.
    Navarre's and Condé's house.

Threshold-scene:

    Seroune's house-door.

Now for an attempt at reconstituting a notion of how they did it.

First, for stage-topography. The stage is an oblong, something less than twice as long as it is deep. The long property-dock side has two large folding doors (no doubt kept open and the spaces hung with curtains) DL (Door Left) and DR (Door Right), not far from its ends. These afford general unlocalized entrance-and-exit, past the central crowd of stage-sitters in front of the blank wall of the property-dock. We call the property-dock side P, and the yard-side Y. The ends of the stage are as usual L and R, that is, Stage Left and Stage Right.

Each of the four corners of the stage is fitted with a trap-opening, affording four entrances from the tiring-house or cellarage beneath: at Stage Left, traps PL and YL; at Stage Right, traps PR and YR.

The two oblong houses, loggias of open post-and-rail construction, stand near the ends L and R, their four ends over the four traps. Each house can be enclosed by drawing curtains. By the same means it can be made into two or more houses.

In these scenes, the house at Stage Right will be employed as two houses: (a) Ramus's study, with a stool and table, over trap YR, and (b) the Admiral's house (referred to as A) over trap PR. This house has a second story or 'above' (A2) reached by an internal stair; it is furnished with a low bed concealing under it a dummy figure of the Admiral. By an arrangement of cords and pulleys, the curtains round A2 can be drawn from stage-level. The house at Stage Left will also serve as two: (a) Navarre's and Condé's house, over trap YL, and (b) Seroune's, over trap PL.

These houses are standing open, transparent, with curtains all drawn back. Expectation—in the encircling audience—sees on a sudden all that Art should hide. The two stagekeepers or curtain-drawers, in black masks, remain on stage for duty throughout. In order to draw a house's four sides of curtains simultaneously, the two stagekeepers go to diagonally-opposite corners, where each pulls the cords of two sides at once.

We take up the action after the poisoning of the Queen Mother of Navarre and the wounding of Admiral Coligny. The French King, Catherine his mother, with Guise, Anjou, and Dumaine, are on stage, plotting the massacre of the Huguenots.

Shortly before line 245 the curtains of the Admiral's two-storied house (A and A2) are closed on four sides, below and above. Inside this concealment, the Admiral, his attendants, and Messenger at once come up through trap PR into A. While the Messenger stays at stage-level, the others mount up into A2, and the Admiral gets into the bed.

At 245 the Messenger meanwhile enters out of A, and tells the King that the Admiral entreats him 'To visit him sick in his bed'. The King agrees: *Exit Messenger* back into the closed A (246–251).

King. Content, I will goe visite the Admiral.   255

The King with his attendants goes to the closed A; they are admitted by the Messenger.

Guise. And I will goe take order for his death.   256

Exeunt DL Guise, Queen Mother, etc. The curtains are now opened above on A2—*Enter* (*i.e.*, discovered) *the*

147

Admirall in his bed—with attendants. The King and his attendants come up by the inside stair and appear above in A2.

King. How fares it with my Lord high Admirall?   257

And so forth; at 277 the King and his attendants descend, the curtains are again closed round A2, the royal party comes out of the closed A, and *Exeunt omnes* DR.

 Enter (DL) *Guise, Anioy, Dumaine, Gonzago, Retes, Montsorrell, and Souldiers to the massacre.*

Guise. Away then, break into the Admirals house.   286
        . . . *Gonzago*   291
  Conduct them thither, and then
  Beset his house that not a man may liue.
Anioy. That charge is mine. Swizers keepe you the
   streets,   294

Anjou sets Switzers,

  And at each corner shall the Kings garde stand.   295

and sets Guard at corners of A.

Gonzago. Come sirs follow me.   296

Exit Gonzago and others with him (into A). As they do so, the curtains are opened on A.

Retes. But look my Lord, ther's some in the Admirals
   house.   301

Curtains are now opened also on A2: *Enter into the Admirals house, and he in his bed.*

Anioy. [*on open stage, below*] In lucky time, come let vs
   keep this lane,
  And slay his seruants that shall issue out.   303

Gonzago comes up into A2.

Gonʒa. Where is the Admirall?
Admi. O let me pray before I dye.   305
Gonʒa. Then pray vnto our Ladye, kisse this crosse.
                                        Stab him.
Admi. O God forgiue my sins. *Dies.*

The Admiral's servants run out of A and are killed by the
Guard. Then Guise calls up from the street below.

Guise. *Gonʒago,* what, is he dead?
Gonʒa. I my Lord.
Guise. Then throw him down.   310

While the Admiral rolls out of sight under the bed, the
dummy figure of the Admiral is thrown down from A2.

Guise. Cheef standard bearer to the Lutheranes,   317
        Thus in despite of thy Religion,
        The Duke of *Guise* stampes on thy liueles bulke.

The dummy figure is then dragged off DR. During
other murders on the open stage, the curtains are closed
round Seroune's house over trap PL and Seroune and his
wife come up into it. Then from DL *Enter Mount-*
sorrell and knocks at Serouns doore. His wife answers unseen from within.

Serouns wife. Who is that which knocks there?   350
Mount. Mountsorrell from the Duke of *Guise.*
Wife. Husband come down, heer's one would speak
        with you
        From the Duke of *Guise.*

Enter Seroune (from his house). While he is being murdered, his wife goes down through trap PL, and curtains

round their house are drawn open as before. Then the curtains are shut round Ramus's study while Seroune's body is dragged off DL, and Ramus comes up unseen through trap YR and sits at his table.

Enter (*i.e.*, discovered on the opening of the curtains) *Ramus in his studie*. Soliloquy, lines 365–368. From DR, *Enter Taleus* (into the study to Ramus).

Tal.	Harke, harke they come, Ile leap out at the window.	373
Ramus.	Sweet *Taleus* stay.	

Enter Gonzago and Retes (from DR as Taleus leaps out).

Gonzago.	Who goes there? . . .	375
Retes.	O let him goe, he is a catholick.	379

Exit Taleus (DL). *Enter Ramus* (from his study).

Gon.	Come *Ramus*, more golde, or thou shalt have the stabbe.

Enter the Guise and Anioy (DR).

Anioy.	Who haue you there?	385
Ret.	Tis *Ramus*, the Kings professor of Logick.	
Guise.	Stab him.	

After thirty lines of dialogue they kill him. Then the curtains are shut round Navarre's and Condé's house over trap YL. While Guise is planning how to separate the tutors from these two princes, Navarre, Condé, and the two schoolmasters come up and take their places inside the closed house.

Anioy.	For that let me alone, Cousin: stay you heer, And when you see me in, then follow hard.	433

He knocketh, and enter the King of Nauarre and Prince of Condy, with their scholmaisters—that is, as one comes to the door to answer the knock, all the curtains round the house are drawn back for discovery.

Anioy. How now my Lords, how fare you?   435

After a line or two, Anjou is in; then *Enter Guise after him.*

Guise. Murder the Hugonets, take those pedantes hence.
Na. Thou traitor *Guise*, lay of thy bloudy hands.
Condy. Come let vs goe tell the King.   445

Navarre and Condé *Exeunt* (DR), as the tutors are murdered.

So much for one preliminary attempt at realizing the resource and suppleness of Shakespeare's stage: an attempt to bring us face to face with a technique developed through centuries of practice, however novel and difficult of belief it may at first appear. For refusal to believe is commonly the first reaction to any revolutionizing discovery: ' 'T ain't so.' And the second, after an interval for assimilation, is 'That's no *discovery*; we always knew it.'

This present discovery—of Shakespeare's arena-stage in the 'wooden O'—has since 1953 undergone the customary term of rejection and disbelief. The second wave, with its chorus of 'Discovery? Nonsense, we knew it all the time', should soon be coming in, and we shall learn who it was that knew it, but has selfishly been keeping his knowledge from the world.

Every informed reader however is well aware that the Elizabethan records have here presented us with something utterly unlike anything which has hitherto filled our minds as a picture of Shakespeare's theatre. The reality which rises before us shows not one feature of resemblance to the fancied 'Globe' of the stage-historians or of the 'restorers'. As a consequence, those of us who can most promptly and efficiently *forget what we thought we knew about it* will be the first to arrive at an understanding of Shakespeare's stage practice.

For consider again the contrasts between fancy and fact:

Whereas we all fancied *one background or scenic wall* and therefore *one audience*—which even when occupying three sides of a jutting stage remains *one audience*—Shakespeare on his tennis-court-like stage in fact employed *two opposing sets of scenes*, and played at once to *two opposed audiences*: 'for if our *other audience* see *You on the stage* depart before we end . . .'.

Whereas we pictured Shakespeare preposterously giving the most advantageous position (where the orchestra stalls now are found) to the 'blunt monster with uncounted heads' standing in the open yard, in fact he played primarily to the select audience sitting close at hand, filling the protected other side of 'the GLOBES faire Ring'—the stools in front of the central property-dock wall, the lords' and gentlemen's rooms and two-penny galleries above. It is not the vulgar 'understanders' in the yard, but these 'hearers of quality' seated conspicuous 'in the stage's front' whom Shakespeare's Chorus addresses:

> the scene
> Is now transported, gentles, to Southampton:
> There is the playhouse now, there must you sit.

> Yet sit and see;
> Minding true things by what their mockeries be.

Whereas our Italianated and conditioned minds fancied his stage with a 'back' or actors' side, over against a 'house' or audience side, his audience in reality occupied *both* sides, and his actors came up *from below*, between them. For although we could imagine his tiring-house nowhere but 'behind' the stage, in fact it was *underneath* the stage, *inside* the stage structure.

Whereas we even imagined Shakespeare relegating his important intimate scenes 'within' and 'above' to a pair of remote pigeon-holes superposed in the imaginary scenic wall, in reality he set them out near the stage-ends, in transparent 'rooms' standing over the trap-doors of entrance.[1]

Whereas our prodigal fancy, in demanding 'backstage production areas', storage rooms, and what not, denied to the spectators a full quarter or more often a third of the whole surrounding building's available seating-space, Shakespeare in fact filled that segment—which, being the shaded southwest side and nearest the stage, naturally contained all the best seats—with high-paying customers. This fact helps to explain why his theatre made money, and was not reduced either to bankruptcy or to dependence on public subvention or 'state aid'.

In short, not one characteristic of his theatre—neither

---

[1] Here we must always remember Professor G. F. Reynolds's well-founded doubts of the use of the inner stage, his proof of the occasional use of simultaneous settings at the Red Bull, and his conviction that these were employed on the other public stages. But his doubts of the *employment* of an 'inner stage' are evidently insufficient to shake his conventional belief in its existence; for he still propagates the common notion of 'a typical stage': 'a main stage ... behind it was a smaller stage shut off by a curtain, and above this smaller stage a balcony'. See his *English Literature in Fact and Story* (1946), 101, 509–510.

153

the two confronted audiences, the employment of the whole side of the building adjoining the stage for seating, the scenes standing in traditional opposition at the ends, the whereabouts of the 'within' and the 'above', the management of the curtains, the location of the stage entrances, nor the position of the tiring-house underneath the stage—has ever been even suspected.

If therefore we are to ascertain Shakespeare's methods of staging and of production, the work lies all ahead. We are in for a radical reappraisal. Appropriately agonizing, at first, no doubt, like the wrench of giving up any popular fallacy. But in the end unimaginably rewarding.

While the present work is already in proof, I learn of Dr William E. Miller's interesting paper, '*Periaktoi* in the Old Blackfriars' (*Mod. Lang. Notes*, January 1959). Dr Miller found that to Abraham Fleming's 1589 version of Virgil's *Georgics* 3. 24—'how curtens theatricall or pagents on the stage / Doo go asside [from former place] their frontiers being turnd'—the translator added in the margin: 'pagent . . . *versilis, siue versatilis* . . . this deuise was not vnlike the motion of late yeares to be seene in the blacke friers.' From this Dr Miller makes two questionable assumptions: (*a*) that the theatre-hating Puritan Fleming is here referring familiarly to the stage of the early Blackfriars Theatre (1576–84), and also (*b*) that his 'motion' means full-size scenic machinery on that stage.

But nothing has ever suggested that the Children acting there employed perspective stage-machinery at any time. Every evidence indeed points the other way. And since the phrase in question is exactly like that in *Every Man Out*—the 'motion of the city of Niniueh . . . to be seene at Fleet-bridge'—it is clear to me that Fleming's 'motion', like Jonson's and Shakespeare's, means as usual nothing else than *puppet-show* or *mechanical peepshow*. He is here reminding his reader how an ingenious inhabitant of the Precinct of the Blackfriars, close to Fleet Bridge—perhaps one of the refugee Continental craftsmen—got money by exhibiting a miniature perspective-stage fitted with the rotating painted prisms which instantaneously changed the scene, as in the expensive court masques and pastorals on the Continent.

VI

IN THE ROUND

UNTIL very recently the control exerted over our imaginations by three centuries of picture-stage has been complete. Before recent performances in the round opened our eyes, we all of us unconsciously took 'a play' of necessity to imply 'a stage at the end'. So natural was it to see the stage there, that even historians—without feeling the need of a scrap of supporting evidence—confidently projected this latter-day image of ours on to the Elizabethans. And the habit is still general today. Instances of it are all too common. Ernest Law, for example, mentally reconstructing the 1604 performance of *Measure for Measure* in Whitehall's Great Hall, unhesitatingly represents Shakespeare furnished with a modern 'box-set', complete with up-to-date tableaux-curtains:

the influence of the shape of the room—oblong, instead of circular or horseshoe—obliging all the audience to be in front of the stage, so that on the drawing aside of the curtains there was produced just that effect of a framed, animated picture—objectively detached from the spectators—which was not completely reached in the public theatres until some two hundred years later.[1]

Sir Edmund Chambers—similarly without evidence—assumes that the stage, both at Court and in the 'private' theatre, stood against one end of the room:

---

[1] *London Topographical Record* VII (1912), 42–43.

The Presence chamber, or at need the great hall, sufficed for the purposes of a play, and here a temporary stage was easily erected against the screen.

The 'private' house, roofed and lit, and with its seats arranged in tiers along three sides of a long room . . .[1]

Professor Hardin Craig, likewise ignoring the absence of any proof, imagines the stage-at-the-end to be self-evident; except that he thinks it was obviously not at the lower end or screen, but at the head or dais:

The convenient custom of placing actors on the platform or dais must quickly have established itself. It was so in the early Blackfriars and, of course, in the halls of schools and colleges.[2]

And Professor Craig is only one of many, no one of whom has submitted evidence of any Elizabethan play ever performed against the end of a room.

So general is this human but quite unscientific propensity to attribute our own ideas to our ancestors, that the question at issue, which is *Where was the Elizabethan stage?*, is not even asked. It is universally begged. And the question preliminary to that one is *Where was the medieval stage?* If we asked that question first, we should at least be approaching the Elizabethans from an historical direction. Even for the modern specialist, as Sir Maurice Powicke reminds us, earnest attention to medieval history is the best preparation.

The students of the medieval theatre most productive and practical are the French, under the inspiring leadership of Gustave Cohen. Indeed, as M. André Veinstein recently pointed out, 'The spirit of study and research is

---

[1] *Shakespeare's England* (1916), 1. 98; *Eliz. Stage*, 2. 355.
[2] Ed. *The Complete Works of Shakespeare* (1951), 30.

at the very heart of the renaissance of the modern French Theatre'; and small wonder, since France produced a great medieval drama. After its own inevitable struggle with the errors of modern preconception, French scholarship is coming to find that the characteristic medieval theatrical principle was the *round*, with the stage in the middle:

> The medieval European theatre [following the Roman example] frequently adopted, for its temporary open-air constructions, the circular form of the amphitheatre. . . . The Cornish 'rounds' perhaps announce the Shakespearean theatre. These medieval borrowings from the antique forms, and these survivals, seem to us to deserve more attention than they have received hitherto.[1]

'The amphitheatre-form was that of the theatre of the Middle Ages much more often than we generally believe,' declares Gustave Cohen in the foreword to the latest edition (1951) of his great work, *L'Histoire de la Mise en Scène*; and he amply proves his statement with the findings of his own and others' recent research.

Preceding chapters in this present study have not only emphasized the fact that in England the amphitheatre-form with the stage in the middle was that of the pageant-production carried on from the Middle Ages, but have also discovered it to be the rule of the Elizabethan public theatre as well. Now what of performances at Court, at the University colleges, at the 'private' or indoor theatres? Were these completely different, adopting the classical or Renaissance single background or 'scenic wall'? Or were they essentially the same, performances in the round, like

---

[1] Hélène Leclerc, *Les origines italiennes de l'architecture théâtrale moderne* (1936), 33–34.

those of the public amphitheatres such as the Curtain and the Globe?

Let us begin with the Elizabethan staging at Court. We know that here the method remained the medieval one of multiple or simultaneous settings. It employed 'apt howses, made of canvasse, Framed, Fashioned and paynted accordingly'. Chambers's treatment of these 'houses' is significant. Having got off to a false start with the customary and almost automatic assumption of a 'façade', he was later forced by the facts to reconsider. As he recognized in his third volume,

> Two localities at opposite ends of the stage could not, obviously, be worked into a continuous architectural façade. They call for something more on the lines of the multiple setting.[1]

But *still imagining the stage standing against a single background or wall*, he never suspected that these houses, like the three-dimensional houses facing each other from the ends of the pageant-stage and the public stage, likewise imply an audience similarly amphitheatrical. For why indeed go to the expense of constructing *framed houses* if your audience does not surround your stage? When one employs a façade-stage for an audience all gathered facing it, flats or at most hinged screens are all one requires.

But the advantages of the amphitheatre are obvious and great. If you do not pre-empt an end of the room, but set your stage with houses out in the middle, you not merely provide more seating- or standing-room (which in these small halls was the controlling requirement), but also bring the play close to more eyes and ears. George

---

[1] *Eliz. Stage*, 3. 43.

Devine gives us the actor-director's considered conclusion: 'The modern auditorium, extending the stage away from the audience, harms the close contact that must have existed in Shakespeare's Globe, and which helped to produce the communal feeling of a shared experience.' The 'round' is the natural form of audience. Left to themselves, people gather round any bit of drama—a dispute, a fist-fight, or a buskers' performance—in a ring.

No doubt three-dimensional houses—the original *scenes* of the medieval stage—being still unfamiliar, are viewed with the suspicion inspired by the unknown. Yet however little understood and even less appreciated to-day, these houses were apt implements of the presented drama, highly developed through centuries of practice. Only ignorance could suppose such constructions crude, flimsy, or otherwise unsatisfactory. For we remember that in the royal Household the Office of Revels and the Office of Tents, Hales, and Pavilions functioned originally under one Master; that throughout the Tudor period they shared one Clerk and one storehouse: that their skilled artificers were cunning in the construction for royalty of portable houses [1] of painted wood and canvas, tents, and 'hales'. The Latin equivalent of *hale*, French *halle*—an oblong pavilion roofed but open on all sides—is significantly given in the *Promptuarium Parvulorum* as *scena*. In a collapsed or unjointed condition these were carried, just as the *scenes* or houses for the players were to Whitehall, on progress and on expeditions overseas, and set up to house the King and his Household.

---

[1] 'The several names given to these Moveing Houses . . . A Tent, or a Sperver. A Hutt. A Booth', etc. Randle Holme, *The Academy of Armoury* (1688), 3. 499.

For the later years of Henry VIII's reign, the accounts preserved among the Loseley papers furnish illustration:

The Kynges Newe Tent of Tymbre . . . the Howses Layde vp at the Charterhouse . . . after his gracious coming from Bulloigne . . . for caryage of the Kynges Hyghnes Tentes, Hales, Pavylyons, Joyned Howses of Tymbre . . . Paynted Clothes of dyvers workes and coloures . . . The kynges lodgynges made of tymbre and paynted in maner of bryck-work . . . Hales and Rounde house, meetly good.[1]

Further documents give measurements. These show that while hales and galleries were oblong (two dimensions), tents were circular (one dimension) [2]—information useful to modern producers of *Julius Caesar* and *Richard III*:

Tents & Hales at the Siege of Terwyn & Tourney [Térou-anne and Tournai].

The King. A house of Timber. The gallery into the Hale 30 ft long 10 ft wide . . . The Tents 20 ft apiece

The Ld Chamberlain. A Hale with a gallery into a tent The Hale 30 ft long 15 ft wide The gallery 12 ft long 7 ft wide The tent 23 ft . . .[3]

Inventories of the same sort were drawn up for Elizabeth's brother Edward VI.

These portable, prefabricated, jointed, open-work 'lodgings' on occasion housed King and Court, and were framed and adorned to the exacting taste of a King who 'exceeded all his progenitors in setting up of sumptuous housing'. To presume that similar ones on a smaller scale, made by the same craftsmen as scenes for actors to enter-

---

[1] H.M.C., *Seventh Report*, App. Pt. 1, 602–604.

[2] The two forms are well illustrated in the woodcut of Tyrone's submission, in John Derricke's *The Image of Irelande*, 1581.

[3] B.M. MS. Addl. 11321, f. 97. Many others are here similarly described for the rest of the Household.

tain the King at Whitehall were less 'meetly good', strong, apt, efficient, and beautiful, would hardly be safe.

As we have seen, the employment of three-dimensional scenes or houses implies an amphitheatre: the audience encircling the performers. Evidence that this arrangement was the rule is amply available; [1] but since none of it has been taken to heart, in reproducing some items of it, I add italics.

Under Henry VII, for a Twelfth Night 'disguising' or 'running mask', 'all the greate hall was . . . staged *Round abowte* with Tymber, that the people myght easely behold'.

Under Henry VIII, for a play by the Chapel, the White Hall 'was scafolded and rayled [*i.e.*, for standing] *on all parts*'. Within Henry's 'theatre' built at Calais, '*rownde abowt by the syds* were made thre loftes one above another for men and women for to stond upon'; and another source repeats that these three galleries stood '*on every syde*'.[2]

Under Elizabeth I, for *Gorboduc*, presented in 1561/62 on a built-up stage both at the Inner Temple and at Whitehall, 'the hall is to be furnished with skaffolds to sit upon, for ladies to behold the sports, *on each* [*i.e.*, *on every*] *side*'. For the Queen's entertainment at the Universities, the arrangement was similarly amphitheatrical. When Elizabeth visited Cambridge in 1564, the Office of Works at her expense prepared King's College Chapel for plays. The stage-and-tiring-house, five foot high, was

---

[1] The early materials were first brought together by T. S. Graves, *The Court and London Theatres* (1913), 44–45.

[2] *Chronicles of London* (ed. Kingsford), 200; Hall, *Chronicle*, 518, 723; *Chronicle of Calais* (Camden Soc.), 29.

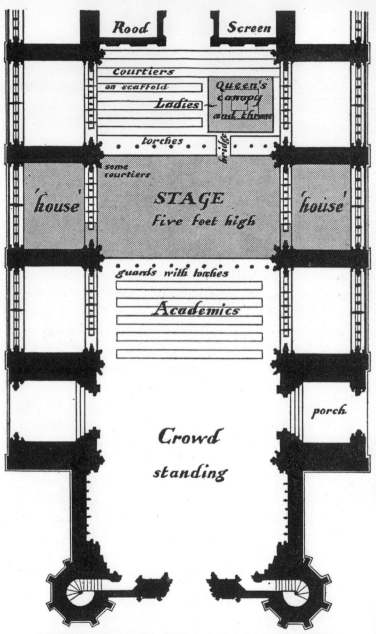

OUTER CHAPEL, KING'S COLLEGE, CAM-
BRIDGE, AS PREPARED FOR PLAYS, 1564

built in length across the outer chapel from wall to wall below the rood screen, 'containing the breadth of the Church from the one side to the other, that the [side] Chappells might serve for Houses' or scenes at the ends of the stage. This length—40 foot—was so great as to require the services of two prompters on the stage.

The Queen (near the south wall) and her ladies and officers (to her right) were placed in elevated positions beyond the upper or rood-screen side of the stage:

In the rood loft, another stage for ladies & gentlemen to stand on. And the two lower tables, under the said rood loft, were greatly enlarged & rayled for the choyce officers of the Court [to stand on].[1]

Thus they faced the lower part of the audience across the open platform, in precisely the same manner as at performances at Court, and as at the Globe the select and conspicuous audience sitting on and 'over the stage' in the lords' rooms and twopenny galleries faced the groundlings and the cheaper galleries. Two years later, when the Queen visited Oxford, the oblong hall of Christ Church presented a similar round. There was a built-up stage-and-tiring-house similarly erected across it, and again with the houses (*palatia*) at the stage-ends; and *all the walls* (*omnes parietes*) were lined with galleries, from which the audience beheld *on every side* (*circumcirca*).

At Whitehall on Twelfth Night 1600/1, 'In the Hall which was richly hanged and degrees [tiers of steps] placed *rownd about it* was the play after supper.'[2] Don

---

[1] Qu. *Eliz. Stage*, I. 226. Chambers's interpretation (p. 227) of the Chapel's arrangement, like his view of the stages at Court, is clearly based on a misconception.

[2] Alnwick Castle, Percy MSS., Letters and Papers VII, 21ᵛ.

Virginio Orsino, who attended as the Queen's guest of honour, concurs in this description with his testimony that '*atorno atorno erano gradi con dame*'—'on every side were steps with ladies'.[1] Thus there were here no galleries, and *Twelfth Night* had its first night on the floor. Had a stage been erected, the Works would have made a charge for it. But for the next Christmas, 1601/2, the Office of Works reports 'framing and setting up a broad Stage *in the middle of the Haull*'.[2]

Since my publication of these documents revealing the customary amphitheatrical disposition of the room for Court and college plays, some few teachers and critics, strangely unaware of any stage-arrangement other than the modern 'picture' or Italianate one, have made extraordinary efforts to resist the fact that the Elizabethans carried on the amphitheatrical method of the Middle Ages.[3] In their view, the Elizabethan eye-witness testimony must at any cost be forced into conformity with the traditional lore of the lecture-room. To accept the new evidence would be much too upsetting. When therefore an Elizabethan says degrees were 'placed rownd about' the Hall, he must be subjected to expert explication and presumed to mean 'on three sides only'. And when Don Virginio Orsino also writes that these same 'degrees with ladies' stood *atorno atorno—on every side—* he cannot be permitted to mean what he says either. Professor Empson nimbly explains it away as a simple matter of psychology: when they say 'four', they really

[1] See *The First Night of 'Twelfth Night'* (1954), 65–67, 229.
[2] P.R.O., E101/504/16.
[3] *E.g.*, Miss M. St Clare Byrne, *Theatre Notebook*, Jan.–Mar. 1955, and Professor William Empson, *The Times Literary Supplement*, 10 December 1954.

mean 'three'. A very convenient formula, if it would work when one hears the Inland Revenue saying 'four'.

An astonishing attempt has even been made[1] to use Bastiano de' Rossi's description of the tiers of seats in the Florentine Sala de' Magistrati,[2] which, writes Rossi, '*circondavano [la sala] intorno intorno infino alla prospettiva*'— 'encompassed [the hall] on every side up to the stage-scene [at the end]'—as evidence that Don Virginio's unqualified *atorno atorno* and the plain English *rownd about* do not mean '*all* around'.

But obviously it proves the precise contrary. Rossi's qualifying limitation *infino alla prospettiva* had to be put in only *because* a plain unqualified *intorno intorno* (like *tout autour* and *ringsumher*) means '*all* around'. This is no more than a point of very elementary grammar.[3] In short, in the Florentine *Sala* of 1585 the seats were *not* all around, because there was a 'perspective' at the end— which for a play in England was first introduced at Oxford in 1605.[4] In the Whitehall Great Hall of 1600/1, set

[1] By Professor A. M. Nagler, *Shakespeare Quarterly*, Autumn 1954.

[2] For the performance of *L'Amico fido*, 1585.

[3] Compare '[Queen Elizabeth's kingdom] è cinto *intorno intorno* dal mare, *fuor che dalla parte che confina con la Scotia*'—'is engirdled *round about* by the sea, *except on the side which borders upon Scotland*'—Cesare Campana, *Dell' Historie del Mondo* (1596), lib. 9, p. 321 (italics mine).
To assume a meaning for Italian expressions without troubling to look them up is inadvisable. In this regard even Sir Edmund Chambers was not impeccable, translating 'case *merlade*' (*i.e.*, 'battlemented') as 'marvellous'. Stranger still was his treatment of Serlio's phrase *mentre la scena e vota di dicitori* (*i.e.*, 'while the stage is empty of players'). Of this he made '*Vuota di dicitori* (tiring-room?)'. *Eliz. Stage*, 3. 4, and 4. 364, 467a.

[4] *Vide infra* in this chapter. Surely Professor Nagler cannot suppose he is discovering this historic innovation nearly five years earlier for the staging of *Twelfth Night* at Whitehall.

with the medieval opposed houses, the seats *were* all around.

And even when the Office of Works makes a charge for 'setting up a broad Stage in the middle of the Haull', a friendly correspondent remains unconvinced that this means central or amphitheatrical staging, for the odd reason that he himself has a fireplace which he confesses he might describe as being 'in the middle of the room', whereas in reality it is at the side. The point overlooked by all these critics is that the Elizabethans fortunately did not share our hazy thinking and our slipshod expression. When they say *middle*, or *round about*, they mean it. For example, in 1562 at the Inner Temple,

Supper ended, the Constable-Marshall presenteth himself with Drummes afore him, mounted upon a Scaffold, born by four men: and goeth three times round about the Harthe, crying out aloud 'A Lorde, a Lorde, &c.' [1]

Similarly at Christmas 1594, into the Great Hall at Gray's Inn

entred the Prince's Champion, all in compleat armour, on horseback, and so came riding round about the fire; and in the midst of the hall stayed, and made his challenge.[2]

Again, Robert Hayman writes in his *Quodlibets*, 1628:

When I was at Lincolns Inne the fashion was, (and I thinke it still) after dinner vpon grand and festivall dayes, some young Gentlemen of the house would take the best guest by the hand, and he the next, and so hand in hand they did solemnly passe about the fire.

---

[1] Qu. W. Dugdale, *Origines Juridiciales*, 153.
[2] 'Gesta Grayorum', pr. Nichols, *Prog. Eliz.*, II (1788).

'Cast in a gallant round, about the hearth they go.'[1]
Like the stage in Whitehall's Great Hall, the medieval
hearth at the Inner Temple, at Gray's Inn, and at Lincoln's Inn stood *in the middle* of the hall—where it remains today at Penshurst Place—beneath the louver in
the roof. It may well have been the age-old central fire
which fixed the traditional form of gathering in these
halls as a 'round'. For the Elizabethans at all events the
middle was still, without modern muddle, explication, or
shuffling, the middle.

And so it remained under James. For Shrove Sunday
1604, when Shakespeare's company played at Court, ten
months before their *Measure for Measure*, the Office of
Works charged 'for making ready the hall . . . with *a
stage in the middle*' and for 'altering of a stage in the hall
to bring it nearer the king'.[2] It is essential to notice here
that they did *not* move the king to bring him nearer the
stage. They *brought the stage nearer the king*. The contrast will be obvious when later in this chapter we find the
first introduction of a stage *at the end of the room*: they
will then be *moving the king*, not the stage. In itself, this
workaday carpenters' description of the hall's amphitheatrical arrangement shows that the stage had no
'back', façade, or scenic wall. For had this stage in the
middle employed that exotic unified background, when
it was moved up the hall to bring it nearer the king, obviously no part of the crowded audience left behind it
could have seen the performance.

And let no one fancy that on play-nights those halls
were anything less than packed. Lords Chamberlain were

---

[1] Drayton, *Poly-Olbion*, 27th Song.
[2] A.O. 1/2418/36. Italics mine.

known to break their white staves over people's heads in their attempts to control the throng. To restrain the expected multitude, in 1601/2 'eight partitions within the Hall end and entries' were framed and set up.[1] By admitting the crowd a few at a time from one partition to the next, the forward pressure could be controlled and prevented from building up the killing power it developed on the Christ Church stairs at Oxford in 1566. The advantageous result of this piece of foresight was that on this occasion the Guard were *not* called in to help the ordinary Yeomen Ushers in keeping the doors. Even within the smaller rooms of York House under Charles I, a similar gate had to be set up to control the crowd. As the French Ambassador Bassompierre reported,

the King and we were led into another room where the assembly was, and one entered it by a kind of Turnstile . . . without any confusion.

Continuing our record of performances in the round, for *Ignoramus* acted before King James and a packed audience of more than two thousand in the Hall of Trinity College, Cambridge, in May 1615, we again find the time-honoured amphitheatrical or court-like arrangement:

the upper end of the Hall, *beyond the stage*, was wholly reserved for the King, and Prince's followers, and for the courtiers.[2]

Manifestly, if the mistakenly-assumed scenic wall or unified background had been there facing the king, the rest

---

[1] E101/504/16. Miss St Clare Byrne makes heavy weather of this simple report of the erection of control-gates at the Hall's screen-end and in the entries to it.

[2] James Tabor, the University Registrary, quoted in Ruggle's *Ignoramus* ed. John S. Hawkins (1787), cxxi. Italics mine.

of the house would all have been sitting and standing un-
seeing behind it. But the stage, like the pageant stage, was
open: no such wall existed. '*Below the stage*' in the hall,
all the academics were accommodated according to their
degrees; the players' houses or multiple settings standing,
as they had always stood, at the *ends* of the transverse
stage.

In precisely the same way, the jointed, removable
theatre ingeniously constructed in 1638 for Queens' College, Cambridge, comprised for the choice audience of
Masters 'The Scaffold at the upper end of the hall, *above
the stage*', together with the Doctors' little fore-gallery at
stage-level, joined to the stage by a bridge.[1] To these
choice scaffold-seats above the 'front' or upper edge of
the box-like stage-and-tiring-house, access was given by
the President's door at the head of the hall, corresponding
to the King's door at Whitehall, and at the public theatres
to the door serving the stage-and-tiring-house and the
lords' and gentlemen's galleries.

When in 1613 Lord Knollys received Queen Anne at
Caversham with Thomas Campion's entertainment and
mask, the seating was the same, the usual Court 'round'—
the luminaries placed where they could both best see and
best be seen:

Supper being ended, her Maiestie, accompanied with many
Lords and Ladies, *came into the Hall* [*sc.* at the upper end,
facing the lower part of the room across the playing-space],
*and rested Her selfe in Her Chaire of State, the Scaffoldes of the
Hall being on all partes filled with beholders of worth. Suddainely
forth came the* Traueller, Gardener, Cynicke, *with the rest of
their crue* . . .[2]

---

[1] Malone Society, *Collections* II pt. 2 (1923), 199. Italics mine.
[2] *Campion*, ed. P. Vivian, 84.

HALL OF QUEENS' COLLEGE, CAMBRIDGE
PERSPECTIVE VIEW OF PERFORMANCE WITH
REMOVABLE THEATRE IN AND AFTER 1638

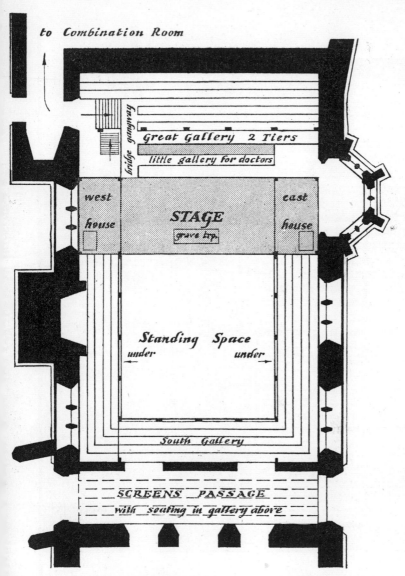

to Combination Room

bridge gangway

Great Gallery 2 Tiers

little gallery for doctors

west house

STAGE
grave trp.

east house

Standing Space
under   under

South Gallery

SCREENS PASSAGE
with seating in gallery above

HALL OF QUEENS' COLLEGE, CAMBRIDGE
PLAN OF REMOVABLE THEATRE

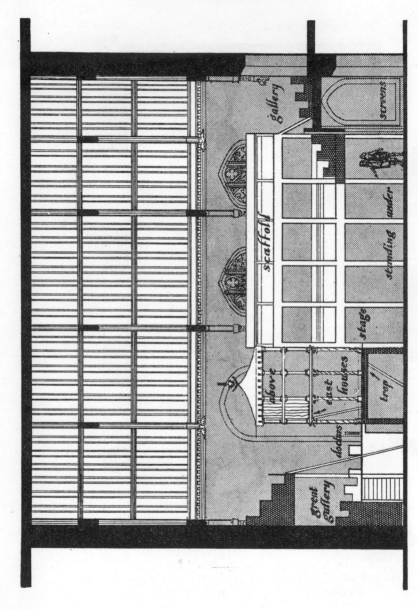

HALL OF QUEENS' COLLEGE, CAMBRIDGE
SECTIONAL VIEW OF REMOVABLE THEATRE

In order to perform before the Queen and the encircling company, the actors in the universal manner came forth from the sides, and acted in the centre.

If we are to get rid of our obsessive and tenacious illusion, we need continually to remind ourselves that the Elizabethans' ancestral and instinctive idea of 'a theatre', like Henry VIII's 'theatre' at Calais, differs utterly from our fixed Italianate picture-stage image. For we have forgotten that what Shakespeare and his contemporaries visualized at the word 'theatre' was a *round*, a *circus*, an *amphitheatre*, with the *stage in the middle*. To their minds, in the universal World—Shakespeare's 'this huge rondure'—the Earth is set as

The centre of the vast circumference,
The flow'ry mantled stage.

The world's a theatre, the earth a stage
Plac't in the midst.

The earth's a stage to heav'ns surrounding ey,
For men to act their partes.

This world a stage deuisëd for the nonce,
be set [*i.e.*, surrounded], and deckt with players.

They . . . are set before all mens eyes, and in the middest of the Theatre of the whole world.

If then the world a Theater present,
As by the roundnesse it appeares most fit,
Built with starre-galleries of hye ascent
In which *Iehoue* doth as spectator sit.[1]

---

[1] Poole, *op. cit.*, 372; Francis Quarles, Bodl. MS. Don. d. 58, f. 13ᵛ; Robert Robinson, Epigrams, Bodl. MS. Rawl. Poet. 218, f. 21; Thomas Knyvett, Camb. MS. Dd. IX. 23, f. 26; *Conferences . . . with Ed. Campion, Jesuit, 1581*, 1584, qu. *O.E.D.*; Thomas Heywood, *An Apologie for Actors* (1612), sig. a4ᵛ.

'The stage, the centre', 'stage in the midst', 'stage surrounded, beset', 'in the midst of the theatre'. Could they describe their theatre-in-the-round more unequivocally? Nashe tells of a banqueting-house 'builte round of green marble like a Theater'. At the Whitehall tournament of 1580, the

Tarrace was *on all sides beset* with Lords, Ladies, and persons of quality . . . by which meane those that beheld the Tarrace in this sort furnished deemed it . . . *a Theater* celestiall.[1]

An amphitheatrical ring in nature strikes Spenser as a 'Theatre':

> a pleasant glade,
> With mountaines round about enuironëd,
> And mighty woods, which did the valley shade,
> And like a stately Theatre it made.[2]

And in common with Francis Bacon, who tells of 'hills that stand encompassed theatre-like', a certain 'C.M.', writing in 1596, describes

a fayre forrest, that was *round about invironed with a circle* of mightie mountaines, like the forme of an artificiall *Theater*, whence *from every several side* the idle beholders sits, and sees the arte of imitating acters.[3]

This description of their theatre in the round is about as far from our former and misguided notion of their audi-

---

[1] William Segar, *Honor, military and civill* (1602), 195. Italics mine.

[2] *F.Q.*, 3.5.39.

[3] Bacon, *Sylva* (1626), sect. 253; C. M., *The Second Part of the Nature of a Woman* (1596), sig. B3 (italics mine). For a most illuminating exploration into the European extent of the Renaissance idea of the world as an amphitheatre, see the late Richard Bernheimer's study 'Theatrum Mundi' in *The Art Bulletin* XXXVI (1956), 225–247.

ence in a segment gathered in front of a scenic wall, or a stage against the end of a room, as one could well get.

Not less instinctive and unmistakable is John Vowell *alias* Hooker in describing St Stephen's Chapel, the House of Commons:

> This House is framed and made like unto a theatre, being four rows of seats one above another, round about the House.

That Vowell—like Orsino, 'C.M.', and the rest—means what he says, *round about*, and not (as modern academic prejudice might wish him to mean) 'on three sides', is shown by the famous engraving of the Commons (1624)[1] sitting round about the House in (now *five*) tiers, which continue unbroken *behind the high-backed canopied chair of the Speaker* on the fourth side or head of the chamber: thus forming a *complete round*—what the Elizabethans called 'a theatre'.

Students of the stage, by the way, who raise modern-minded objections against occasionally-blocked 'sight-lines' might study this theatre in the round with profit. Egalitarians in our day assume that by right every Member in his seat should be in a position to catch the Speaker's eye. This picture proves that in Shakespeare's time such a 'right' was unknown. Obviously those Members shown sitting behind the great Chair's high back could neither see Mr Speaker nor be seen by him. Some indeed could not see some of the front-benchers. Did the gross injustice of being placed out of sight move them to refuse to sit in the House? Not at all. They could still

---

[1] Vowell's description and the engraving are both reproduced in Sir John Neale's *The Elizabethan House of Commons* (1949), 364, 365. In 1571 Vowell was M.P. for Exeter.

hear, and they could still vote. The sanctity of sight-lines is a modern invention.

'Build thy House round with Galleries, Like to a Play-house.' In the printed satires on the Roundhead Parliament, it was this patent fact—that this 'theatre' of law-makers with its continuous tiers of crowded benches en-circling the protagonists haranguing and disputing across the central floor, vividly *reminded every reader of the amphi-theatrical playhouses*—which gave these Cavalier gibes their sting:

The onely Play-house is at Westminster.

Since you haue satt, your play is almost done.

The Stage at Westminster, where the two Houses now Act.

On *saturday* last the house acted their parts against all stage-players, commanding the boxes, stages, and seates, (except their own) to be made unserviceable for further acting.

The Parliament play-house is sufficient to lead the Kingdome a daunce.

They are exquisite Tragedians, and play their parts to the amazement of all mankind.

But your own Play-houses at Westminster . . . are the only Stages where Players must come.

An Act made upon the Stage at Westminster.[1]

The 'stage' of the amphitheatrical 'Parliament playhouse' was the eight-foot-wide alley or central floor of wood,

---

[1] See my *Commonwealth and Restoration Stage* (1928), 12, 14, 19, 31, 39, 46.

standing a few inches high upon the stone flags. And a Member in rising to speak 'took the floor' by setting one foot upon the edge of this long platform.[1]

In Restoration England the disposition of Guildhall for London's entertainment of Charles II and his Parliament (1660) remained similarly court-like, amphitheatrical, with the players in the middle:

> The King sat under a state at the upper end of the hall in the middle of the table, the Duke of York at the end on the [King's] right hand, and the Duke of Gloucester on the left: a degree lower (divided with a rail), were four tables, two on each side of the hall, for the Lords, and a degree lower than that, six tables, three on each side, for the Commons: . . . and long galleries *round the hall* full of women; after dinner there was some pastime by men habited like lawyers, soldiers, countrymen, &c., which took up the rest of the day.[2]

Circular arrangement for the King is the reverse of accidental or occasional. For in the history of royalty, the terms *Court* and *Circle* are well-nigh synonymous. Dr Johnson defines *Circle* as 'An assembly surrounding the principal person', as the King at Court. *The Times* today publishes the 'Court Circular'. Symbolism inevitably played its powerful part. The perfect circle is a 'type of God',[3] and the divinity that 'doth hedge a king' is represented in the crown, 'the circle of my glory'.[4] Since

---

[1] See the Seal of 1651, reproduced in Maurice Hastings, *Parliament House*, 1950.

[2] Sutherland MSS., H.M.C. *Fifth Report*, App., 154*b*. Italics mine.

[3] Donne, Verse Letter to the Countess of Bedford.

[4] *King John*, 5.1.2. And see Dr Honigmann's illustrative notes, New Arden ed., p. 119.

'the perfect'st *figure* is the *round*', the ring of courtiers formed

> The King and Queenes Court, which is circular
> And perfect.[1]

At the Palace of Richmond, Christmas 1599, Gloriana's glistening circle round the Queen and the players of *Old Fortunatus* inspires rapture in the Epilogue:

> When I entred first
> The circle of this bright celestiall Sphaere,
> I wept for ioy.

More than thirty years earlier at Whitehall, the Prologue of *Damon and Pithias* had stood likewise surrounded by the Circle:

> On euerie syde, wheras I glaunce my rouynge eye,
> Silence in all eares bent I playnly doe espie

—just as the contemporary French Court at Fontaine-bleau sat encircling a performance of *Genièvre*:

> une jeune presse
> De tous costez sur lez tapis tendus.[2]

---

[1] *Jonson* (ed. Simpson), 10. 320; and cf. *Dryden* (ed. Summers), 3. 527*n.*:

> [the Queen] in private mourns,
> And prayes, and to the Circle then returns.
> *The Conquest of Granada*, 4.3.

> This is not *Lisbonne*, nor the Circle this,
> Where, like a Statue, thou hast stood besieg'd,
> By Sycophants and Fools, the growth of Courts:
> Where thy gull'd eyes, in all the gawdy round,
> Met nothing but a lye in every face.
> *Don Sebastian*, Act 4.

[2] G. Lanson, *Revue d'Hist. Litt.*, 10. 422.

These repeated expressions, 'circle', 'sphere', 'on all sides', refer to the surrounding audience, not to the shape of the room or theatre. Historians unaware that plays in pre-Restoration England were normally produced 'in the round' have more than once stumbled over such phrases, mistakenly imagining them to imply a round building, which they do not. To clear our ideas before considering further illustrations, it will be useful to draw up a list of theatres according to shapes.

Round, or approximately so:

> St Paul's, Theatre, Curtain, Rose, First Globe, Swan, Second Globe, Hope, and (probably) Cockpit in Drury Lane and Second Fortune.

Square:

> First Fortune, Red Bull.

Square or oblong:

> Boar's Head and all the other inn-yard playhouses.

Oblong:

> Palace Halls, College Halls and Chapels, Inns of Court Halls, City Company Halls, First and Second Blackfriars, Whitefriars, Salisbury Court, Gibbons's Tennis Court.

We have, first, a group of passages [1] from plays acted at the Curtain, the Rose, the Globe, referring to the round internal shape of the building: 'this cockpit . . . this wooden O', 'this round circumference', 'this small circumference', 'we ring this round', 'this throngèd round . . . this faire-fild Globe', 'the GLOBES faire ring';

---

[1] Qu. *Eliz. Stage*, 2. 524.

SHAKESPEARE'S WOODEN O

and for the octagonal St Paul's, the ancient Chapter House, 'If any spirit breathes within this round'.[1] Two others may refer either to the building or to the audience surrounding: 'all this fair circuit . . . this round', and 'When the proud Round on ev'ry side hath rung'.[2]

The Prologue to Dekker's *The Whore of Babylon* and the first act of *The Roaring Girl* reflect the square shape of the Fortune: 'The Charmes of Silence through this Square be throwne' and 'Within one square a thousand heads are laid'.

When, however, performances in oblong halls present us with the 'round', the encircling auditory is unmistakable. Thus for Middleton's *Mayor of Quinborough* at the Blackfriars, the Prologue promises to produce what

> best may please this round faire ring
> With sparkleing iudgments Circled in.

And for Randolph's *Muses' Looking Glass* in the same oblong theatre, Roscius the Epilogue addresses the

> Ladyes fair,
> And Gentle-youths; And others too who ere
> Have fill'd this Orbe.

Similarly, in the oblong Salisbury Court, the Prologues flatter

> This noble Auditory, who like a Spheare
> . . . sit round.

> . . . what a lustre's here?
> How many Starres deck this our little spheare?[3]

---

[1] Marston, *Antonio's Revenge.*
[2] *A Warning for Fair Women*; Drayton, *Works* (ed. Hebel), 2. 334.
[3] Marmion, *A Fine Companion*; Sharpe, *The Noble Stranger.*

Precisely the same is true of the amphitheatrical productions in oblong college halls. On the Christ Church
stage at Oxford, Goffe's Orestes pictures not only his
own performance in the round, but the same at the professional theatres:

> And now ye fiends of hell, each take a place
> as 'twere spectators at a first dayes play . . .
> Be all my senses circled in with Fiends . . .
> for all lights else
> vanish from out this Centre, be this room fraught
> so full of mischief, may make the Fabrick crack.[1]

And Prologues and Epilogues to other academic plays
address the 'Ladies and gentle youths' seated in 'the
Orbe'; 'we shall present to night Vnto this Round'; 'But
you, that fill the Orbe'.[2] We find the amphitheatre of
1564 in King's College Chapel maintained in oblong
halls of Cambridge colleges three generations later under
Charles—in Emmanuel, Trinity, and Queens':

> 'O how gladly I behold you in a ring round about! Be this
>   our circle.'
> that mirth
> Which fits this long dead round.
> 'Enchanting poesy . . . enter thy circle.' [3]

In sum, the Circle round the Sovereign at Court, and
the circle round the actors at the play irresistibly recalled
each other. As John Donne tells Sir Henry Wotton,

---

[1] *The Tragedie of Orestes*, 4.7.
[2] ?Goffe, *The Careless Shepherdess*; Zouche, *The Sophister*.
[3] 'O quàm vos κυκλοθεν Intueor lubens, hic noster esto circulus'
William Mewe, *Pseudomagia*; Thomas Randolph, *Aristippus*;
'Circulum ingredere tuum. . . . Poesis incantans' Edward Kemp,
verses to Peter Hausted's *Senile Odium*.

in my youths giddiest dayes
When to be like the Court, was a playes praise,
Playes were not so like Courts, as Courts are like playes.

And Courts are Theaters, where some men play
Princes, some slaves.

And Shakespeare shows us the Court, the circle, and
the player in it:

within the hollow crown
That rounds the mortal temples of a king
Keeps Death his court . . .
Allowing him a breath, a little scene
To monarchize, be fear'd, and kill with looks.[1]

Acting Cartwright's *The Lady Errant* at some great
house, the Prologue compares its audience of choice
beauties surrounding him with the Circle at Court:

This honour'd Ring presents us here
Glories as rich and fresh as there;
And it may under Question fall,
Which is more Court, this, or *White-Hall*.

No matter what the shape of the room happened to be,
the plays were by custom and tradition performed amphi-
theatrically, in the round.

Shortly after Shakespeare's death, the greatest theatrical enterprise of the seventeenth century was set on foot
and for at least fifteen years continued to be actively
pressed. The project was to build 'King James his
Amphitheatre', all of stone and brick, 'to hould Twelue
thousand Spectators at the least' (four times as many as
the Globe). In this great oval in Lincoln's Inn Fields it
was planned first to give '*Tragedies, Comedies,* and

---

[1] *Ric. II*, 3.2.160–165.

Histories, Acted both in *Latine* and *English*, full of high State, and Royall Representmentes with many variable and delightfull properties'.[1] Here was a plan to challenge the magnificence of Rome in building, and the huge rings of their own forefathers for acted plays—such as the famous Quarry or Quarrel at Shrewsbury:

> There is a ground new made theator wyse
> Both deepe and hye in goodlie auncient guise:
> Where well may sit ten thousand men at ease,
> And yet the one the other not displease.
> . . .
> A grounde most apt, and they that sit above
> At once in vewe all this may see for love;
> At Ashton's playe, who hadde behelde thys then
> Might well have seen there twentie thousand men.[2]

No question but that shows and plays in the round in His Majesty's Amphitheatre would have recalled glories both Roman and Old English. But like the National Theatre today, it was talked of and not built.

If anything can free our minds of the mistaken picture of Elizabethan staging which has ruled us since the beginnings of study, it is the leading dramatists themselves, describing their audience as a *circumference*, a *full ring*:

> sit in a full Theater, and you will thinke you see so many lines drawne from the circumference of so many eares, whiles the *Actor* is the *Center*.

> No chamber-comedies . . . we'll show no pastime till after dinner, and that in a full ring of good people, the best, the noblest.[3]

---

[1] See my paper, 'The Projected Amphitheatre', *Shakespeare Survey* II (1949), 24–35.
[2] Thomas Churchyard, *The Worthines of Wales*, 1587.
[3] Webster, *Characters*, 1615; Middleton, *The Spanish Gypsy*, 2.1.

All the evidence of that staging already presented and to be presented reveals one universal method: namely, the oblong stage or playing-place was set in front of the select audience which faced down the room from the 'head', its scenes or hangings occupied the stage-ends left and right, and the general audience filled the rest of the room. This is to present plays in the round. And it is still 'in the round' whether the lighting be natural or artificial, whether the room which surrounds the stage be round, square, or oblong.

Since in all such diverse rooms the method was essentially one, no basis in fact exists for drawing contrasts, or indeed for finding material differences between productions outdoors and indoors, between the methods of the so-called 'public' and 'private' theatres. After 1608 Shakespeare's company gave its plays in summer in the round 'public' Globe, and in winter in the oblong 'private' Blackfriars. The type of audience expected must always influence the playwright's choice of subject and his handling of it. *Richard III* was not written for the ladies of the Court, and *The Tempest* was not composed to content the rowdy patrons of the Red Bull. And variations in playing conditions naturally imposed some minor differences. When immediately following a grand ball the actors had to play on the cleared tile floor (*e.g., Twelfth Night*), they were without a built-up stage, and could have no entrances through traps, or ghosts or devils appearing through the floor. Or when in 1588 the new stage built for a small and crowded palace hall at Richmond was but 14 foot square, interior scenes were hardly practicable. But these variations are matters of detail, and of no effect upon the basic method of production, which was not modern and Italianate, to a segment of audience, but medieval, to an audience all round.

It was in Jacobean Oxford that the exotic picture-stage for a play first appeared, taking the end of the room and forcing the audience out of its customary 'round'. And it was coldly received. At Christ Church for James I in 1605 this Italian novelty of changeable scenery for a play was introduced for the first time, by Inigo Jones. Since the 'perspective' could be viewed only from one side, the experiment obliged King and courtiers to surrender their traditional place at the head above the stage, and to join the inferior audience below it.

The result was not happy. To begin with, the lords 'utterly disliked the stage', pointing out since now 'the King was so placed' (with his back to the body of the house) that 'the auditory could see but his cheek only'. This depressing limitation to the enjoyment of the many who came rather to see the King than the play was never presented by the habitual 'round', in which he faced the house from the other side of the stage. And when they moved him farther back so as to be seen by more people, the King (now 28 foot distant from the stage) complained that he couldn't hear anything. No such unfortunate innovation was however repeated at the exercises which followed in St Mary's Church. Here the King was restored to his customary state, 'with his back towards the Quire', facing the congregation.[1]

Scouts from Cambridge took careful note of this Christ Church rebuff of Inigo's. As we have seen, in their subsequent performances for James and Charles, the Cambridge colleges never fell into the Oxford error, but

---

[1] Nichols, *Progresses of James I*, 1. 528–539.

maintained the ancient and well-tried 'round', to the satisfaction of all.

To every rule may be found an exception to test or prove it. The exception to the ruling 'round' for plays in England made its appearance in 1630. In that year Inigo Jones, encouraged by the welcome enjoyed by his importation of Continental scenes and machines for masques at Court, went farther, and imported an Italian neo-classical stage, of the sort employed by the Dutch Rederijkers or Chambers of Rhetoric. That is to say, he built for King Charles in the Cockpit-in-Court a small-sized imitation of Palladio's Teatro Olimpico of Vicenza, with a permanent two-storied façade-stage of arches. It was Palladio's Teatro of which Dudley Carleton wrote, that 'at Vicenta the 4th day of March will be shewes in that theater worth the seeing'.[1] Jones's derivative Cock-pit thus introduced a background-stage, radically differing from the English open or amphitheatrical stages of all the theatres. Although this presented a clean break with the native tradition, the attempt might not have proved utterly abortive had anyone been found to compose either neo-classical plays or 'shows' suitable for it.

But English drama, it soon became evident, was neither to be written for this alien 'architect's stage', nor suited to be acted on it. The only word for the construction is 'artificial'. It had no place in the tradition of English drama or of English staging, and the best comment on this ill-judged foreign borrowing is the fact that nothing of the kind was ever tried again.

No one could have been more wrong-headed than the anonymous academic with his Greek lines in *Jonsonus*

[1] Venice, 21 Jan. 1610/11 N.S. P.R.O., S.P. 99/7/30.

Virbius (1638), prophesying a bright future for English neo-classical drama at the Cockpit-in-Court, which he fondly thought would supersede the 'still barefoot stage' (*planipedia*)—the open platform of London's commercial theatres:

[*The Muse addresses the infant Jonson*]

'Hail, hope of the still barefoot stage, in which you, leading with slipper or buskin, will drive Greece and Rome mad with envy, as you rejoice in the crown of a new-built theatre, with the changing of a platform for marble arches.' She said, and flying off, put a brick into the hands of the child, as a token of sounder building.[1]

Unfettered by the Baroque marble-arched background, the English stage remained until the Restoration medieval and amphitheatrical, still able to show Hell at one end and Heaven at the other, embracing between them the 'World' or 'Court' for the trial of man's soul.

Can anyone be expected to believe that the traditionally romantic English drama of 'lamentable tragedy mixed full of pleasant mirth' could come to life out of the classical background of arches which the Chambers of Rhetoric employed for their rigid *tableaux* and set explanatory speeches? Poles apart from the Dutch academic with his shows, his rhetorical descriptions, and his formal arches is the English dramatic poet

whose breast, filled by the Muses
With raptures, into a second[2] them infuses:

---

[1] Anon. (?R. Brideoake), Greek verses in *Jonsonus Virbius* (1638), No. 33, ll. 12–18. See *Jonson* ed. Herford and Simpson, 11. 481. Dr Simpson kindly gave me this translation.

[2] *I.e.*, a second breast—the actor's.

Can give an actor sorrow, rage, joy, passion,
Whilst he again, by selfsame agitation
   Commands the hearers, sometimes drawing out teares,
   Then smiles, and fills them both with hopes and fears [1]

—the Englishman who

in this quallitie is most vaine, indiscreete, and out of order;
he fyrst groundes his worke on impossibilities: then in three
howers ronnes he throwe the worlde: marryes, gets Children,
makes Children men, men to conquer kingdomes, murder
monsters, and bringeth Gods from Heaven and fetcheth
Divels from Hel,[2]

with the result that the romantic poetry and the 'impossible' action of the English Elizabethan plays are still
alive today, while the contemporary *tableaux vivants* and
academic exercises presented on the classical stages of the
Rederijkers have for centuries been deader than mutton.

It was in the ominous reign of Charles I, who squan-
dered even more gold than his father had done on ruin-
ously expensive court masques with their Italianate scenic
stages and machines, that degenerating popular taste took
the infection from the Court. The public too began to
itch for spectacle—for the

                gawdy show
    Of boords and canvass, wrought by *Inigo*

—instead of the drama served by their traditional amphitheatres. No matter that this foreign stage-in-depth,
made for scenic masque and opera, at once reduced the
seating-space available; for no one should need to be told

---

[1] Dekker, Prologue to *If it be not good the Devil is in it.*
[2] George Whetstone, epistle dedicatory to his *Promos and Cassandra.*

that 'at the sumptuous masques performed at James's court and Charles's there was no room and no view for spectators behind the stage'.[1] One has only to compare the Hall at Whitehall set with tiers of degrees round about it for *Twelfth Night* with the same Hall prepared with a stage-in-depth for the scenic masque *Florimène* (1635) to realize the magnitude of the loss. That room could accommodate nearly twice as many people at an open-stage play as it could at a scenic masque. And if Trinity at Cambridge in 1615 had imported one of Jones's scenic stages-in-depth for *Ignoramus*, well nigh half of the two thousand and more who heard and saw it 'in the round' would never have got in.

Nevertheless the demand grew for shows, made out of the 'painting and carpentry' which, as Jonson rightly says, are 'the Soule of Masque'. The able dramatist—Jonson, Lope de Vega, Dryden—recognizes the encroaching architect, decorator, and scene-designer as his natural enemy.

> Mighty Showes!
> The Eloquence of Masques! What need prose
> Or Verse, or Sense . . .?[2]

The more show, the less drama. A child or an imbecile is pleased with a show. It takes a brain to enjoy a play.

> The Wise *Italians* first invented show;
> Thence, into *France* the Noble Pageant past;
> 'Tis *England*'s Credit to be cozn'd last.[3]

---

[1] Professor F. P. Wilson, 'The Elizabethan Theatre', *Neophilologus* 39 (1955), 52.
[2] Jonson, *Expostulation with Inigo Jones.*
[3] Dryden, Prologue to *Albion and Albanius.*

But cozened it was in the end, like the rest. And after 1630 the telltale symptoms began to appear in the occasional pre-empting of extensive space from the end of the hall not merely for masques such as *Florimène*, but also for *plays* backed with the new Italianate deep scenic stages.

Examples are Heywood's *Love's Mistress* before the royal pair at Denmark House on the King's birthday 19 November 1634, when 'Mr Inego Jones . . . to every Act, nay almost to every Sceane . . . gave such an extraordinary Luster; upon every occasion changing the stage, to the admiration of all the Spectators'; Henry Killigrew's *The Conspiracy* (*Pallantus and Eudora*), acted at York House with 'Scenes fitted to every Passage of it' in 1634/5, to celebrate Lord Pembroke's marriage; William Strode's *Passions Calmed* in 1636 before the King at Christ Church, Oxford, 'on a goodly stage reaching from the upper end of the Hall almost to the hearth place',[1] complete with quick-changing perspective scenes. And on the following night William Cartwright's *Royal Slave* with its own scenes on the same stage was so well received that by command the set was taken to Hampton Court for a repeat performance at the Palace. William Habington followed in 1640 with his play *Cleodora*, staged in the Great Hall of Whitehall with full Italianate scenery.

As for the commercial theatres, we have the problem of Thomas Nabbes and his *Microcosmos*—not however a play but a 'moral masque'—in 1637 at the Salisbury Court. It is possible that in this small oblong theatre he may have achieved something in the manner of the spectacular unified Italianate scene; and if so, it was an effort

---

[1] Anthony à Wood, *Annals*, 1. 409.

at the kind of thing Sir William Davenant was evidently meditating when in 1639 he secured a patent to build a new theatre in Fleet Street.[1] This was to be at most 120 foot square; in it he would present 'scenes' and 'musical entertainments'—that is, opera—as well as plays.[2] Had the Civil Wars not come between him and his hopes, the unified objective Italianate stage might well have supervened for plays in the English commercial theatre some twenty years earlier than it actually did.

Even after the delayed and revolutionary advent of the exotic scenery on Davenant's stage at Lincoln's Inn Fields, the first few years of the Restoration saw two Theatres Royal still maintaining the native English stage of Shakespeare, playing to an audience encircling the actors. These were Killigrew's Theatre Royal in Vere Street (Gibbons's Tennis Court) and Whitehall's ancient theatre: the Great Hall, where plays had been acted 'in the circle' ever since the days of Cardinal Wolsey.

The invading Italian perspective scenery put an end to Shakespeare's stage, offering 'show' in the place of wit.

> With what strange ease a play may now be writ,
> When the best half's compos'd by painting it! [3]

To both these theatres that end came soon—to Vere Street in 1663, and to Whitehall in 1665. When in that latter year Charles II built his permanent scenic stage,

---

[1] Rymer, *Foedera*, 20. 377.

[2] The Cockpit in Drury Lane—being in all probability circular —offered little scope for the erection of any kind of perspective stage. The 'right Scoene', 'left Scoene', and 'middle Scoene' mentioned in Nabbes's *Covent Garden* (acted there in 1632) are no more than a variation of the usual multiple scenes or houses of the native amphitheatrical stage.

[3] Prologue to Thomas Rawlins's *Tunbridge Wells*, 1678.

taking up more than a third of the Hall's length, the 'old stage' was however left in the centre: made over to provide him with a central seat from which view the changing 'perspectives' through the new proscenium arch. But before they went, two messages from those amphitheatrical stages—one in a Prologue, the other in an Epilogue—now sound in our ears like a farewell. At Gibbons's Tennis Court shortly after the Restoration, Jonson's *Alchemist* was once more played in the traditional 'circle'; and addressing the ring, its Prologue ends,

> A thousand Eyes dart raies into our Hearts . . .
> Where shines such Glory in so bright a Sphere.[1]

And similarly from Whitehall's stage-in-the-centre, before the players left it for ever, we hear the Epilogue to Tuke's *The Adventures of Five Hours* telling Charles II seated in the ring that

> This shining circle then will all sit mute
> 'Till one pronounce from you *Le Roi le veut.*

---

[1] Pr. C. H. Wilkinson, *Proceedings and Papers of the Oxford Bibliographical Society*, 1. 281–282.

VII

OPPOSITION

As we have seen, the open pageant stage which preceded the Elizabethan had its scenic entrances directly opposed at the ends of the oblong, left and right—a transverse axis. And everybody knows that the Restoration stage, which immediately followed the Elizabethan—although alien movable scenery had turned its best open side into a 'back' enclosed by a proscenium arch—on its remaining open half still maintained the transverse axis: entrance doors with window-stages over them, directly opposed at the ends, left and right (see next page for illustration).

The obvious inference is that on the open Elizabethan stage, which chronologically came between the two, the entrances were the same as they were both before and after: as described in 1594—Hell's 'ground-worke at the one end of the stage' and 'at the other end in opposition . . . a faire Castle'.

However obvious this conclusion now appears, our Italianate preconception of staging-in-depth against a unified background has successfully concealed the truth during almost two centuries of study. Unaware that the traditional method of production was 'in the round' with audience on both sides, and that on the built-up Elizabethan stage the players entered from the tiring-house underneath, students could imagine the entrances nowhere but 'at the back'. Yet the Elizabethan evidence of the transverse axis, of scenic entrances facing from

N   193

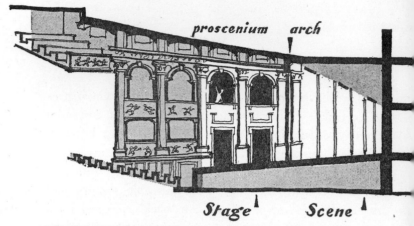

proscenium arch

Stage   Scene

SECTIONAL SKETCH OF WREN'S DRURY LANE

Notice traditional entrances and 'aboves' opposed on open stage. Behind arch and curtain, the foreign perspective scenery has been added.

the ends, has always been staring at us from the plays.

In the Elizabethan staging at Court Sir Edmund Chambers found 'houses opposed' so frequently and undeniably as to oblige him to abandon his first mistaken assumption of an Italian stage.[1] And when we turn to the various 'private' or indoor theatres, it is clear that scenes were placed in opposition here just as at Court. We have already seen that at Paul's for Percy's *Necromantes* two players ascend *to either end of the stage from within*—that is, through traps at the stage-ends. Similarly at the Whitefriars, Jonson's *Epicoene* (4.5.30) has two 'studies' or small rooms with doors set one at each end of the stage. A few further examples will suffice:

On the stage Mercurie *from one end*, Ceres *from another meete.*

---

[1] *Eliz. Stage*, 3. 33–34.

Enter Malevole *and* Maquerelle, *at seuerall doores opposite.*
Enter the Queene . . . *at the one end of the stage, and the* Duke
. . . *at the other end of the stage.*[1]

But the great 'public' playhouses as well—such as the
Globe and the Red Bull, whose long platforms as we
know stood out with two ends and yard-side free from
contact with the house—show precisely the same employment of opposed scenes, with characters often
directed to 'passe ouer the Stage' from entrances at the
stage-ends:

Enter at one end John Lincolne . . . *at the other end enters*
Fraunces.

From one end of the Stage enters an antique . . . *from the other
end of the Stage enter another antique.*

Enter Stukeley *at the further end of the stage* . . . *Two trumpets
sound at either end.*

Enters Lust, *bringing forth* Browne *and* Roger, *at one ende*
Mistres Sanders *and* Mistres Drurie *at the other.*

Enter Terentius . . . Regulus, Trio, *and* others, *on different
sides.*

Enter Spungius, Hircius, *ragged, at opposite doors.*[2]

On the Globe's stage *The Merry Devil of Edmonton* (5.1
and 5.3) requires two inns facing from opposite ends.
Mine host Blague of the George refers to his rival as
'mine overthwart neighbour'.

---

[1] Wilson, *The Cobler's Prophecy* 1.3 (?Paul's); Marston, *The
Malcontent* 5.1 (Blackfriars, 1604); Markham and Machin, *The
dumbe Knight* 4.1 (Whitefriars, 1633).
[2] *Sir Thomas More*, 1.1; *John a Kent and John a Cumber*, 3.1;
The Life and Death of Captain Thomas Stukeley, 245, 2382; *A
Warning for Faire Women*, 2 (Curtain or Globe, *ca.* 1599) Jonson,
Sejanus 3.400 (Globe, 1603); Massinger and Dekker, *The Virgin
Martyr* 3.3 (Red Bull, *ca.* 1620).

The presence of such unquestionably opposed settings on these open oblong stages was extremely awkward for the usual and unwarranted assumption of a 'scenic wall'. So awkward, that in an attempt to accommodate them its apologists were driven to invent doors 'obliquely placed' in the property-dock wall. This is desperate indeed, for that wall is shown perfectly flat in the drawing of the circular Swan; and in the square Fortune and the square Red Bull it would also be perfectly flat.

The one thing which made the plays' clear requirement of opposed settings on these stages puzzling was of course the mistaken notion that the tiring-house was situated 'at the back'. But since we have learned that in actuality the tiring-house was located underneath the stage, with two trap-entrances at each end, opposed settings placed over them appear both natural and obvious.

In sum, entrances from scenes at the opposite ends are common to all the Elizabethan stages, Court, 'private', and 'public'. And our discovery that the Elizabethans universally maintained the traditional transverse axis shows us why the arrangement and action of their stages reminded them of tennis courts, and suggested the opposed sides for a game at chess. That the same 'scenes opposed' held the stage in Spain's amphitheatrical *corrales* is evident from Lope de Vega's protest at their over-elaboration: 'There's no chessboard like the stage's hangings.' [1]

This scenic confrontation maintained the visual ground for that essential of the drama—conflict. Almost too common and familiar are the Elizabethan displays of

---

[1] 'No hay tabla de ajedrez como su lienzo.' Dedication of *Lo fingido verdadero*.

'two mighty opposites'. In *The Three Lords and Three Ladies of London* we have the London Lords facing their (Spanish) opponents Shealty [*i.e.*, Mariolatry], Pride, and Tyrannie. These

march once about the stage, then stand and viewe the Lords of London, *who shall martch towardes them, and they giue backe, then the Lords of* London *wheele about to their standing, and th'other come againe into their places.*

Antony and Cleopatra 2.6 again presents the adversaries:

Enter Pompey *and* Menas *at one side, with drum and trumpet; at the other,* Caesar, Antony, Lepidus . . . *with Soldiers marching.*

And in William Rowley's *A Shoo-maker a Gentleman* 3.3:

Enter Dioclesian, *the Eagle borne before him at one doore, at the other,* Huldrick *and* Rodrick, *Kings of the Goths and Vandalls, with their Army.*

Heaven's Walls—the house at Stage Right with its upper story—was the traditional location for sieges and for scenes on the 'upper stage'. That the place of the music room—always 'above'—was also on the Walls is shown by Jasper Mayne's 'Thou laidst no sieges to the *Musique-Roome*'.[1] But the house opposed at the Hell end, Stage Left, could be similarly supplied with an 'above'. For example, in *The Tragedy of Claudius Tiberius Nero* (sig. C4ᵛ):

Enter Caligula *at one end of the stage, and* Sejanus *at the other end below.* Julia *at one end aloft, and* Tiberius Nero *at the other.*

---

[1] *Jonsonus Virbius*, 1638.

Four isolated characters in four distinct 'rooms' on two levels. Later in the same play the 'above' is again employed as the Walls:

Germanicus and Piso scale the walls, Germanicus is repulst at the first assault.

Since the post-supported framework for the Walls stood fore-and-aft over the traps near the end of the stage, it was perfectly feasible to show the *inside of the city wall* at the same time as its outside which faced the adversary —something quite impossible to the 'façade-stage' so long and so erroneously imagined. In Heywood's *Four Prentices* at the Red Bull, the Christians besiege the Persians holding Jerusalem. A crowd of defiant Persians flourish their standard on the walls. The Christians attack; and after one repulse 'Guy and Eustace climbe vp the wals, beate the Pagans', set up their own shields, and bring away the enemy's flags. Then we see and hear the beaten pagans *within the city* encouraging themselves to a rally, and returning to defend the walls. In the upshot they sally out of the city and fight centre-stage.

Shakespeare employs this simultaneous showing of the inside and the outside of the city in the Orleans of his *1 Henry VI*. In 1.4 the siege is presented, the opposed houses showing respectively the walls of Orleans near one end of the stage, and the English-held barbican, 'tower', or 'turrets' in the suburbs, near the other end, with the 'field' between. A cannon-shot fired across the stage from the Orleans walls kills Lord Salisbury and Sir Thomas Gargrave on the 'tower'.

Then in 2.1 the English advance across the 'field' with

scaling ladders for a night assault. *The English scale the walls ... and all enter the town ... The French leap over the Walls in their shirts*—and in the 'field' discuss the venturous and desperate surprise attack. From the walls, *Enter an English* Soldier, *crying* 'A Talbot! a Talbot!' *They fly, leaving their clothes behind.* Hereupon (2.2) *Enter* Talbot [*and others*] *Within the Town*—that is, at the end of the stage *behind the walls*, which point Talbot describes as 'the market-place, The middle centre of this cursed town'.[1]

This convenient space between the fore-and-aft 'house' and the very end of the stage—used by Heywood and Shakespeare as 'the inside of the city'—we find elsewhere realistically employed as the 'backside' or garden of a house. And since both Walls and houses are transparent when 'opened', action behind them at the end of the stage is visible to all.

Jonson's comedies offer several examples of this 'backside' or garden, either mentioned or shown,[2] notably in *The Case is Altered.* For this play the Milanese palace, exhibiting both state-apartments and servants' hall, is set near one end of the stage, simultaneously with the house of the beggar Jaques de Prie near the other. Scenes are presented both before and behind de Prie's lowly house, with action shifting immediately from 3.4 at its front to 3.5 on its 'backside'.

---

[1] Although Chambers (3. 97) recognizes that these scenes in *1 Henry VI* 'seem to me clearly to point to walls standing across the main stage', they failed to shake his belief in the erroneously-assumed scenic wall imagined at the 'back'.

[2] See the notes in the Simpsons' edition on *Every Man Out* 2.4.87; *The Case is Altered* 4.8.1; *Poetaster* 2.1.12; *Eastward Ho* 5.1.85.

This 'back' or outer side's facilities for realism, on any stage public or private, were too advantageous to be neglected. In *The Great Duke of Florence*,[1] Act 5, Sanazzaro, locked in an upstairs room, 'looks back' out of the window on hearing hoofbeats, exclaiming,

> A goodly troop! this back-part of my prison
> Allows me liberty to see and know them.

Shortly afterwards the troop enters on foot as outside the house. Act 5 of Heywood's *If you know not me* presents a similar example.

An instance still more vivid—in which the strip between the back of the fore-and-aft house and the very end of the stage is employed as a city street—is found in *The Captain*, 5.2.[2] To play a trick on Jacomo, who is below in the street behind the house, the characters in the upstairs room instruct the Wench to go to the back window and empty a chamber-pot on him. The audience both sees the violent effects of this, and watches the Wench describing them to the others behind her in the room.

Fab. Look out then if you can see him.
Wench. Yes I see him, and by my troth he stands so faire I could not hold were he my father; his hat's off too, and he's scratching his head.
Fab. O wash that hand I prethee.
Wench. God send thee good luck, this the second time I have thrown thee out to-day, ha, ha, ha, just on's head.

---

[1] By Massinger and Ford, Cockpit in Drury Lane.
[2] A Globe–Blackfriars play by Fletcher, also presented at Court in the winter of 1612–13.

Fran. Alas!

Fab. What does he now?

Wench. He gathers stones, God's light, he breakes all the
street windowes.

Jacomo [*below*]. Whores, Bawds, your windowes, your windowes.

Wench. Now he is breaking all the low windowes with his
sword. Excellent sport. Now he's beating a fellow that
laugh'd at him. Truely the man takes it patiently; now
he goes down the street gravely, looking on each side,
there's not one more dare laugh.

Action in the first Quarto of *Romeo and Juliet* employs
the upper windows of the Capulet house, both front and
back. Act 3 Scene 5 begins *Enter Romeo and Iuliet at the
window*, for their scene in front. Later, with the speech
(supplied in the Folio) 'Then window let day in, and let
life out', Juliet opens the window at the back, facing the
end of the stage, for Romeo to climb out; and *he goeth
downe*, continuing the scene from the ground behind the
house (compare page 273 below).

And in the two final acts of *Antony and Cleopatra*
Shakespeare takes full advantage in similar fashion of
both sides of the Egyptian queen's famous 'monument'.
From the opening of 4.13, when *Enter Cleopatra and her
Maides aloft* and she says, 'O Charmian, I will never go
from hence', the upper room of the monument is the
scene of all the action involving Cleopatra. The dying
Antony, the invading Proculeius with his Guards, Dola-
bella, Caesar and his train, the Clown with the asps, and
finally Caesar again, to view the bodies and to close
the play—all these in turn appear in the monument
'above'.

First, bringing news of Antony, *Enter Diomed*,

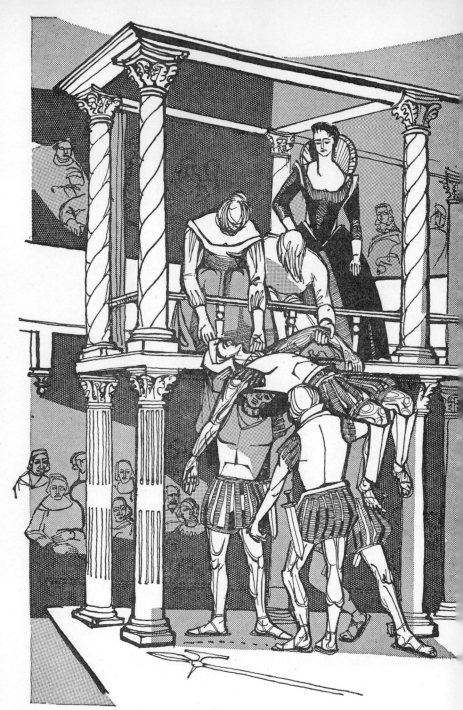

THEY HEAVE ANTONY ALOFT TO CLEOPATRA

between the back of the locked monument and the end of the stage, and Cleopatra hails him from aloft:

Cleo. How now? is he dead?
Diom. His death's vpon him, but not dead.
    Looke out o'th other side your Monument,
    His Guard haue brought him thither.

> *Enter* [to the front of the monument] *Antony and the Guard.*

Here follows the famous directed action in which *They heaue Antony aloft to Cleopatra,* in obvious contrast to the description in North's Plutarch. This unmistakable business provides the clearest indication I have found of the elevation of the upper floor of the 'house'. It could not have been raised more than six or six-and-a-half foot, to permit the Guard to heave Antony up to arms' length and within reach of the five or more boy-actresses above, and with their aid to get him safely in, on to the upper floor. We find this reachable height corroborated by a passage in Massinger's Globe–Blackfriars play *The Picture* 4.2, where from stage-level the servants hand up implements to Ubaldo and Ricardo, imprisoned above in two adjoining rooms. This moderate height also suits the 'leaping from the walls'—as the French in *1 Henry VI*, young Arthur in *King John*, and Forrest from 'above' in Heywood's *Fortune by Land and Sea*—a feat dangerous if not impossible, had the 'above' been twelve foot up, as theorists have firmly believed it was. The back of Cleopatra's monument is employed again for the 'surprise', when Gallus enters from behind while Proculeius holds Cleopatra in conversation.

The commonly-held theory that all the great final

passages of this tragedy were somehow exhibited in a remote pigeon-hole-stage in a 'scenic wall' at the back, set
more than fifty foot distant from the nearest facing gallery
seats, and raised twelve foot above the stage floor, requiring the manipulation of a block-and-tackle for hoisting
the hero like a bale of goods into a warehouse, shows how
far the uncritical acceptance of a preconception can lead
us into absurdity.

What we have just observed—the facility of realistic
front-side and back-side offered by these houses extending fore-and-aft near the stage-ends—was but one of the
effects of which they were capable. Another striking one
was the ability to present a character in a room 'above',
gazing down obliquely upon a scene shown at stage-
level in a downstairs room *in the same house*. This was
accomplished by making an 'upstairs' over one part only
of the oblong house, and leaving the room for ground-
floor action uncovered, without ceiling or roof. It is thus
in Ford's *Love's Sacrifice*, Act 5, that we are shown the
furious Fiormonda witnessing the achievement of her
deadly revenge on Fernando, who slighted her love, and
on Biancha, her successful rival:

Enter aboue, Fiormonda.

Fior. Now fly revenge . . .
> That I, en-sphear'd aboue, may crosse the race
> Of Loue despis'd, and triumph o're their graues,
> Who scorne the low-bent thraldome of my heart.

> *A Curtaine drawne, below are discouered Biancha in her
> night attire, leaning on a Cushion at a Table, holding
> Fernando by the hand.*

From her post above, Fiormonda sees all, even after
the doors to the room below are 'shut up' (though the

audience still sees the interior), and comments on the action throughout—the arrest of Fernando and the murder of Biancha by the Duke.

Fletcher brings this same scenic resource into play with powerful effect in Act 2 Scene 4 of his already-quoted *The Captain*. Angelo, in love with Lelia, bribes her maid to place him where he can see down into the room, on his promising 'not to stir, or speake'. Accordingly, *Enter Angelo above*, where he remains in full view of the audience. Then both Angelo and the audience witness, in the unroofed and transparent room adjoining below, Lelia's lascivious wooing of a reluctant old man (her own disguised father). After the maid is sent out, *Father locks the doore* and Lelia recognizes him. When even this appalling discovery fails to check her wickedness, her father resolves to kill her. *Father draws his sword*. From aloft, *Angelo discovers himself* to them.

Angelo. Hold reverend Sir, for honour of your age.
Father. Whoe's that? . . .
    What art thou, and how cam'st thou to that place?
Angelo.   . . . let me in,
    And I protest I will not hinder you
    In any act you wish, more then by word,
    If so I can perswade you; that I will not
    Use violence, I'le throw my sword down to you. . . .
Father.   . . . throw down thy sword.
Angelo.   There 'tis.

During Lelia's six lines of soliloquy, Angelo descends to the room adjoining, and the father *lets in Angelo and lockes the doore* again.

In *Henry VIII* 5.2 [1] Shakespeare shows us the King

---

[1] Acted at the Globe 29 June 1613.

and Dr Butts privately looking down from a window above the palace Council Chamber into the lobby at Archbishop Cranmer forced by the malice of his enemies to wait amongst pages and pursuivants before the Council Chamber door. The arrangement here is similar to that in *Love's Sacrifice* and *The Captain*.

We have just seen how in one oblong house two levels adjacent, not superposed—that is, the ground floor and an 'above' commanding a view of it—were shown together. But the versatile fore-and-aft house, with certain additions, could also present scenes realistically as 'aboard ship'. Here the stage-level end of the house, not surrounded with posts but railed in, represents the ship's deck. Its open trap provides the companion-way down to the 'hold'. The other end of the house, built up with framework, is the cabin, whose railed flat roof serves for the quarterdeck or poop. Set in the main deck is a lofty post for the mast, with a platform some fifteen or twenty foot up, reached by a taut rope-ladder, for the 'main top'.

Thus in the second act of Fletcher and Massinger's *The Double Marriage*, on to the main deck *Enter Boteswain and Gunner* from the cabin; and the Boatswain steps to the trap-hatchway and hails down it.

Botes. Ho, in the hold.

          Enter a Boy [*up the companion*].
Boy. Here, here.
Botes. To th' main top boy.

     Exit Boy [*climbing to the main top*]. . . .
    Enter [*up through a cabin hatchway to the poop-
    deck*] *Duke of Sessa above and his daughter Martia
    like an Amazon.*

They talk down from the poop to the main deck.

Botes. Call up the Master, and all the Mates.
> *Enter below [up the companion from the hold] the*
> *Master and Saylers . . .*
Boy above. A Sayle, a Sayle. . . .
Mast. Up, up, another,
> And give more certain signes.
> > *Exit Saylor [climbing to the main top].*

In another shipboard scene, Heywood's *Fortune by Land and Sea* Act 4, a Boy climbs to the main top.

When both the ground-floor room and the 'above' over it were open or uncurtained, the interior stairs leading up were naturally seen from all sides, as in Cleopatra's monument. Here follow a few illustrations of the use of visible interior stairs.

The murderous Merry (in Yarington's *Two Lamentable Tragedies*) plans to lure his neighbour Beech up to his upper floor and kill him from behind on the landing:

> And therefore I place the hammer here
> And take it as I follow Beech up staires . . .

When the unsuspecting Beech comes, Merry bids him 'Goe up these staires, your friends do stay above', and we see him pick up the hammer as he mounts close after his victim. Similarly in *Look About You* (sc. 23) people are shown climbing the stairs to an upper floor. At the Globe *A Yorkshire Tragedy* exhibits Calverley's mad violence to his family 'above' in his own house, including his throwing his child's nurse down the stairs:

> I'll break your clamour with your neck: down staires!
> Tumble, tumble headlong! so!

In *Titus Andronicus* 5.2 Tamora and her sons enter. *They knock and Titus opens his studie doore,* which is 'above', for Tamora twice bids him 'come downe'; and when he complies, says, 'See heere he comes'.

Marlowe's *The Jew of Malta* Act 5 shows the oblong two-storied house, with internal stairs and the usual cellar-traps at both its ends, as the rich Jew's residence. Barabas imparts to Ferneze his plan to invite Calymath and his fellow-bashaws up to a floor in his gallery made collapsible, and then Ferneze is to cut the cable and plunge them to their deaths in a cauldron prepared in the open cellar-trap directly beneath, in the closed room at ground-floor level. Ferneze warns the Turks of the plot; then while Barabas is standing above on his treacherous floor inviting them up, Ferneze cuts the cable and drops him into his own cauldron. Barabas is seen to drop from above, but his actual plunge into the pot is to be surmised; for when the curtains encircling the room below are opened, his head only is visible above the floor: he speaks, grimaces in agony, and expires.

> *Enter* [Barabas] *with a Hammar aboue, very busie.* . . . .
> *Bar.* Are all the Cranes and Pulleyes sure?
> *Serv.* All fast. . . . .
> *Bar.* There, Carpenters, diuide that gold amongst you: . ..
>   Downe to the Celler, taste of all my wines.
> *Carp.* We shall, my Lord, and thanke you.
>
>   *Exeunt* [Carpenters, *down from above at the other end,*
>   *and again down through the cellar-trap there.*] . . .
>
> *Bar.* [*confiding his plan to Ferneze*]
>
>   Now as for *Calymath* and his consorts,
>   Here haue I made a dainty Gallery,
>   The floors whereof, this Cable being cut,

Doth fall asunder; so that it doth sinke
Into a deepe pit past recovery. . . .

Enter Calymath and Bashawes [having been warned].

Caly. Come, my Companion-Bashawes, see I pray
How busie *Barrabas* is there aboue
To entertaine vs in his Gallery;
Let vs salute him. [*louder*] Saue thee, *Barabas*. . . .
Bar. Will't please thee, mighty *Selim-Calymath*,
To ascend our homely stayres? . . .

A charge, the cable cut,
A Caldron discouered.

At this point we may advantageously consider the Elizabethans' frequent use of the 'room' at stage-level to represent an upstairs room or a bed-chamber, and the open floor-trap to the tiring-house as stairs leading down to the street level. Thus *A Chaste Maid in Cheapside*, acted at the Swan, has (3.2) *A bed thrust out upon the stage*; *Allwit's wife in it*, and visitors come up through the opening in the floor as into a bedroom from downstairs. Richard Brome's *The Northern Lass* 2.2 similarly shows the stage-level as the first floor of Mrs Traipswell's house, with the trap-stairs as leading down to the street level:

Enter Beavis [up the trap from below] . . .

Tra. O, are you come? where's the Knight?
Be. He stayes below, and will'd me to come up first. . . .
Tra. [*to Constance*] . . . go you to your Chamber. . . .

Ex. Con. [climbing to the 'above'].

In the next scene Mrs Traipswell goes up to join Constance, and at her suggestion *She sings above*.

We have already noticed the instance in *2 Henry IV*

2.4 where Pistol appears up through the floor-trap as from downstairs, and on becoming insufferable is driven down again by Falstaff. Such scenes in taverns were favourites, making great play with some patrons arriving from below, and others entertaining themselves above. Brome provides a lively example of it in *The Covent-Garden Weeded* 2.2:

> *Vintner.* You are welcome, Gentlemen . . . (*he rings the bell*) shew up into the Phoenix . . . Carry up a Jordan for the Maidenhead, and a quart of white muskadine for the blew Bore. (*Run down the staires.*) . . . (*Fiddlers below [under the stage] tuning. Knock above, and a pot thrown.*) Why boyes, drawer, rogues, take up, (*below*) By and by, by and by, (*above*) Wine, Tobaccho.

In Dryden's *The Mistaken Husband*[1] 1.2 Learcut's servants Thomas and Isbel are separating for the night.

> *Thomas.* Do you go that ways to bed? [*Exit Isbel.*] I'll make down this way [*approaches the trap*].
> *Learcut.* [*below*] Are my knaves all deaf? shall I be murdered here? why *Thomas, Andrew*——
> > *To him* Learcut *coming up stairs he justles* Thomas *and falls on his knees, frighted.*

A century earlier, *Tancred and Gismund* had been performed at Court on a built-up stage-and-tiring-house; and in the Prelude to Act 4, through an open trap *from underneath the stage ascendeth Guiszard and he helpeth up Gismund.* The Induction to Beaumont's *The Knight of the Burning Pestle* (1607) exhibits similar action, when the Citizen is on the stage among the stool-holders and

---

[1] Acted early in the Restoration on an Elizabethan stage.

his Wife and Rafe are inside it, at the bottom of the trap-
stairs:

Wife below Rafe below.
Wife. Husband, shall I come up husband?
Citizen. I cunny. Rafe helpe your mistresse this way: pray
  gentlemen make her a little roome, I pray you, sir, lend
  me your hand to help up my wife . . . Boy, let my wife
  and I have a cupple stooles . . . Come up Rafe.

Preparation of one oblong house as two adjoining
rooms at stage-level readily accommodates the action indicated in many plays. A familiar example is *2 Henry IV*
4.4 and 5 (actually one continued scene), where the King
says 'Beare me hence Into some other chamber', the Lords
go to 'the other roome', and later say of the Prince, 'He
came not through the chamber where we staide'. Two
adjoining rooms are also vividly exhibited in Marston's
What You Will, Act 2: *Enter [i.e., Discovered] a Schole-
maister, draws the curtain behind with . . . schole-boyes
sitting with bookes in their hands.* That is, rooms A and B,
separated by a curtain, are shown completely enclosed.
For the action *Enter a Schole-maister*, the stagekeepers
draw three sides of A to reveal him. Then when he *draws
the curtain behind* to show the adjoining room, they simultaneously draw open the remaining three sides of B.
Exactly similar is the action in *Thomas Lord Cromwell* 3.2,
where 'Cromwell shuts the dore' to his (outer) room, then,
opening an inner one, reveals Hodge sitting 'in the study'.
This room behind is evidently shown as the 'place behind
the stage' (see 'stage' meaning 'booth', p. 140 above) in
Greene's *Alphonsus*: Mahomet's 'sacred seate'. And for
two adjoining rooms 'above', the stage direction for the

scene of gallantry in Jonson's *The Devil is an Ass* 2.6.38 is sufficiently precise: *This* Scene *is acted at two windo's, as out of two contiguous buildings.*

So much then for action shown with the traps from below, in one or two rooms at stage level, on the visible internal stairs, and in a room or rooms above—in a 'house' set fore-and-aft near one end of the stage. Now for a few interesting scenes which utilize houses at both the stage-ends.

A famous one of these—one impossible to be shown by the hypothetical 'alcove stage', and which therefore has annoyed all its apologists—is prescribed at the beginning of Peele's *David and Bethsabe*. Here the Prologue, finishing his speech,

> *drawes a curtaine, and discouers Bethsabe with her maid bathing ouer a spring: she sings, and David sits aboue vewing her.*

With the actual Elizabethan opposed 'houses', nothing could be more obvious than the setting here: the low, curtainable place for the bathing-spring at Stage Right (Prologue's side), and the monarch's gallery above at Stage Left opposite.

This is no more than the familiar arrangement for opposed settings at Court performances pointed out by Sir Edmund Chambers,[1] in which a commentator, 'presenters', or spectators are shown 'above' at one end, witnessing the play. In *The Rare Triumphs of Love and Fortune*, the speeches show the action. At the end of Act

---

[1] *The Rare Triumphs of Love and Fortune* and Lyly's *The Woman in the Moon. Eliẓ. Stage* 3. 45–46, and compare 3. 91–93.

DAVID SITS ABOVE VIEWING HER

1 Jupiter—above, in Heaven at Stage Right—tells the gods with him,

> Take up your places here to work your will. . . .
> Vulcan [*below, on stage*]. They are set sunning like a crow
> in a gutter.
> What, are they gone? . . .
> Are not these a sort of good, mannerly gods to get
> them away?

Even while Vulcan is calling attention to the row of gods sitting above at Stage Right, the curtains are shut on them: 'What, are they gone?'

But when Chambers notices the same on the public stages—*The Battle of Alcazar*, *James IV*, *A Looking Glass for London*, *The Taming of a Shrew*, and especially *The Spanish Tragedy*, where the Duke and his Court enter and then climb up to a gallery to see Hieronimo's 'play within the play'—it is only the usual mistaken preconception of a scenic wall with 'alcove stages', and the failure to realize that all performances were in the round, which prevent him from seeing that *opposition* was as obligatory on the public stages as it was at Court. For by no method other than that of opposed settings is it possible to present such scenes to spectators placed on both the long sides of the stage.

Especially for battle-scenes, one favourite treatment of the 'house' opposed to the Walls was to prepare it as a 'mount', sometimes no doubt with an external ramp for ascent.[1] Heywood's *The Rape of Lucrece* at the Red Bull has the city walls at one end, and a hill in opposition at

---

[1] Such a ramp, or easy external stairs from aloft, certainly seems indicated in 1.4 of Thomas Goffe's *The Courageous Turk, or*

the other. In Marston's *Sophonisba* (3.2) at Blackfriars, *Scipio leads his traine up to the mount*; and everyone recalls Pindarus's climbing the 'hill' in *Julius Caesar* 5.3 to report the progress of the fight to Cassius. By contrast, in *Bonduca* 5.2 it is 'a steep rock i' th' woods' where Caratach is at bay, lowering young Hengo over the cliff by a belt to get them food; later, the Romans surmount the rock from its other side.

Both hill and opposed city-walls come into play in staging Samson's unique feat on leaving the Philistine Gaza (*Judges* 16. 3), when he 'took the doors of the gate of the city, and the two posts, and . . . carried them up to the top of a hill that is before Hebron'.[1] The *Simson* of Hans Sachs, written 1556, bears the express stage direction *Simson nimbt das thor vnnd geht ab*.[2] Here he evidently

---

Amurath the first, played at Christ Church, Oxford, between 1609 and 1618:

A Masque.

Enter from aloft two Torch-bearers, then Jupiter *and* Juno, *and two Torch-bearers more, then* Mars *and* Venus, *and two Torch-bearers more, then* Apollo *and* Pallas, *and two more Torch-bearers, then* Neptune *and* Diana. *Whilst they are descending*, Cupid, *hanging in the Ayre, sings to soft Musicke this Song . . .*

[1] This celebrated Biblical exploit, which excited Don Adriano de Armado's imagination (*Love's Labour's Lost* 1.2), was a literary commonplace: 'Where's that strong man that did so many kill? . . . That carried *Asah* gates to *Hebron* hill' (Samuel Rowlands, *A terrible battell betwixt Time and Death*); '*Sampson* that pull'd the Gates of *Gaza* downe' (John Taylor, *The Sculler*, Epigram 37); and of course Milton, *Samson Agonistes* 146–148. A carved misericord at Ripon shows the hero with one of the gates on his left shoulder, the other under his right arm. See M. R. Anderson, *Misericords* (Penguin), plate 11. The author points out that Samson was associated with the Resurrection, and that this carving and another were 'closely copied from the woodcuts of a fifteenth-century *Biblia Pauperum* printed in the Netherlands'.

[2] Qu. Max Herrmann, *Forschungen zur deutsche Theatergeschichte* (1914), 69–70.

carries the gates off the stage, not up a visible hill. About the London performance in 1567 at the Red Lion, Stepney, of 'the playe, which is called the story of Sampson' we have no details.[1] But another performance of a *Samson*, with the exploit fully shown on the stage, is reported in Middleton's *Family of Love* 1.3, where some characters have just been to a play, in which they 'saw Sampson bear the town-gates on his neck from the lower to the upper stage'. The muscular actor bore the gates—property ones, like the 'Canvas stone' of Hercules Furens [2]—from the city walls or Hell at Stage Left (the lower) up the 'hill of Hebron' or Heaven above at Stage Right (the upper stage).

Since the Spanish stage closely resembled the Elizabethan, it is not surprising that settings such as we have been considering—two scenes 'above' opposed, the use of one upper scene's back and front, as Cleopatra's monument or Caratach's rock—are found paralleled in stage directions from Spanish plays. Among those pointed out by Dr N. D. Shergold are the following:

in *La fuerza de la verdad* by D. Francisco de Malespina there is to be a hill on either side of the stage: 'Van subiendo por vno de los montes que avrà a los lados del teatro'. It was possible to descend from the hill on two sides in *El valiente Campuzano* by Fernando de Zárate: 'Por vn lado del monte baxen Campuzano, y Pimento de Soldados . . . Por el otro lado del monte baxe la Cartuxa', and two staircases lead down to the stage from *lo alto* in Fernández de Mesa's play *Cada uno*

---

[1] Records of the Carpenters' Company, qu. Chambers, *Eliz. Stage*, 2. 379.

[2] See Beaumont and Fletcher Folio (1647), sig. b2ᵛ.

con su igual: 'Ha de auer vn bosque con dos escaleras q[ue] baxan al tablado'.[1]

And among the many evidences of this similarity quoted by H. A. Rennert [2] we find two 'aboves' at opposite ends (*corredores de arriba*) shown as castles upon which the adversaries in turn display their banners:

saca Silveria sobre los corredores de arriba, a un lado una bandera . . . Al otro lado saca arriba Olivenza otra bandera.[3]

In another, a Turkish man-of-war is unveiled above at one end; then at the other in opposition a Maltese galley:

En una parte de lo alto del teatro se vea una Galeote Turca . . . y en la popa Moros . . . Disparando se descubre otra cortina en la otra parte, y se vea una galera de S. Juan.[4]

Houses set facing each other from the stage-ends offered a most impressive means of showing the magic revelation to characters at one place of a scene being enacted far away. Greene's *Friar Bacon and Friar Bungay* 2.3 affords an excellent example of this resource. Within the Friar's transparent cell, Edward is bidden to peer through 'this glasse prospective' trained at the cell-wall, but in the direction of the other end of the stage. Then both he and the audience see the far-off scene unveiled with its actors living and moving. A magic 'television'

[1] Dr Shergold has generously permitted me these quotations from page 270 of his valuable unpublished dissertation 'The Staging of Secular Drama in Spain, 1550–1700', Cambridge University, 1953.

[2] *The Spanish Stage in the Time of Lope de Vega* (1909), 85n. 1; 'The Staging of Lope de Vega's Comedies' *Revue Hispanique* XV (1907), 471.

[3] Tirso de Molina, *Doña Beatriz de Silva*, Act 1.

[4] Lope de Vega, *El Amete de Toledo* (before 1617), Act 1.

or precisely the same sort is realistically conjured up in Chapman's *Bussy D'Ambois* 4.2.

Each of the ends could be divided up into as many as three houses, thus affording realistic simultaneous or multiple settings—such as were provided at Court performances—for plays requiring many locations. Thus at one end of the Fortune stage for *The Roaring Girl* are presented *The three shops open in ranke*. And a similar setting at one end of the Blackfriars stage for *Eastward Ho* has *Enter Maister Touch-stone and Quick-silver at severall dores . . . At the middle dore, enter Golding, discovering a gold-smiths shoppe*, while at the other end are prepared Sir Petronel's house, Security's house, and the Blue Anchor Tavern. In a few cases, in addition to the normal and usual entrances opposed at the stage-ends, we do find on both public and private stages, a property-dock door pressed into service as the 'middle door'.[1] But the customary crowd of stage-sitters along that wall and the elevated stage-boxes above them were far from encouraging a property-dock door's frequent employment as a localized piece of scenery.

If anyone should be tempted to doubt that three set 'houses' could be accommodated at one end of the Blackfriars stage, built in a hall 46 foot wide, one has only to consider the 1631–32 performance of Hausted's *Senile Odium* in the Hall of Queens' College, Cambridge. Here the length of a stage built up across the room, including end-houses, was limited to the 28-foot width of the hall. The depth of the stage is conjectural; but that built at Woodstock in 1621 for Holyday's *Technogamia* measured 24 by 16 foot.[2] Similar proportions would give the Queens'

---

[1] See *Eliz. Stage* 3.74n. 1, and 132n. 1.   [2] P.R.O., E351/3254.

College stage a depth of about 18 foot. Possibly it was somewhat more. But on some such depth as that, for *Senile Odium*, six separate houses were simultaneously set, three at each end, one of them furnished with an 'above' for action at a window. Separation between two neighbouring houses is indicated in 3.8, where one of them has a 'back door somewhat facing' the other house.[1]

Here an interesting question suggests itself. How did the colleges present their plays when they could not afford a complete removable theatre such as Queens' College, Cambridge, purchased in 1638 (pp. 170–172 above)— built-up tiring-house-and-stage with end-houses, and scaffolded galleries to set up against all four sides of the hall? Sometimes a built-up stage could be afforded;[2] at other times ingenuity supplied some of the lack. Records reveal that one ready method was to have the dining tables moved together to make a stage across the hall.[3] In some cases they paid for the erection or building of houses for the stage-ends;[4] but in others for this purpose of scenic entrances they more economically employed the

---

[1] *Aurelius [to Eugenius]*. Nostin' tu posticum vestrum aliquando in aedes spectans Ludovici . . .?

[2] 'Joani Dowse pro bidui sua opera cum famulo diruentibus scenam in aula ac reponentibus res illas in lignario' (Queens', 1540–41); 'for framing yᵉ stage' (Trinity, 1570–71); 'for making the stage at the playes' (Trinity, 1586 87). Malone Society *Collections* II, pt. 2 (1923), 184, 167, 169.

[3] For plays at Christ's College, Cambridge, in 1551–52 the carpenter was paid 'for removing yᵉ tables in yᵉ haull & setting yᵉᵐ vp agein with yᵉ houses'. *Ibid.*, 206.

[4] 'pro erigendis domibus eiusdem comoediae' (Queens', 1545–46); 'for makynge howses for yᵉ players' (Trinity, 1556–57); 'for making houses at the Comaedie' (Corpus Christi, 1581–82); 'for paynting the stage . . . for paynting the Sayleirs [*i.e.*, the *celures* or roofs of the houses]' (Trinity, 1614–15). *Ibid.*, 185, 159, 210, 172.

available pieces of furniture called *portals*. To understand just what these portals were, we should first distinguish the two kinds: the outward portal (what the French call *avant-portail*), a porch outside a main door,[1] and the inward portal, 'A space within the door of a room, partitioned off, and containing an inner door' or 'a little square corner of a Room, shifted off from the rest of the Room by the Wainscot'.[2]

What they used was inward portals—roofed frames with a door or hangings (*portières*), usually set up in a room 'before a door, to keep off the wind'.[3] Obviously these were excellently suited to serve as houses or scenic elements for entrances, set at the ends of the table-stage. The 'Colledge stuff' for plays at St John's College, Cambridge, in Henry VIII's time included three 'portals' of wainscot, along with two tables, 'hanginges of owlde red sai', a great chest and 'a great cofer' containing 'plaiars raiment' and 'plaiars apparell'.[4]

The medieval-Elizabethan houses opposed at the stage-ends persisted in the Latin-play productions of Westminster School into modern times. In the most recent illustrated account of them, however, Mr Richard Southern [5] erroneously concludes that this medieval method came in with 'classic-type plays'; and also misled by the common false assumption of a scenic wall at the

---

[1] Compare 'The two Portals that ietted out before these Posternes, had their sides open foure seuerall wayes', Dekker, *The Magnificent Entertainment*.

[2] *O.E.D.*, s.v. Portal 2. (*obsolete*).

[3] Cotgrave's dictionary on *Portail* or *Oste-vent*. Compare the Spanish *cancel*, and the modern French *tambour*.

[4] R. F. Scott, *Notes from College Records*, Fourth Series, 275.

[5] 'The "Houses" of the Westminster Play', *Theatre Notebook* 3 (1948–9), 46–52.

'back' of the Elizabethan platform, he fails to see that these houses at Westminster are a continuation of the universal arrangement of the native English stage described by Sir Philip Sidney—'Asia of the one side, and Affrick of the other'. On the public stages too the medieval 'houses opposed' survived well-nigh into living memory. Outside the curtain on the stage of the Surrey Theatre in the 1850s, writes Clement Scott, facing from each end stood 'to all intents and purposes a little house'. And he goes on,

> It was fascinating to a child to see on either side of the stage proper a little green door with brass knockers and handles, and over each door a window with lace curtains and a balcony with flower pots in it.[1]

The uncurtained, open stage—frequently miscalled 'forestage' or 'apron'—is nothing but *the original stage of the Medievals and the Elizabethans*. Progressively encroached upon since 1660 by the exotic perspective 'scene' first introduced at its 'throne' side (which we now call the 'back'), all that survives of it in some theatres is the slender slice between the curtain and the footlights, and in others, nothing at all. Even its historic name, *proscenium*, has been forgotten—the name which means 'that which stands in front of the "houses" (*scenae*)'.

To close this treatment of the Elizabethan stage-technique of end-houses on a lighter note, I may again compare the contemporary similar methods maintained in Spain. To look up the term 'stage hand' in a modern English–Spanish dictionary is to find *metemuertos*, literally 'corpse-remover'. We need hardly remind ourselves

---

[1] Qu. M. Summers, *The Restoration Theatre* (1934), 143.

that on the arena-stage of Lope de Vega and of Shakespeare, if the fatally-wounded could not manage (as
Clenardo does in *El Caballero de Illescas*) to fall dead
'within'—that is, into one of the 'houses' standing over
traps at the stage-ends—the 'bearers' or stage hands had
to be on the spot to carry or drag such bodies 'in' to those
hangings.

Occasionally, to be sure, the action required the
player, as Gloucester or Hamlet, to 'throw thy bodie in
another roome', or to 'lug the guts into the neighbour
room'. Hamlet's punning 'Come sir, to draw toward an
end with you' suggests the action: 'From his mother's
closet he hath dragged him' 'toward an *end*'—to the hangings at the other *end* of the oblong 'house', where under
their momentary shelter Polonius can promptly come to
life and get down into the tiring-house through the trap.

The late W. J. Lawrence [1] saw a situation in Shirley's
The Cardinal in which he found it 'impossible to divine
how the bodies littering the rush-strewn boards were
cleared away'. Of four men alone on the stage, three are
killed; and the fourth decamps, remarking of the third
victim, 'I must not stay to bury him'. Lawrence asks
what became of the bodies, since 'it is hardly conceivable
that each . . . took care to fall back through the rear-stage
curtains. Yet what other solution is admittable?' It
would perhaps have helped him to know that there was
no 'rear stage', and that the presence of hangings at both
ends of the stage made things somewhat easier. But Body
Number Three at least is certainly still lying visible on
the stage when the survivor goes off. Just another routine
job for the *metemuertos* or bearers.

[1] *Those Nut-cracking Elizabethans* (1935), 75.

'I TOOK THEE FOR THY BETTER'

These 'mutes' are as rarely mentioned or spoken to as those ever-present and 'necessary attendants of the stage' the curtain-drawers or stagekeepers. But everyone re-calls the profane speech given to Nell Gwynn, lying dead on the open stage at the close of Dryden's *Tyrannick Love*, 'Spoken by Mrs *Ellen*, when she was to be carried off dead by the Bearers':

To the   Hold, are you mad? you damn'd confounded Dog,
Bearer.   I am to rise and speak the Epilogue.

When on the Italianated English stage the proscenium arch had at length encroached sufficiently far, its front curtain simplified the problem of corpse-removal. You could drop the curtain on a final scene of carnage, and the corpses could rise and walk off unassisted. But on their open *tablado* the stage hands of Spain had carried off the dead into the *corredores* or end-houses for so many generations that in our latter day, when both in England and in Spain the need for bearers to clear the boards of bodies has long been forgotten, they are still *metemuertos*.

VIII

STAGE-SITTERS AND LORDS' ROOM

Two of the unmistakable and characteristic features of a production at an Elizabethan public theatre are the crowd of stool-holders sitting on the stage, and the spectators over it in elevated boxes known as 'the lords' room'. As W. J. Lawrence pointed out,

> Of the four known views of early non-scenic theatres, three show incontestably that spectators sat in elevated boxes at the back of the stage.

But since this is the location of the theoretical 'balcony stage', and what is more, a position from which it is physically impossible to see into the hypothetical 'inner stage' beneath, it is small wonder that theorists hitherto have joined in an effort to argue the 'lords' room' out of existence.

Let us consider first the stage-sitters—what Chambers called 'the throng of feathered and restless gallants'—who customarily graced the Globe's 'crowded stage'.[1] In pages preceding we have seen enough of the actual common system of staging with end-houses to realize how mistaken the theory was which obliged historians to assume that the stool-holders sat out along the ends of the stage. The awkward question whether any gentleman in his right mind would pay a high price to sit out as an annoying obstruction to the unruly groundlings' view, his silk or velvet outside inviting apples, eggs, and stones

---

[1] Henry Hutton, *Follie's Anatomie* (1619), sig. B2ᵛ.

from those below, and exposed to wet from gusty showers blown under the eaves of the 'cover', does not seem to have been asked. And unhappily for the 'central inner stage' theory, the contemporary evidence shows that 'at the ends' is just where these gentlemen did *not* sit.

The familiar *locus* is Dekker's prescription for the Gull's behaviour in the playhouse:

let our Gallant . . . presently advance himselfe up to the Throne of the Stage. I meane not into the Lords roome [1] . . . But on the very Rushes where the Commedy is to daunce, yea and under the state of *Cambises* himselfe must our fethered *Estridge*, like a peece of Ordnance be planted valiantly (because impudently) beating downe the mewes and hisses of the opposed rascality.

That is to say, he and his like sat *centrally* at the 'ground-front' [2] of the property-dock, under the lords' room, *facing* the 'opposed rascality' massed in the yard across the stage. Had they sat at the stage-ends, they would have been neither in the dancing-area nor 'enthroned'. Their two parties would have been *opposed* not to the rascality, but to each other. The contrast between the

---

[1] 'I meane not into the Lords roome (which is now [1609] but the Stages Suburbs): no, those boxes, by the iniquity of custome, conspiracy of waiting-women and Gentleman-Ushers, that there sweat together, and the covetousnes of Sharers, are contemptibly thrust into the reare, and much new Satten is there dambd, by being smothred to death in darknesse.'
This passage means that gentlemen at this date scornfully prefer to sit openly on the stage below, rather than to be crowded above in the lords' room with loose courtiers of more wealth than wit, who by extra payment have contrived to pre-empt those select boxes for an amorous crush. 'Suburbs' connoted 'assignations' or 'brothels'.
[2] For 'ground' meaning 'stage-level', see the English Wagner Book's description of Hell (at Stage Left) as a 'ground-worke'.

amphitheatrical Elizabethan method, with the stage-sitters facing forward conspicuous from the central property-dock wall, and the façade-stage, where to see the play they must sit at the two ends facing inward, is manifest.[1]

We find the public amphitheatre's choice southwest side adjoining the stage, containing the lords' room or boxes, galleries, and the commanding central 'front' for the stage-sitters, thus described in the induction to *Lady Alimony*:

be . . . our *boxes* by ladies of quality . . . crowdingly furnished? our *galleries* and *ground-front* answerably to their pay completed? [Italics mine.]

And later the less select remainder of the house, beyond the outward side of the stage, is reported:

Besides, sir, all our galleries and ground-stands are long ago furnished. The groundlings within the yard grow infinitely unruly.

The august central station of the stool-holders between the opposed 'houses' or end-scenes shows itself from the days of Elizabeth to those of Charles I:

Throne your selfe in state on the stage, as other Gentlemen use Sir.[2]

---

[1] For a picture of spectators sitting at the ends of Molière's stage, see the print of a scene from Brécourt's *La Noce de Village*, acted 1666, reproduced in Abry, Audic, et Crouzet, *Hist. ill. de la litt. française* (1916), 156; and for similar sitting at the stage-ends of the Lincoln's Inn Fields Theatre in 1728 see Hogarth's painting of *The Beggar's Opera*. No stage-sitting whatever had been permitted in the reign of King Charles II. See M. Summers, *The Restoration Theatre* (1934), 54–62.

[2] Jonson, Induction to *Cynthia's Revels*, 1601.

The world . . . unto a Theater comparëd is,
Upon which stage the goddes spectatours sitt,
And mortals act their partes.[1]

[Knights of the Garter] sit in the Center
Of common stage Playes.[2]

For these central stage-sitters, whom latter-day theorists
of 'scenic wall' staging must deplore, relegate 'by all
logical analysis' to the fringes, and in practice banish alto-
gether as an impossible nuisance, in reality adorned the
stage as the magistral bench of 'Judges [who] sit to doom
each Play': the *dramatic critics*, whose displeasure is
dreaded, and whose favour is ever sedulously courted
with provision of the most advantageous seats:

Player. Watch at the doors before the Play begins,
And make low congies to the cruel Criticks
As they come in.[3]

Who silent sits on stage, each players part
With judgement sound to harken and behold.[4]

By your leave Gentlemen. You Wits o' th' age,
You that both furnisht have, and judg'd the Stage,
You, who the Poet and the Actors fright [5] . . .

A sound realism will replace the mythical 'inner stage'
with these magistrates of wit, sitting 'on the Stage at
Black-friars, or the *Cock-pit*, to arraigne Playes dailie'.
And at the public theatres, backed by the other gentles in

---

[1] R. C., *The Time's Whistle* (ca. 1615). E.E.T.S. (1871), 126.
[2] ?John Eliot, *Poems* (1658), 77.
[3] Davenant, *The Play-house to be Lett*, Act 1.
[4] *Anon.*, B.M. MS. Addl. 10110, f. 207.
[5] Henry Harington, Beaumont and Fletcher Folio (1647), sig. f4ᵛ.

the southwest galleries, they presided 'in the Center Of common stage Playes', 'under the state of *Cambises*' at the head of the open court, like a tribunal: 'you sit The Lord and Judge of all fresh wit',[1] 'when your comedies and enterludes have entred their actions', hearing plays as if they were pleas—the amusing or impassioned exchanges between adversaries confronted like two 'hemispheres' left and right before them on the tennis-court-like platform.

> Come, boy, the other Pipe. They say
> The Tragedy's to come,
> Still Musick but divides the Play;
> The last Act crowns the sum. . . .
>
> The Plot begins to dawn: I see
> The parts in clouds divide;
> Each Hemisphere darts enmity,
> And th' ruin of a side.[2]

'Below the bar'—down beyond the stage-rails—a heaving press of the populace thronged the *parterre* or body of the court as on a Star Chamber day at Westminster, but here far more enthralled by the dramatic poet who

> Can draw, with adamantine pen, ev'n creatures
> Forg'd out o' th' hammer, on tiptoe to reach up

---

[1] Suckling, *Fragmenta Aurea* (1646), 35. From this commanding 'throne' side, the introduction of Italianate perspective scenery drove them and the other gentles across the stage to the pit below, where they still sit to this day:

> But, gentlemen, you that as judges sit
> In the star-chamber of the house, the pit . . .

Thomas Jordan, *A Prologue to introduce the first woman that came to act on the stage, in the tragedy called* The Moor of Venice.

[2] 'Mercurius Britannicus' for 19–26 October 1652. Obviously by a Cavalier (possibly D. Border), counterfeiting an issue of the Parliament newsbook.

And, from rare silence, clap their brawny hands
T'applaud what their charm'd soul scarce understands.[1]

And in tragedy, how irresistibly wrought by the crises
of passion even these 'judges' on the stage found themselves, is witnessed to by Thomas Palmer in his praise of
Fletcher:

> Like Scenes, we shifted Passions, and that so,
> Who only came to see, turn'd Actors too.
> How didst thou sway the Theatre! make us feele
> The Players wounds were true, and their swords, steele!
> Nay, stranger yet, how often did I know
> When the Spectators ran to save the blow?
> Frozen with griefe we could not stir away
> Untill the Epilogue told us 'twas a Play.[2]

It was on the Elizabethan open stage, 'circled about with
wonder of all eyes', a stage intimately embracing both
performer and public, that the dramatic poet developed a
psychological power able to send a critic leaping from his
judicial seat to the rescue of a threatened character.

So much for the centrally-seated stool-holders, who
corroborate the de Witt sketch in showing that the
'inner stage' is a myth invented by ignorance. As for the
lords' room over their heads, the conspicuous central
boxes over the stage shown filled with spectators in the
de Witt drawing—this, when not prostituted to base
uses for a premium, was the choice objective of the
social climbers. Fastidious Briske, for one, who talks

as if he had . . . ta'ne tabacco with them, over the stage, i' the
lords roome.[3]

---

[1] Dekker, Prologue to *If it be not good the Devil is in it*, 1612.
[2] Beaumont and Fletcher Folio (1647), sig. f2ᵛ.
[3] Jonson, *Every Man Out . . .* 2.3.191.

> See you him yonder, who sits o're the stage,
> With the Tobacco-pipe now at his mouth?
> It is *Cornelius* that brave gallant youth
> Who is new printed to this fangled age.[1]

> One that sat over the stage [2] . . .

Ben Jonson himself (as 'Horace') is warned against venturing on the stage after his play is ended 'to exchange curtezies, and complements with Gallants in the Lordes roomes'.[3]

Leading actors on a busman's holiday characteristically made a point of exhibiting themselves in this 'best and most conspicuous place':

> The [Mogul] King sits out like a player in the gallery over a stage to be seene.[4]

And the actor Richard Perkins, a principal Queen Anne's man, complacently confesses in 1612:

> Still when I come to playes, I love to sit,
> That all may see me, in a publike place:
> Even in the stages front.[5]

Here again we have the head-on collision between the fully amphitheatrical arrangement of the actual Elizabethan stage and our illusory Italianate notion of it. Like the East Indian king, 'in the gallery over a stage to be seene', Perkins is showing himself to all from the centrally-placed lords' room, above the 'ground-front' of the

---

[1] Guilpin, *Skialetheia* (1598), sig. B4.
[2] Dekker, 'The 45 Iest' in *Iests to make you merrie*, 1607.
[3] *Idem*, *Satiromastix*, sig. M.
[4] Sir Thomas Roe, 14 February 1615/16, qu. C. C. Stopes, *Southampton* (1922), 379.
[5] Verses to Heywood's *Apology for Actors*, sig. a3.

critics, facing directly across the open stage towards the yard. Since his, the inward side, is the best spectator-side of the house, he properly calls his position 'the stages front'; just as its outward edge, bounded by the low-paying groundlings, to whom the actors more often turn their backs, is properly the 'back'.

If we would see Shakespeare's stage as the 'quality' and the critics saw it, we must once and for all leave the position in the distant cheaper galleries or with the rascality, from which we have been imagining Perkins's place as the 'back'. In the lords' room on the expensive, sheltered, and commanding side above the critics, he is in fact sitting conspicuous in the 'best place' in the stage's front. Stage Left is his left, Stage Right his right. It is the 'understanders' in the yard and the far-off gallery-sitters behind them who are at the back.

The artist who drew for us the stage of the Globe showing the scene at Middleton's *A Game at Chess*[1] took up his standpoint in this gentlemen's 'front'. He shows us the Black House and 'Hell' (which is always at Stage Left) *at the left of the picture*. And the actors, entering from the hangings at the stage-ends, of course play more to this select audience than they do to the 'stinkards' below: just as they do at Court to royalty's seat, the upper end, and at the colleges of the Universities to the dais-head above the stage, where Masters and Doctors preside.

It is by no accident that this central head of the room 'in the stage's front' was seen as the judgment-seat 'where the goddes spectatours sitt', and was called the 'state' or 'throne'. For the throne was the stage's traditional central feature, dating from the days of the mysteries, and

---

[1] See Frontispiece.

still flourishing as late as 1658 on the stage of the Amsterdam Schouwburg. The *domus* or *sedes* of the King or Judge (*e.g.*, Herod, Pilate) held the centre. Heaven stood at his extreme right, and Hell at his extreme left—where it remained on Shakespeare's stage, and where it is still located on the English stage today.

The centre of the stage described in the English Wagner Book of 1594 is dominated by the traditional 'high Throne . . . prowdly placed'. Obviously, it is *forward* to this 'throne' (surrounded, as Dekker implies, by the 'court' of gentlemen-critics) that the Elizabethan Prologue, entering at Stage Right, makes his 'three lowly obeisances'—as he does to the Throne when acting at Court; and not, as our mistaken and Italianate theory would grotesquely have him do, to the rascality back in the yard below.

As we have already noticed, the contemporary Spanish stage of the *corrales* remained, like the Elizabethan English, medieval and amphitheatrical, a plastic stage. In 1623 the Spanish term for 'a theater where comedies are represented' is the descriptive *un coliseo*, a circus.[1]

Its persistent medievalism is one of the countless manifestations of Spain's tenacious adherence to the traditional, the customary, the popular.[2]

Like Shakespeare's, Lope de Vega's stage had no unified 'scenic wall', either with or without recesses. And again like Shakespeare's, in the place of a 'scenic wall' it showed not only boxes for the *gente principal* in the best side of the house, next to and over the stage, but also the central

---

[1] Percivale-Minsheu's *Dictionary*.
[2] W. H. Shoemaker, *The Multiple Stage in Spain* . . . (1935), 125.

'state', as well as the *lienços* or hangings which curtained the open, pillared *corredores* right and left at the stage-ends:

> Below in the middle of the yard was the stage or platform, with a 'state' at the head, and, at the two sides, old curtains of painted cloth or figured silk, with openings for the entrance of the players. With these curtains everything was represented—sea and land, country and city, house and forest, hall and hovel, except in the plays with stage-machines and *apariencias*.[1]

In England, as in Spain, tradition dies hard. In the Middle Ages the dais-centre by the best seats at the head of the stage was the place of the king's or judge's court. In the days of Cervantes and of Shakespeare the *dosel*, the throne or 'state', was still there in the stage's front, backed by the *aposento del Consejo* or 'lords' room' above. And when, after the great days of the drama were done, Italian influence at last diminished Spain's open stage to 'one side' by the introduction of the back-scene, this latter took its name, *foro*, from that same feature, centuries old: '*Foro*, court of justice; (*theatr.*) background, drop-scene'.

Again like the Elizabethan English, the Spanish theatres-in-the-round had a door or doors serving the

---

[1] 'En el centro bajo del corral estaba la escena ó tablado con dosel ["*Dosel de seda*, a hanging of silke, under which the kings or great personages sit"—Percivale-Minsheu] en el fondo y cortinas de indiana ó damasco antiguas por uno y otro lado con huecos para la salida de los comediantes. Con estas cortinas se figuraba todo, mar y tierra, campo y ciudad, casa y bosque, sala y choza, salvo en las comedias de tramoyas y apariencias.'

A. Sánchez Moguel on the early *corrales* of Madrid, in his *Estudio sobre . . . Calderón*, qu. José Sánchez Arjona, *El Teatro en Sevilla* (1887), 140.

select stage-and-tiring-house side of the house, opposite
the public gate. At the Corral del Coliseo, Seville, 1612,
for example, records speak of

the doors very close to the stage and tiring-house which
admitted the spectators.[1]

Also at Seville's Corral de la Montería, 1628,

A small door, situated facing the main one, and adjoining the
stage, gave access to the [four] rooms reserved for the
Governor of the Castle and some other dignitaries who held
office there.[2]

This select over-the-stage correspondent to the English
theatre's lords' room is described for the Corral de la
Olivera in Valencia, rebuilt 1618:

At the balcony level appeared a loge for spectators: they
called it sometimes *aposento del balco*, sometimes *aposento del
vestuario*. A roof covered it, flattened as much as possible so
as not to mask the windows opened in the back wall.[3]

In similar fashion, and like the Boar's Head's 'said
weste galleryes over the said Stage', the London Globe's
choice southwest or stage-side was entered by the second
or tiring-house-and-stage door, placed opposite the

---

[1] 'las puertas que daban paso á los espectadores muy próximas
al tablado y vestuario.' J. Sánchez Arjona, *Anales del Teatro en
Sevilla* (1898), 152.

[2] 'Una pequeña puerta, situada frente á la principal, y junto al
escenario, daba entrada á los [cuatros] aposentos reservados para el
Alcaide del Alcázar y algunos otros ministros que tenían oficio en
ella.' *Idem, El Teatro en Sevilla*, 140.

[3] 'Au niveau même du balcon, une loge s'ouvrait où les spec-
tateurs étaient admis: on la nommait tantôt *aposento del balco*,
tantôt *aposento del vestuario*. Un toit la couvrait, qu'on avait sur-
baissé le plus possible pour ne point masquer les fenêtres ouvertes
dans le mur du fond.' Henri Mérimée, *op. cit.*, 43.

(northeast) main door. And this whole side of the theatre was far from being wasted on the curtained 'acting areas', storage-rooms, and work-rooms imagined by the modern mind's eye Italianated. With the one exception of the property-dock (with stage-sitters crowded in front of its wall), from stage-level up it was all properly and profitably employed in galleries protected against sun, wind, and rain for the wealthiest patrons 'in the stage's front'. And overhead, large windows in the lofty gable-ends of the 'hut' passed southwest light through the whitewashed joists of its open floor to illuminate the broad stage beneath the high rain-cover.

Hemmed in thus above on every hand by packed galleries, and below by a crowd of sitters on its best side and on the others by the multitudinous upturned faces of the groundlings, the Elizabethan public stage seemed to float like an island on an inland sea. As 'Sir Alexander' in *The Roaring Girl*, the player standing on the Fortune's stage describes what he sees round about him:

> Nay, when you look into my galleries . . .
> Within one square a thousand heads are laid,
> So close that all of heads the room seems made . . .
> The very [stage-]floor, as 't were, waves to and fro,
> And, like a floating island, seems to move
> Upon a sea bound in with shores above.[1]

---

[1] Pointed out by M. W. Sampson, *Modern Language Notes*, June 1915.

IX

RIGHTEOUS HEAVEN AND
SINISTER HELL

> ... and now in little space
> The confines met of empyrean Heaven
> And of this World, and on the left hand Hell.[1]
> *Paradise Lost.*

> [Judas] a two-fold path descries,
> One leading up a hill, Repentance' way,
> And (as more worthy) on the right hand lay:
> The other headlong, steep, and liken'd well
> Unto the path which tendeth down to hell.
> William Browne, *Britannia's Pastorals.*

> You ...
> That have the office opposite to Saint Peter,
> And keepes the gate of hell.
> *Othello.*

IN earlier chapters it has been sufficiently established that the Elizabethan stage was arranged and equipped to show Heaven and Hell facing each other from the stage-ends. Such *loca* or *sedes* have no place in any Renaissance 'scenic wall', but are properties retained from the medieval amphitheatre—its multiple or 'simultaneous' settings, its free-standing 'places' or 'houses'. 'At Mons in 1501, as at Valenciennes in 1547, Hell ... is at the extremity opposed to Paradise'.[2] In *The Harrowing*

---

[1] 'In the Midrash Tehillim XC, it is expressly stated that Hell (Gehenna) is on the left hand of God.' E. C. Baldwin, *Mod. Lang. Notes* 40 (1925), 251.

[2] Cohen, *op. cit.,* XXI.

of Hell, the Chester Whitsun play, Christ in triumph invades Hell, delivers its prisoners, and takes them to Heaven. In order to body forth the antithesis of Good and Evil, or of Angel and Devil, Heaven and Hell *had* to stand opposed at the ends of the medieval-Elizabethan platform. Clearly, this inescapable duality of religion, of Hell Mouth opposed to Paradise, cannot manifest itself in any secular, humanistic façade of palaces, arches, or connected house-fronts.

Although in our latter-day Christmas pantomimes the devils still come up with flash and smoke, no 'reg'lar-built, all-fired Hell' survives in the foreground of our modern mental landscape.[1] But it would be foolish to forget that for the Elizabethans the infernal fire burned ever-present, as it had done for their forefathers when the Cooks of Chester presented *The Harrowing of Hell*. At the terrible climax of Marlowe's tragedy, Faustus, crying 'Ugly hell, gape not!' is carried alive to the everlasting flames, 'And burnëd is Apollo's laurel-bough'. In Caroline times John Earle is confident with his infernal metaphor: '*A Cooke:* The Kitchen is his Hell, and hee the Divell in it.' Not less real were the fires of Purgatory in which Hamlet's father was 'confined to fast'.

By means of built-up stages, Hell was shown both at Court and in the public theatres. For *Gorboduc*, Whitehall in 1562 was able to present three furies coming up

---

[1] How vivid by contrast was the Hell-vision of our ancestors, who could read a detailed guide-book, beginning

Ignis, et Algor, Stridor, et Horror, Lacrima, Vermis,
Malleus, et Fetor, Spes perdita, Vincula, Fames,
Esse, carere Deo, Tenebre, Vox, Mors sine Morte ...

B.M. MS. Harley 1801, f. 105b.

'from under the stage, as though out of hell'; and for *Gismund of Salerne* (February 1566), Greenwich Palace was furnished both with a Hell for Megaera and a Heaven for Cupid. We find both 'hell, and hell-mowthe' supplied as stage properties at Whitehall in 1571–72, and 'heaven' and 'hell' mentioned by the Clerk of the Revels in 1574–75. At the Rose on Bankside in 1598 Henslowe inventories 'j [one] Hell-mought'; and as we have seen, the English Wagner Book of 1594 mentions as a customary feature of the public theatre 'at the one end of the Stage . . . the teeth of this Hels mouth far out stretching'. 'Hell is discovered' in Scene xvi of the amplified *Doctor Faustus*; and recalling his personal torment with heckling and disorder on the stage of the Hope, John Taylor the Water-Poet exclaims,

> What I endur'd vpon that earthly hell
> My tongue or pen cannot describe it well.[1]

For, as Dekker testifies, Hell was 'under everie one or their stages'.[2] Bounding the ends of the boards left and right, Hell and Heaven embraced the stage and all the absorbing scenes enacted upon it. As the actor Estoutevile (Stutevile, Stutfield) assures the prolific playwright Heywood, 'thou wilt still Make all 'twixt heaven & hell flow from thy quill'.

Deeply ingrained in the ancestral mind of England, the outward symbolism of religion's antithesis or dualism has become so much a matter of second nature as to be overlooked. From the beginning the Lords Spiritual took the Sovereign's right, the 'upper' hand. In Chaucer's time

---

[1] 'Taylors Reuenge', *Works* (1630), Second pagination, 146a.
[2] *Newes from Hell*, 1606.

we find 'The Clergy then placing themselves on the
Right-hand, and the Nobility on the Left-hand of the
King, according to the ancient custom of the High Court
of Parliament . . .'[1] If (especially after the Reformation)
it seems a bit hard on the nobles at the Sovereign's left to
equate them with Hell—and they might retort with
'Reason is our Soules left hand, Faith her right'[2]—the
faithful have the last word with the camel and the needle's
eye. The Temporal or Money Power cannot refute
Gospel.

Pluto, god of gold, ruled the nether regions. As Milton
observes, 'Let none admire That riches grow in Hell';
and Donne sings of Cupid,

> He's an infernal god, and under ground,
> With *Pluto* dwells, where gold and fire abound.[3]

John Webster pictures Pluto's rising out of the time-
honoured Hell trap at Stage Left in *The Duchess of
Malfi* 3.2:

> Pluto the god of riches . . . when he's sent One [*i.e.*, on]
> the Divells arrand, he rides poast, and comes in by scuttles.

The Oxford English Dictionary (s.v. *Scuttle*), forgetting
stage convention, here amusingly mistakes the sense. It
represents Webster's majestic Dis or Pluto as *scuttling in*,
with 'a short, hurried run'. But the *scuttles* which Pluto

---

[1] *A True Historical Relation of that Memorable Parliament* [of
10 Ric. II], 1641. Reprinted by J. Morgan, *Phoenix Britannicus*
(1732), 392.
[2] Donne, Verse Letter to the Countess of Bedford.
[3] For Pluto-Plutus, see F. L. Lucas's excellent note, *The Complete Works of John Webster* (1927), 2. 167; and Dr Percy Simpson,
Studies in Shakespearean Drama (1955), 11.

comes in by are nothing else than the ancient and indispensable 'cuts' in the stage—the traps or 'risings', the
entrances from below:

> *Opens the Scuttle, . . . pulls up to him* Learcut.[1]

This *scuttle* is the Old French *escoutille*, Port. *escotilha*,
Span. *escotillón*:

> *Enter by the scuttle or trap* (por el escotillón) *the
> demon Pillan.*[2]

'When in the scene they invoked the demons, these came
up quite tranquilly by the stairs of the scuttles (*escotillones*) or
openings in the stage.' [3]

And when Edward Alleyn as Marlowe's conjuring Faustus cries '*surgat Mephistophilis!*' it is up through the open
Hell trap at Stage Left that the frightful fiend emerges
from the tiring-house. Ordered down again to change his
horrible shape for something better, he sinks—and eight
lines later once more comes in by the scuttle, now trans-
formed as a Franciscan friar.

We have already remarked that the amphitheatrical
arrangement gave the important spectators sitting on the
'Throne' or lords' room side of the stage the same view
of it as that of the 'King'. Hell (Stage Left) was at their
left, Heaven (Stage Right) at their right. Early French
plays show this clearly. The positions of the actors in *Le*

---

[1] Dryden, *The Mistaken Husband* 5.1. The first instance of
scuttle in the sense of 'run' recorded in the *O.E.D.* is dated 1712,
a century later than *The Duchess of Malfi.*
[2] Lope de Vega, *Arauco domado*, Act 1.
[3] Ricardo Sepúlveda, *El Corral de la Pacheca* (1888), 11.

Mystère d'Adam (thirteenth century) are indicated according to Stage Right and Left; and addressing the élite on the Throne side, the Presenter of *Le Mystère de Saint Vincent* (1476) says, '*Premier voiez la en droit paradis*'—pointing to Heaven at Stage Right, *their* right.[1]

All this is made obvious by Fouquet's famous miniature showing the amphitheatrical presentation about 1450 of *Le Mystère de Sainte Apolline*.[2] Here the numerous select ladies of the open-air audience sit conspicuous in the protected gallery adjoining the central Throne. Heaven rises therefore at their extreme right, and Hell Mouth gapes at their left. In order to be able to show both scenery, actors, and the splendid 'gentles' of the encircling audience, the artist has necessarily taken up his stand with the populace on the lower, the 'yard' or 'parquet' side. From this outside point he naturally sees and draws Heaven at the left and Hell at the right, which is the reverse or improper view: that of the London 'understanders' in the yard and of the occupants of the cheaper northeast galleries behind them at the Globe.

It is revealing to mark this reverse or 'back' point of view of 'the vulgar sort' catered for in the illustrated broadside ballads hawked to the man in the street. For example, in the woodcut adorning *The Lady Pecunia's Journey unto Hell*, Hell Mouth is shown *at the right*, as it always appeared to the groundlings. In another, Hell Mouth is again at the right, God at the left; and in a third, the Devil appears once more at the right.[3]

---

[1] Cohen, *op. cit.*, 76; and cf. 59.

[2] *Idem*, XIV and plate facing page 86.

[3] See the reproductions in H. E. Rollins, *Cavalier and Puritan* (1923), 335, 214, and *The Pack of Autolycus* (1927), 78.

That the lords at the court of James I observed the same ancient decorum—of howling Hell at Stage Left and harmonious Heaven at Stage Right—is evident by Campion's *Lords' Maske* (1613):

> On the left hand from the seate was a Caue, and on the right a thicket, out of which came Orpheus . . . Mania, the Goddesse of madness, appears wildly out of her caue.

This question of 'whose left is the real or proper left' we find sharply settled by Mistress Indulgence in the play *Apollo Shroving*,[1] when telling her maid Jugge Rubbish how to hold up the mirror for her upper-class use:

Ind. Thou spitefull baggage, more yet on the left hand.
   Is *that* thy left hand?
Jug. Heere's my left hand.
Ind. I, but the other side is *my* left hand. You must conforme
   your eyes and hands to your Mistresse, and forget which
   is your owne right or left.

Just like Jugge Rubbish, the populace and the gallery-sitters on the yard side, the outside of the Elizabethan stages, although they *saw* Sinister Hell at their right, had to forget their own right and left, and conform their eyes to their 'masters', the gentry sitting opposite, filling the expensive 'front' or 'inside'.

It is no accident that by the English, whose stage remained amphitheatrical until the Restoration, Stage Left (Hell station, Prompt Side) is still called 'Left', while the French, who much earlier changed to the one-side or façade stage, have long called the same side 'Right'.[2] For

---

[1] By William Hawkins, 1627 (ed. H. J. Rhoads, 1936), 4.3.
[2] See Cohen, *op. cit.*, 38, 59.

what governs usage here is the point of view of the director—French, *metteur en scène, animateur*. He conducts the rehearsal from what will be the position of the important spectators. If the staging is modern, Italianate, one-side, the director must take his stand with the unified audience, and see Stage Left at his right. He is taking the objective, the outsiders' view of the scenic situation. If on the other hand the staging is amphitheatrical, with the important spectators on the upper or Throne side of the stage, the director stands there. He takes the insiders' view of the proceedings, and Stage Left is his left.

Since the French are logical to a fault, and their actors (like Jugge Rubbish) must conform their hands to their masters, on the French stage their left is 'Right', and the French describe Hell—which is always at Stage Left—as standing at the 'Right'. But the medieval terminology still maintained in the English-speaking theatre shows how much longer the English stage remained amphitheatrical, its audience divided. Facing the 'vulgar sort' across the open oblong platform, the master-part of the audience sat like courtiers by the 'King' or Throne. Like the ladies at *Sainte Apolline*, they were the 'gentles', the audience *par excellence*. As insiders, Stage Right (Heaven) was *their* right, Stage Left (Hell) *their* left. After centuries of continuous habit and use, the English nomenclature was fixed: not to be shaken by the reversal logically called for when the exotic unified or 'scenic wall' stage-setting was at length adopted after 1660, and the 'gentles' thereby obliged to move across and join the 'general', the outsiders, on the lower or pit side of the stage. And to this day, when at the Christmas pantomimes in London the imps and devils appear from their

244

unchanging, age-old Hell-station, it is still called 'Stage Left', even when royalty is in the 'one-side' audience.

And even in the earlier-changing France, how little the Renaissance had affected the popular stage during close on two hundred years after the *mystères* of the fifteenth century has of late been strikingly demonstrated by Professor Raymond Lebègue.[1] He shows us a play, the *Martire de la glorieuse Ste. Reine d'Alize*, published 1687 —ten years, as he reminds us, after Racine's *Phèdre*—on being produced at the small provincial town of Alise (Côte d'Or). Although admitting the exotic modern in the form of a back-drop, its 'simultaneous' setting (as shown by the stage-directions, of which I here translate passages) still exhibits the transverse axis of the medieval-Elizabethan theatre: 'scenes' or 'places' opposed, together with entrances, at the ends of the oblong stage, left and right:

Arrangement of the Stage.

On the right side of the Stage [*i.e.*, Stage Left, Hell] at the end, must be raised an Idol of Jupiter . . . beside it . . . there must be a Hell Mouth whence the Devils come forth. . . .

At the other end of the Stage [*i.e.*, Stage Right, Heaven] . . . three Crosses . . . and three trees . . . Among these three trees . . . a little Cell, which shall be the retreat and prison of Sainte Reine.

In the middle of the Stage there must be a Throne . . .

The Hangings must have two entrances: the one by the Statue [Stage Left, Hell] . . . the other by the Crosses [Stage Right, Heaven], where Sainte Reine will enter.

In short, everything is exactly the same as it was in the fourteenth century; but the important audience has

---

[1] 'Quelques Survivances de la Mise en Scène Médiévale' in *Mélanges . . . offerts à Gustave Cohen* (1950), 219–221.

moved from the stage's 'front' or Throne side across into
the pit: the migration which causes Hell, remaining at
Stage Left, to be now logically called 'Right', even in the
conservative and provincial Alise.

An English word-picture of similar multiple scenes
opposed in the Elizabethan circus-theatre, as they appeared to the contemporary mind's eye, is drawn for us
by John Norden [1] during the great Queen's lifetime.
Here is his portrayal of the drama of England under the
Catholic, heretic-burning Mary Tudor, who 'broke
Religion's frame': [2]

> She pul'd it downe, and did erect the stage
> Whereon was plaid the tragedy of *rage*:
> It stoode not long, the Actors partes were done,
> And they went out, *Eliƶaes* part begun,
> And all applaud her, and her equipage.
>
> Began it now? a part she playd before,
> Not of an Agent, but a patient:
> She silent sate, and heard the Lions rore,
> Like captiv'd *Daniel* in a dreadfull tent.
> Her part was not like daughter of a King
> To whome *All hayle*, the truest subjects bring.
> Curtaines were drawne to sit in all mens view,
> Prince-like attended: Shee with bloudy crew
> Guarded as guilty: cover'd with *loves* wing.

---

[1] *A pensiue soules delight* (1603), sig. B4ᵛ.
[2] Compare True Religion's speech:

> 'With this sharp sword . . .
> A cruell Lady pearcd me to the heart . . .
> Her name was Mary that did act this part:
> But e're she kilde me she was slaine by death,
> And I revivd'e by young Elizabeth.'
>
> R. C., *The Time's Whistle*, 'Somnium', ll. 79–84.

As Queen Elizabeth said in 1586, 'we Princes, I tell you, are set on stages, in the sight and view of all the world'. Accordingly, 'set before all mens eyes and in the middest of the Theatre of the whole world', Norden's second stanza presents to the encircling audience the stage of England under Catholic Mary, with young Elizabeth a 'captiv'd Daniel' [1] sitting imprisoned 'in a dreadful tent'.

Contrast and opposition form the soul of the setting in 'this throngëd round'. At Stage Left (Hell) stands the stately and gloomy curtained house representing Mary's Spanish Court. Facing it from the other end, at Stage Right (Heaven), stands the 'dreadful tent' holding 'This Phoenix of the world, the worthiest *Dame* That ever acted on the Stage of Fame' [2]—the young Elizabeth, or True Religion Oppressed.

Then, discovery. The curtains encircling are drawn away in turn for each 'to sit in all mens view', conspicuous from every side of the amphitheatre. First, at the Hell end (Stage Left) the opening curtains disclose the Protestant-burning [3] Queen Mary, 'Prince-like attended' by her black court of enemy priests and Spaniards. When this baleful sight has had its long moment to sink in, from the Heaven end opposite comes the contrasted opening of

---

[1] '*Daniel* and I are envied both, because
We give that honour to the King of heaven
Which others unto Images have given.'
Christopher Lever, *Queen Elizabeths Teares*, 1607.
[2] J. L., *An Elegie vpon Elizabeth*, 1603.
[3] 'Some three hundred men and women were burned in less than four years [under Mary] . . . On the average, four Catholics suffered for every year of Elizabeth's reign, as against 56 Protestants for every year of Mary.' G. M. Trevelyan, *History of England* (1926), 321, 363.

the 'dreadful tent'. Elizabeth the Prisoner appears in view, 'She with bloudy crew guarded as guilty'.[1] But—with an angel or minister of grace appearing over her head from 'above'—she is 'cover'd with *loves* wing'.[2] A year before Norden's publication, Richard Vennar had decoyed a throng to the amphitheatrical Swan Playhouse with a playbill announcing *England's Joy*; in Scene IX of which Queen Elizabeth 'is taken vp into Heauen, when presently appeares, a Throne of blessed Soules, and beneath vnder the Stage is set forth with strange fireworkes, diuers blacke and damned Soules'.

It is his own and his readers' familiarity with the physical conditions of the actual public stage which gives Norden the features of his picture. Throughout the reign of James I those conditions continued without any change, as we have seen by the staging in 1624 before packed audiences at the Globe of Middleton's *A Game at Chess*.

To close this chapter on the Elizabethan stage's traditional and typical opposition of Heaven to Hell, we may now turn to consider two important features intimately involved with it: the 'music' and the prompter.

Whereabouts in Shakespeare's arena-playhouse are we to visualize the theatre-orchestra and the singers as sitting? Having forgotten that on his open oblong the

---

[1]   'I am, (alas) into this prison cast,
          And (God he knowes) without deserving cause:
          And I among such Lions now am plac'd,
          As watch to seaze my body in their pawes . . .'
                                                        Lever, *ibid.*
[2]   'Then sith that we so like to *Daniel* are,
          God will as well for us as *Daniel* care.'
                                                        Ibid.

Elizabethan actor had 'a heaven and a hell of his own', and attempted to squeeze him—like the Dormouse into the teapot—into a couple of remote pigeon-holes, it is little wonder that we have not known where the indispensable 'music' was placed. Plainly, it was somewhere 'above' or 'aloft', for by immemorial theatrical custom the musicians occupied a platform, a 'room', or a gallery elevated above the main stage. '*Pulpitum* . . . The higher part of the stage, where the Musitians were' (Littleton); '*Poulpitre* . . . a room for Musicians in the upper part of a Stage' (Cotgrave); '*Jubé* . . . a high place made for singers, or other Musitians, over stages, &c.' (*idem*).

As W. J. Lawrence wrote, after reviewing the evidence from the plays,[1]

It is to be clearly deduced . . . that the music room was situated at an elevation, that it was fronted by curtains, and that it was occasionally used as a place of dramatic action. If this is not sufficient proof of its precise locality, if it fails to identify it with the curtained upper stage, I despair of ever winning acceptance for the best substantiated of theories.[2]

Lawrence's conclusion was perfectly sound, except that the 'curtained upper room' was not, as hitherto imagined,

---

[1] In Marston's *Malcontent* 1.2 the music is above in Malevole's chamber, and in his *Sophonisba* Act 4 there is *soft musick above*; in ?Webster's *The Thracian Wonder* 4, 182, 186, we have *Pythia above . . . speaks in the Musick-room behinde the Curtains*; in William Rowley's *A Shoo-maker a Gentleman* 1.3, *Musicke heere descends*; in Massinger's *The Bondman* 3.3, the music is 'in yon window'; and in his *City Madam* Act 4, *Musick come down*; in Walter Mountfort's *The Launching of the Mary*, ll. 245 and 2791, *musique aloft*; and in Richard Brome's *The Novella* 5.1, 'Goe up to the Bride-chamber. There is musick.'

[2] *The Physical Conditions of the Elizabethan Public Playhouse* (1927), 92.

a recess aloft in a scenic wall at the 'back', but the upper part of the 'house' (*alto, corredor de arriba*) or Heaven— 'the place wherein the bloudlesse skirmishes are so often perfourmed on the Stage, the Wals'—standing at the end (Stage Right) in opposition to Hell.[1] Manifest corroboration for this is supplied by Jasper Mayne's line, 'Thou laidst no sieges to the *Musique-Roome*'.[2]

Thus elevated, the 'music' did not materially block the surrounding audience's view of action on the stage. In the small, octagonal St Paul's—the ancient Chapter House, internal diameter about 37 foot—they were perched on a curtained platform atop a mast (like the Roman *Meniana*), called a *music tree*: 'Vpon euerie branch sat a consort of singers, so that euerie tree shewed like a Musick roome.' *'While the measure is dancing, Andrugios ghost is placed betwixt the musick houses.' 'While the act is playing, . . . Tiberio climbs the tree, and is received Above by Dulcimel, Philocalia . . .'* [3]

Heaven, with its singing planets and its angelic bands and choirs, has ever been inseparable from music; [4] and

---

[1] This Heaven staged opposite to Hell is of course completely distinct from the high rain-cover or 'shadow' with its central 'hut' —'The couerings of the stage, which we call the heauens' (Heywood, *Apology for Actors*)—for which Cotgrave gives the French '*Volerie* . . . a place ouer a stage which we call the Heauen': the modern fly-gallery.

[2] *Jonsonus Virbius*, 1638.

[3] Dekker, *The Belman of London*, 1608; Marston, *Antonio's Revenge* 5.5; idem, *The Fawne*, before Act 5.

[4] 'Ful of heuenysshe melodye' Chaucer, *Troilus and Criseyde* 5.1813; 'With all the troupes seraphicall Which in the heavenly bower Melodiously, with one accord Ebuccinate God's power' Thomas Newton, *An Epitaph upon . . . Lady Knowles*, 1568; 'There's not the smallest orb which thou behold'st But in his motion, like an angel sings' *The Merchant of Venice* 5.1.56–57; 'Heaven is music' Thomas Campion, *Observations in the Art of*

on the mirroring stage the music must necessarily sound *de coelo histrionio*—from the players' Heaven. A glance at Fouquet's familiar miniature of the production-in-the-round of *Le Mystère de Sainte Apolline* shows that

> Where the bright Seraphim in burning row
> Their loud uplifted angel-trumpets blow

is in Heaven above at Stage Right; and in the painting of the indoor performance at Montbrison 1588 of Loys Papon's triumphant *Pastorelle* [1] we again see the 'music' in precisely the same position—in a balcony over the entrance at Stage Right.

The Elizabethan playhouse-musicians, 'those ayrey soules that grace our Cittie Theaters',[2] similarly perched aloft on the Walls of Heaven at Stage Right; and it was doubtless to encurtain their 'music of the spheres' that the Admiral's men employed their 'cloth of the Sone & Mone'. The hangings of the players' Heaven, its sun and moon, and the sieges of its Walls are all reflected in Nashe's *Christs Teares Ouer Jerusalem*, 1593:

> God shall haue nere a Tabernacle or retyring place in your Citty, which hee shall not be vndermined and desolated out of. The Sun & Moone (perplexed [*i.e.*, anguished] with the spectacle) shall flye farther vpward into Heauen, and be afraide least (when the besiegers haue ended be-lowe) they next sack them [3] . . .

English Poesie; 'An Antipathy as dissonant As heauen and hell, the musique of the spheares, Comparde with gnashings, and the howls below' William Rowley, *All's Lost by Lust* 2.1.108–110.

[1] *Pastorelle sur la Victoire obtenue contre les Alemands . . . Representée le Vintseptiesme jour de Fevrier 1588.* B.M. MS. Harley 4325.

[2] Henry Glapthorne, *The Lady Mother* 2.1.

[3] *Works* (ed. McKerrow), 2. 48–49.

Richard Bernard's *The Birthe of Hercules*, acted at a Cambridge college between 1595 and 1598, had for the musicians 'a players' Heaven, clearly distinguished with moon and stars'; and in the fifth act 'Music, either of trumpets or organs, is heard as though beginning, from the players' Heaven' and 'Here the choir is heard singing as from Heaven'.[1]

On the open, uncurtained outward half of the English Restoration stage, which retained the Elizabethan opposed entrances with the 'aboves' over them, the music was still kept at the post of Heaven. In 1667 at the crowded Duke's Theatre, Lincoln's Inn Fields, Pepys says he was 'forced to sit in the side belcone over against the musique-room'. And 'a very ancient stage-veteran, who had his information from Bowman, the contemporary of Betterton', told Malone that 'the band . . . sat in an upper balcony, over what is now called the stage-box'.

Turning now to the problem of the prompter or book-holder, we ask, where was he placed so that he could be heard on an open oblong stage 43 ft. by 27½ ft.—an area of 1182 sq. ft.—and also in the tiring-house? This practical problem would baffle anyone who believed that the tiring-house was *behind* the stage, as it baffled Sir Edmund Chambers.[2]

Now however that we know it was *underneath* the stage, the chief difficulty vanishes. The prompter could

---

[1] B.M. MS. Addl. 28722. 'Ad comoediae magnificentiam apprime conferet vt coelum Histrionium sit luna & stellis perspicue distinctum' (f. 4). 'The soft musick with the song begun by Jupiter . . . Audiatur quasi incipiens musica vel buccinarum vel organorum, de coelo histrionio' 'hic Chorus audiatur cantans quasi de coelo' (f. 32).

[2] *William Shakespeare* (1930), 1. 106–107.

station himself—his head showing above the floor—in one of the four trap-openings near the corners of the stage, and by ducking down be heard in the tiring-house as well. The well-known allusion to prompting from the tiring-house in *Cynthia's Revels* [1] I find corroborated by Richard Brathwait, 'The Booke-holder stands in the Tyring-house; but the Action must be presented on the Stage',[2] and by Torriano's definition of the Italian *soffiare*: [3] 'to prompt as Players do one to another from the tiring room to the Stage'. Moreover, since the corner-traps were the entrances from the tiring-house to the open, curtainable 'houses' standing over them, 'Siparius'—the book-holder's name in *Lady Alimony*—is further corroboration; for *Siparium* is 'a curtain round about, or hanging canopy, of the little houses in stage-plays'.[4]

Yet the question remains, Which of the four corner-traps was the prompter's station? In the English-speaking theatre of today, Prompt Corner by tradition stands L.1.E.—downstage Left. This is the age-old Hell Corner, where the devils still emerge in Christmas pantomimes. And when once we begin to suspect that this traditional location of the prompter in Hell Corner may be centuries old, corroboration appears from every quarter.

First, the gaping 'ground-work' of Hell Mouth offers the most strategic position for communication between the stage and the tiring-house underneath. Indeed the

---

[1] Induction, 158 ff.: 'We are not so officiously befriended by him [the author] as to have his presence in the Tiring-house, to prompt us aloud, stampe at the Booke-holder . . .'

[2] *A Survey of History* (1638), 217.

[3] In his enlarged edition (1659) of Florio's dictionary.

[4] See page 141 above.

prompter's post in this infernal region among devils and tormentors may well have increased the deep-rooted association between 'prompting' and 'evil':

The deuel foluand & promttand.[1]

> ... the stage
> Whereon they act their enuies stratagemes:
> And that the prompter of their practises [2] ...

> ... by a subtill prompt of the divill.[3]

The Italian for 'prompter' is *suggeritore*, 'the suggester'; and Hexham's English–Dutch dictionary translates 'a suggestion of the devill' as *een in-gevinge des duyvels* and 'a prompter' as *een in-gever*. Chaucer presents 'suggestioun of the feend', 'the suggestioun of the Devel'; the Elizabethan John Carpenter, 'the flesh (which he [the devil] also suggesteth)'; [4] and with Shakespeare the usual sense of *suggestions* is similarly 'temptations'.

The acted drama no doubt affords more illustrations beyond the two following which I have noticed: first, in a play much influenced by *Hamlet*, Goffe's *Tragedie of Orestes*. In 3.5 Orestes and Pylades approach the enchantress Canidia's cave, obviously at the Hell end of the stage. Then *Sound infernal Musick*, and *Enter Canidia*.

Orest. Protect us O ye Ministers of heaven,
    stand neare me my good *Genius*, my soul hath lost
    his humane function, at this hellish sight.

---

[1] 'a1340 Hampole *Psalter* xxxiv 7', qu. *O.E.D.*
[2] John Norden, *op. cit.*, F2ᵛ.
[3] J. Payne, *Royall Exchange* (1597), 27.
[4] *The Parson's Tale* I. 330, 350; *A Preparative to Contentation* (1597), 176.

And when the witch presses them to speak, the equally-aghast Pylades exclaims,

> Prompt us some Ghost.

Does not this thought occur to the author because it was from this hellish region that stage-promptings always came? Prince Hamlet, with his powerful 'cue for passion', is prompted to his revenge not only by the usual Hell, but by Heaven too.

Another piece of evidence comes from a prologue [1] spoken at Drury Lane in 1697, in which the comedian Haines addresses the prompter in his Hell Corner:

> *Do you hear? You Prompter! You may spare your pains,*
> *The Devil shall hearken to you, before* Jo Hains.

On the Spanish stage also in 1762 the prompter's place was at the Hell end, for

his head appeared through a little trap-door . . . and I first took him for a ghost or a devil, just ready to ascend to these upper regions,

wrote the English ambassador's chaplain, used to seeing 'risings' from Stage Left, the infernal end of the London stages. [2] In Garrick's practice the Ghost of Caesar appeared at this Prompt Side (Stage Left), and sank down again through a trap. The Closet-scene Ghost in *Hamlet* is pictured in Rowe's *Shakespeare* (1709) appearing similarly at Stage Left or Prompt Side: a piece of business exactly maintained nearly two centuries later both in Louis

---

[1] To John Dennis's *A Plot and No Plot.*
[2] The Rev. Mr Clarke, in *The Theatrical Review* (May 1763), 178, qu. W. J. Lawrence, *Old Theatre Days and Ways* (1935), 28.

James's production of 1882 and in Lawrence Barrett's of 1887.[1]

It may be possible to follow the fascinating topic of the prompter at Hell Corner a step farther. For the cruel work at Hell Mouth, the Devil was expertly assisted by butcherly fiends in red or flame-coloured 'skincoats'—the *tortores* or tormentors. As Dekker says of a prison, 'it is hell it selfe . . . the officers of it tormentors'.[2] At Canterbury in 1543 a charge was made for 'making of Cloaths for the tormentors in the play'.[3] But it looks very much as though in addition to the live tormentors (and perhaps to keep down salaries), lay-figures of the same were painted and set up by Hell Mouth. For the Play of St George at Bassingbourne, Cambridge, in 1511 the churchwardens paid 'for painting three fanchoms [?phantoms] and four tormentors'.[4]

I put it forward as more than a probable conjecture that the ancient prompter at Hell Corner habitually screened himself behind these painted tormentors; for still today *Tormentors* on the stage are defined as 'Painted flats or curtains placed right behind the proscenium [arch] to mask from the audience the prompter'.[5] And something closely resembling this has recently been discovered by historians of the French theatre on their own modern stage. They have found that *le manteau d'Arlequin*—a narrow red drapery precisely corresponding to

---

[1] This evidence out of prompt-books is drawn from Professor Arthur C. Sprague's valuable work *Shakespeare and the Actors* (1944), 325, 379, 129.

[2] *Iests to make you merrie* (1607), 'The description of a Prison'.

[3] H.M.C. *Ninth Report*, App. 153*b*.

[4] Warton, *Hist. Eng. Poetry*, 3. 326.

[5] W. G. Fay, *A Short Glossary of Theatrical Terms*, 1930.

the English stage's tormentor in location and use—is a corruption of the medieval *le chape d'Hellekin*: 'the jaw of Hell',[1] and has nothing to do either with capes or cloaks or with Harlequin.[2]

---

[1] 'First, Hell-mouth, with a nether chap.' Among properties listed for the Mystery of Tobit at Lincoln, 1563, qu. *The Gentleman's Magazine*, June 1787.

[2] See O. Driesen, *Der Ursprung des Harlekin* (1904), 66–86; and Cohen, *op. cit.*, 95–97.

X

ORIENTATION

First of all, towards the East, Heaven.

BEYOND the necessity of showing Heaven at the right of the Throne, 'and on the left hand Hell', there was however another requirement to be met for a Christian nation of countrymen and seafarers living by sun and wind, as compass-wise as Synge's Christy Mahon[1]— namely, *orientation*. Everyone knows that orientation controlled the planning of churches. But how many have realized how far not only royal courts, but the theatres— which took up and carried on the drama from the ecclesiastics—maintained the custom?

First, for the courts. The engraving of Queen Elizabeth's Parliament sitting in Westminster's White Hall or Court of Requests, with the canopied Queen at the south or 'good' end, shows the Clergy seated at her right, at the east or 'Heaven'.[2] A detailed account of a later Parliament in this same hall, which includes description of the amphitheatrical seating round the full circumference, is that by John Noies, M.P., of the great scene enacted there in June 1610, showing the same orientation:

I have here sent unto you the maner of the Creation of Prince Henrie. First that great roome, which is called the

---

[1] 'I gave a lep to the east. Then I turned around with my back to the north.' *The Playboy of the Western World*, Act 2.
[2] Reproduced from Sir Simonds D'Ewes, *Journals of the Parliaments of Queen Elizabeth* (1682) as frontispiece to Sir John Neale's *The Elizabethan House of Commons*, 1949.

Courte of Requests, was hanged rounde about with cloths of
Arrasse with five or six benches or foormes one above another
rounde about the house [*i.e.*, 'scafolded . . . *on all parts*' as it had
been for a play under Henry VIII], and in the middes of the
house there was as it were an allie rayled on eache side for a
cleare passage to goe in and out. At the upper ende [*south*] was
the kinges throne with a riche canopie over his head, on his
right hand [*east*] sate the Lorde Chauncelor, and at his leaft
hand [*west*] the Lorde Treasurer. . . . The Lord Bishoppes
sate on the right hande, and the judges and barrons on the leaft
hande.[1]

And in the Great Hall at Whitehall, likewise built due
south and north, Queen Elizabeth similarly sat at the head,
the 'good' or 'holy' south. Before her at Shakespeare's
presentation of *Twelfth Night*, Olivia's house stood inevitably at her right, at the heavenly east ('Now heaven
walks on earth'), that of the love-melancholic Orsino at
her left, 'due west', in the dark declining Occident.

The common traditional orientation of churches, scene
of liturgical drama, with altar and the 'good' side at the
east and south, the 'bad' or devil's side at the north or
west,[2] was inevitably continued in the public arenas of the

---

[1] H.M.C., *Various* 3. 259, from B.M. MS. Addl. 46842. Italics
mine.
[2] 'Evil appeareth out of the north', *Jeremiah* 6.1; Olaus Magnus
says the Devil has his seat in the north, *Compend. Hist.*, 51; '*Ab
aquilone omne malum*', Peele, *The Hunting of Cupid*, 29; 'There hath
been an old saying that all evils rise out of the north', Richard
Barckley, *The Felicitie of Man* (1598), 327. Old churches had a
door in the north wall, opened at baptisms and Communions 'to
let the devil out'. To show their contempt for orthodox ways,
the Puritans of Emmanuel College, Cambridge, built their chapel
with its head to the north, the devil's side, earning Corbet's satire:

> Just like the chapel ominous
> I' the college called God with us:

miracles and the mysteries. For staging the 1474 Passion de Rouen, the direction reads *Premierment vers Orient, Paradis*. 'Heaven, placed at the eastern end of the stage, is separated by all the rest of the scenery from Hell'—which is a monstrous Mouth 'opening and shutting at need'. And for *Le Mystère des Trois Doms* at Romans, 1509, *y avoit paradis devers le levant et enfer au couchant*.[1] In the Donaueschingen Passion, the Lucerne Easter Play, and *The Castle of Perseverance*, Heaven was placed at the east, Hell at the north or west. And with the setting thus oriented, the select audience was accommodated at the south: which is doubly good—first because it is the 'holy' place, and second because it is the best spectator-side, with its back to the sun.

Not only Passion plays but pageantry too gave proper and realistic regard to the points of the compass. The shows to adorn the Entry of the Duc d'Anjou into Antwerp in 1581 afford a characteristic instance. Riding north (from the 'good' south, the sun at his back) on what is now the Rue Haute Rivage, the Duke found Heaven presented at the Rue Reynders to his right *at the east*, and Hell at the Marché au Lin to his left *at the west*:

[On the second day, the Duke proceeding northward] along the said street of Saint Michaell to the great marketsted ... there were two pageants more prepared, which were devised both in one daie; the one was Mount Parnassus, whereon sat Apollo, apparelled like the sun, and accompanied with the

---

Which *truly* doth stand much awry,
Just north and south, *yes verily*.

When the Puritans lost control at Emmanuel, another chapel, more decently oriented, was promptly built.

[1] D. C. Stuart, *Stage Decoration in France in the Middle Ages* (1910), 116, 118, 175.

nine Muses plaieng upon diverse kinds of instruments, and with sweet voice singing a certeine ditie togither, written in commendation of his Highnesse. This pageant was in the street called the High-street over against the street named Reiner-street [*i.e.*, on the right hand, east]. Right over against this pageant was an other on the side of the street called the Flax-market [left, west], which was a mossie rocke overgrowen with drie and withered trees, wherein appeared a cave verie hideous, darke, and drierie to behold, and in the same laie lurking the three helhoundes Discord, Violence, and Tyrannie [1] . . .

When Charles II passed through London to his coronation, the music was again properly stationed in the heavenly quarter: 'On the East-side, Winde-Musick.' [2]

With a growing suspicion that this essential significant orientation—not merely of churches and royal halls, but of open-air Passion plays and pageantry as well—was continued in the theatres, let us look first at the 'public' playhouses such as the Globe, which 'lay partly open to the weather'.

Evidently, in facing the question of the weather we are outside the realm of academic or closet-fancy about Shakespeare's theatre. We confront a stubborn reality. The Elizabethan builders of those open-air playhouses unquestionably had to give as much careful thought to the prevailing direction of sun, wind, and rain as the designers of open-air arenas and stadiums do today. But has any student of the Elizabethan stage paid attention to the fundamental fact of the weather? Every modern self-styled 'replica' of Shakespeare's theatre which shelters its central *parterre* under a roof, and resorts to artificial

---

[1] Reprinted by J. Nichols, *Prog. Eliz.* (1788), 2. 188–189.
[2] John Ogilby, *His Majesty's Entertainment* . . . (1662), 16.

lighting, burkes the unavoidable conditions, the primary problems which the actual Globe had to meet and solve. Roof your 'reproduction' in, and at one stroke you destroy your most valuable clues in the search for Shakespeare's stage-methods.

But if someone—following the accepted theory that the Globe's stage was backed by a scenic wall with little central alcove-stages in it—*should* venture to build an honest open-air reproduction, its best seats would admittedly be those directly facing the stage, in the centre of the first and second galleries across the unroofed yard. In almost all the imagined 'reproductions', indeed, this is the standpoint from which we are offered the best view of the presumed 'Elizabethan stage'; and in Mr C. W. Hodges's engaging fantasy [1] it is similarly just there that he places the spectral set of scholars waiting in the dark for light on Shakespeare's stage. And since in all open-air grandstands the best places must be in the southwest quarter, backs to the afternoon sun and the prevailing wind, our reproducer would have to orient his 'Globe' with its stage at the northeast side: not only to face the best seats at the southwest, but also to slant some direct daylight under the lofty 'cover' into the remote but all-important doors and alcove-stages fifty-five foot distant from the nearest of those seats. [2]

From this planned orientation with stage at the northeast, required by the curious theory that Elizabethan staging was (like our own) picture-like or 'one-side', let

---

[1] *The Globe Restored* (1953), 85.

[2] It is by no accident that photographs of toy models of theoretical 'Globes' are taken with the stage at the northeast, with southwest 'sunlight' striking in to their scenic-wall alcoves at the back. For alcoves so distant, such illumination is certainly indispensable.

THE SECOND GLOBE AND THE HOPE OR
BEAR-GARDEN

In this engraving of the view by Wenzel Hollar, the labels on the two
playhouses are mistakenly interchanged.

us turn to examine the actual placing of the stage which Shakespeare's company used.

The authority here—indeed the only evidence worth considering—is Wenzel Hollar's famous 'Long View' of the Bankside, 1647, looking westward from the tower of St Saviour's Church, and showing both the Globe and the Hope Theatres. Hollar's sighting, as a ruler laid on W. W. Braines's excellent plan of the Globe property shows, was about one point north of west, or, to speak by the card, west-by-north. In Hollar's original drawing[1] the position of the famous theatre's two external staircases (entered only from within the house)—one placed almost due east and the other almost due north, left and right of the main entrance-door—and the situation and roof-lines of the 'hut', all point to one fact. Namely, that Shakespeare-and-company put their stage *not at the northeast side*, where if prevalent theory were correct it would have to stand, but at the side *directly opposite*.

That is, they set it *at the southwest*, with the afternoon sun and the southwesterly wind and rain striking directly across into what according to the 'scenic-wall stage' theory would be the best seats: those facing and opposite the stage. And the same is true of the neighbouring Hope, with its stage placed slightly more southerly.

Is it not astonishing that we have contrived to imagine Shakespeare not merely as offering the best position in his theatre to the penny stinkards, and as setting his important intimate scenes 'within' or 'above' at a distance of

---

[1] As Braines noticed, the names of 'The Globe' and of the 'Beere bayting h[ouse]' (The Hope) were mistakenly interchanged in the engraving. The misnomers deceived not only Dr Joseph Q. Adams (*Shakespearean Playhouses*, 1917), but also a writer as recent as Dr John C. Adams (*The Globe Playhouse*, 1943).

more than fifty-five foot from the nearest best seats, but on top of that as obliging the high-paying occupants of those seats to squint into the direct afternoon sun and to absorb the wind-driven shower? Yet such theatrical absurdities are the inescapable implications of the 'scenic wall and inner stage' theory when once applied to the actual Globe.

And what of other open-air theatres? Consider the great and historic Boar's Head inn-yard[1] outside Aldgate, extending north-by-west out of Whitechapel High Street. This inn-yard theatre, the earliest on record, had been in use for plays before Queen Elizabeth came to the throne; and at the close of the century multitudes flocked to it to see Lord Derby's Men in the tremendously popular play of *Edward IV* or 'Shore's Wife'.

In the summer of 1599 Richard Samuel was at great expense remodelling the theatre built in the quadrangular yard of the Boar's Head, with its stage and tiring-house, and with new timber galleries *on all its four sides*: which shows that this playhouse too was a circus, an amphitheatre, a 'wooden O'. Query, on which of the four sides do we now discover that the stage was placed? Answer 'on the *west*':

the stage tyreing howse & galleries on the west side of the greate yarde
the said weste galleryes over the said Stage [2]

[1] William Cavendish (1592–1676), 'the brave Marquesse of *Newcastle*, which made the fine playes', writes at the Restoration to Charles II about 'severall Playe Houses . . . in my Time . . . Some Played, att the Bores heade, & att the Curtin In the feildes & some att the Hope whiche Is the Beare Garden'—Sandford A. Strong, *Catalogue of Letters at Welbeck* (1903), 226.

[2] From a newly-discovered suit about the Boar's Head Theatre, *Woodliff v. Browne et Jurdaine* (1603), uncalendared Proceedings of the Court of Requests, P.R.O., Req. 2/466, Pt. II.

That yard's 'west' in point of fact lay more nearly west-by-south: so that (just as in the Globe) those who occupied the galleries opposite the stage (which seats according to theory should be the best) found themselves somewhat north of east, bedazzled by the direct rays of the afternoon sun. Not an enviable position.

We now know that the stages of the Globe, the Hope, and the Boar's Head—all open-air theatres—all stood at or near the southwest: that is, on the one good spectator-side of the building, its wall backing to the sun and rain, like the pavilion at Lord's or the boxes at the Yankee Stadium. Three other inn-yard playhouses, the Cross Keys, the Bell, and the Black Bull in Gracechurch Street–Bishopsgate (which runs somewhat east of north), all lay *west* of the street. This indicates that in any case their stages were not placed at the east, for that was the public-entrance side. And the galleries and stage of the celebrated Red Bull were similarly built (1605) in a square inn-yard whose public gate stood, like the Globe's, at the northeast.[1]

When one considers the quantities of inn-yards in Elizabethan London in which theatres could have been built, it is a significant indication against *easterly* stage-placing to find that these four inn-yards, selected and flourishing as playhouses, all lay west or southwest of their public entrance-gates. As for the first two theatres built in England, 'whereof the one is called the Courtein, the other the Theatre' near Holywell, according to Stow

---

[1] See Martin Slater's petition for a company at the Red Bull, which he says was formerly 'a square court in an inn': the first evidence found which shows the shape of the Red Bull Theatre. H.M.C., *Cecil Papers* 17 (1938), 234.

(1598), they also were 'both standing on the Southwest side toward the field': indicating approach to the main gate from the road at the east or northeast.

Like the round Globe, the square Fortune had but two entrance doors, set at opposite sides of the house: [1] the one at the northeast, access by the alley from Whitecross Street, the other at the southwest, access from Golden Lane. That the latter, the southwest, was the choice stage, stage-gallery, and lords' room side appears by the fact that the 'carriage trade' rolled up not into Whitecross Street, but into Golden Lane at the southwest:

there were above six-score Coaches on the last Thursday in Golden Lane to heare the Players at the Fortune. [2]

But to consider only the stages of the Globe, the Hope, and the Boar's Head. Documentary evidence shows them placed in the southwest quarter: an orientation directly contrary to that demanded by the usual theory that the Elizabethans used a scenic wall. As we have remarked, if that theory were sound, with its necessary implication that the best seats for seeing the production were those facing it across the yard, those best seats would certainly be found at the southwest, backs to the sun. On the contrary, however, in the real Globe, Hope, and Boar's Head those seats opposite the stage in fact lay at or near the northeast, taking the afternoon sun's glare or the wind-driven shower right in their faces. They were some of the worst seats in the house.

---

[1] 'At the Fortune in Golding Lane ... this day [2 October 1643] there was set a strong guard of Pikes and muskets on both gates of the Play-house.' *The Weekly Account*, 4 October 1643. B.M. Burney 17.

[2] *The Kingdome's Weekly Intelligencer*, 18–25 January 1648. B.M. E.423.23.

If the Elizabethan theatre-builders were not consistently idiotic, the modern assumption that theirs was a façade-stage is an illusion. How misleading that illusion is, appears when we are told by the theorist that (as in our present-day theatres) 'about a fourth' of the house —'that portion opposite the entering door—was devoted to the uses of production'.[1] Here indeed is enormous faith: to believe that the Globe could still accommodate three thousand persons or more (as it did for *A Game at Chess*) *after cutting down its available seating space by twenty-five per cent.* What is more, in the actual Globe this very fourth part opposite the entering door was the *southwest or stage-side, the only really good side for spectators.* Yet theory expects us to believe that the good side was the one side denied to them. To pursue a radical misconception is infallibly to arrive sooner or later at the preposterous.

Any theory of stage-practice at these open-air theatres —unless indeed it be one of the 'preconceived notions taken upon trust and increasing in absurdity with increase of age'—must square not only with common sense but with human nature, and with the economics of the theatre. On the whole a reasonable mind will allow that the best and most costly seats should be the best (*a*) for protection from dazzling sun and foul weather, (*b*) for hearing, (*c*) for seeing, and (*d*) for being seen. In these theatres, of which the Globe was one, the side affording protection from sun, wind, and rain was the southwest. The side

---

[1] 'A third' would be a more accurate statement. J. C. Adams's diagrams (*Globe Playhouse* 53, 242, 309) show the space wasted as a *third*, and Chambers's (*Eliz. Stage* 3. 84, 85) as *more than a third* of the house.

closest to the stage for hearing was the southwest. The side nearest to the stage for seeing was the southwest. The conspicuous side, which the less-favoured in the yard and the distant northeast galleries beheld when looking at the southwest-standing stage, was the southwest. In short, in every respect it was obviously the most valuable and important spectator-side of the house. None but a Shakespeare insane, a bedlam Burbage, or a modern theorist self-deceived would throw it away on 'the uses of production'.

As one would expect, contemporary prices show that places on the stage itself, and those in the boxes and galleries in this southwest, next-to-the-stage side of the house containing all the best seats, were the most profitable to the sharers and owners. As to their value at the Boar's Head, I now discover two statements of 1603 made in the Court of Requests in the dispute about the profits 'arising from the said weste galleryes over the said Stage'. Robert Browne, the actor-manager of Derby's Men—in possession of the 'Stage, tyrynge howse and galleries on the west side of the great yarde'—is here stated to have paid the owner of these west galleries at the rate of five pounds a week; and Richard Samuel, the previous tenant, had paid to the former owner 'half the profits' arising from 'the said weste galleryes over the said Stage at such tyme or tymes as there shoulde be any playes or Comodyes acted and played upon the Stage aforesaid'.

Let us consider this weekly five pounds or 'half-profits'. We may arrive at a rough notion of how much it represented by recalling that at this date the average wages of a 'hired man' or utility-actor-on-salary were some 6s. 8d. a week. If one may trust the equation, the ten pounds total weekly profits of the west or over-the-stage galleries were equivalent to the combined salaries of some thirty utility-actors, or to the entrance-fees of twenty-four hundred penny groundlings in the yard. A very considerable sum: the yearly stipend of some professors at Oxford was no more. And needless to say, not a penny of it would ever have been seen had these 'weste galleryes over the said Stage' been devoted to alcove stages and 'the uses of production'.

The absurdity of imagining that in the Boar's Head, the Fortune, or the Red Bull, areas of these lucrative over-the-stage galleries were taken to provide an 'inner' or a 'balcony' stage is obvious when we recall that these theatres were all quadrangular or square. To *all* the high-paying spectators seated in that protected, best side of the quadrangle, any scene enacted in such a place would be completely invisible.[1]

---

[1] With a persistency worthy of a better cause, Professor C. J. Sisson still contrives to believe in the existence of alcove stages 'inner' and 'upper' (*New Readings in Shakespeare*, 1956, 1. 34 and 2. 219). His paper of more than twenty years ago on the Boar's Head (*Life and Letters Today*, Winter 1936–37), although published without references, evidently utilized material contained in two sets of Chancery Town Depositions: *Samwel v. Woodliff* C24/278/71, and *Browne v. Woodliff et al.*, C24/290/3.

He was unaware of the Court of Requests proceeding to which I have called attention, which shows that the west galleries over the stage were not (as he fancies) a balcony 'which provided the upper stage', but highly lucrative spectator-galleries. As we have seen, the discovery of this suit excludes any possibility of alcove-stages in the galleries over the stage in the quadrangular Boar's Head Theatre.

An earlier and livelier proceeding in Star Chamber (*Samuel v. Langley et al.*, 1600, Sta. Cha. 5/S74/3 and 5/S13/8) contains Samuel's interesting charge that Francis Langley and his backers came armed to the Boar's Head on 16 December 1599, 'in the night time about seven of the clock', and 'intending to murder and kill your subject [Samuel] and his son . . . did in the dark throw divers

Since these open-air amphitheatres necessarily had their best spectator-side adjoining the oblong stage in the southwest quarter—some more southerly, some more westerly—it becomes clear that the ends of those stages thereby maintained the medieval and proper orientation of Hell and Heaven. At Stage Left, Hell, the corners of the stage stood north and west; at Stage Right, Heaven, east and south.

In our general modern vagueness and ignorance in these matters, we need constantly to remind ourselves that the compass-bearings of Heaven and Hell in the universe and on the stage were second nature to our ancestors, who lived not by electric light but by the sun.[1] As that 'great Frequenter of Plays' John Donne wrote,

> Most other Courts, alas, are like to hell . . .
> Here zeale and love growne one, all clouds disgest,
> And make our Court an everlasting East.[2]

And when the actor playing Bernardo mentioned the 'star that's westward from the pole', he unquestionably

---

daggers and other weapons . . . which weapons, hardly missing your said subject and his son, did stick in the walls of the said house'.

Langley, who built and owned the Swan Playhouse, though he here indignantly denies all dagger-throwing, was obviously bent on extending his theatrical profits to include a share in those of the Boar's Head. For Shakespeare's earlier association with him in his quarrel with Justice Gardiner, see my *Shakespeare versus Shallow*, 1931.

[1] Numbers of people today, who ride or drive along busy roads to their day's work, have not realized that when they have a choice it is far preferable to live *east* rather than west from their work, which keeps the sun at their backs both going and coming, instead of directly in their eyes.

[2] *Ecclogue* (1613), an epithalamion.

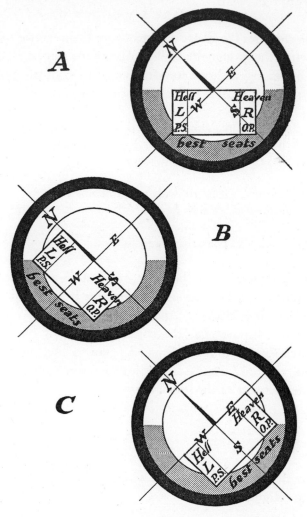

ORIENTATION OF OPEN-AIR THEATRES

Figure *A* shows the siting of the Globe's stage. This was also approximately that of the Hope, the Boar's Head, and the Fortune.

Figures *B* and *C* show how far the stage-position could deviate to the west or south while still keeping the best seats in the shaded segment.

pointed from the Elsinore platform to the northwest sky beyond the prompter's Hell Corner of the stage.

In dealing with the imaginative lighting of the open-air theatres, Professor F. P. Wilson writes,

As the late John Palmer neatly if unfairly put it, where a modern stage-manager calls for two reds, back stage, O.P. side, Shakespeare gave his audience:

> But look, the morn, with russet mantle clad,
> Walks o'er the dew of yon high eastward [eastern] hill.

There was no visible dawn, no visible hill.[1]

No; but there *was* a 'high' or *exact* east,[2] and Horatio pointed to it, over the yard-corner Stage Right, Opposite Prompt side, Heaven. And this same 'high east' comes into the dispute over the correct bearing of the mid-March sunrise in *Julius Caesar* 2.1. In settling the question, not only does Casca point his sword toward the eastern corner of the stage, but his line

> the high East
> Stands as the Capitoll, directly heere

also shows that the Capitol was set at the yard-end of Stage Right, Heaven.

---

[1] 'The Elizabethan Theatre' *Neophilologus* 39 (1955), 49, citing Palmer's *The Future of the Theatre* (1913), 64.

[2] The hill due east from the Elsinore Kronborg lies across the Sound, behind Helsingborg. At a distance of more than three miles its elevation of 125 foot is certainly not enough to qualify it as a *high* hill. But certainly it is a *high-eastward* hill—a hill standing exactly east, as Horatio says.

When Sir Thomas More comes to his execution, we have

Moore.   Point me the block; I nere was heere before.
Hangman. To the east side, my lord.
Moore.   Then to the east
           We goe to sigh; that ore, to sleepe in rest.[1]

On the stage he goes to his death at the east end, Heaven, where his true soul will 'sleep in rest'.[2]

Like Abigail's entrance above in Act 2 of *The Jew of Malta*, greeted by her father below with

> But stay, what starre shines yonder in the *East*?
> The Loadestarre of my life, if *Abigall* . . .

Juliet at her window is also inevitably above at the easterly, heavenly Stage Right. Romeo hails her appearance like a lover and a poet:

> But soft, what light through yonder window breaks?
> It is the East, and *Iuliet* is the Sunne.

But afterward when the two are together there, it is the dawn imagined in the eastern sky beyond the chamber which parts them:

> . . . look Loue what enuious streakes
> Do lace the seuering Cloudes in yonder East . . .

---

[1] *Sir Thomas More* 5.4.127–130.

[2] The Plow Boys' ancient Revesby Sword Play showed the same:

Pickle Herring. We shall take your head from your body, and you will be dead.
Fool. If I must die, I will dye with my face to the light, for all you!

J. M. Manly, *Specimens of Pre-Shakespearean Drama*, 1. 301.

When on the morning of 1 March 1877 Jack McCall came to the gallows at Yankton, South Dakota, for his murder of Wild Bill Hickok, 'He placed himself in the center of the platform, facing east, and gazed out over the throng.' Quoted from *Dakotan and Press* by W. E. Connelley, *Wild Bill and his Era* (1933), 213.

And it is the *back* window, facing that dawn, which she opens for Romeo to descend:

> Then window let day in, and let life out.

As Shakespeare repeatedly made clear in his *Twelfth Night* presented in the Great Hall at Whitehall, it was not only in the open-air theatres that the audience was fully aware of the points of the compass. And this fact is further manifested by plays performed in the round both in the Hall of Queens' College, Cambridge, and in the London Blackfriars, both of which halls stand similarly south and north. Peter Hausted prescribes the following action for the performance of his play *The Rivall Friends* in 1632 on the Queens' College stage extending across the hall east and west:

> Venus (being Phosphorus as well as Vesper) appearing at a window above as risen [in the west], calling to Sol, who lay in Thetis' lap at the east side of the stage, canopied with an azure curtain; at the first word that Venus sang, the curtain was drawn away and they discovered.[1]

In ecclesiastical fashion, the Blackfriars' great upper Frater—the Parliament chamber of Henry VIII—was properly oriented. The lower end (public entry and screen) was at the ominous north, the upper or dais-end at the 'good' south. When it was made an amphitheatre for plays, the stage, built in front of the head-galleries facing down the room, extended across east and west.[2]

---

[1] In 5.11 of this play, the houses at the stage-ends, entered as usual by corner-traps from the cellarage or tiring-house, are illustrated by the direction *all four come out at the four corners of the stage.*

[2] Professor C. W. Wallace's discovered document on the Blackfriars Theatre mentions the paving needing repair along the east

Here again, as in Shakespeare's *Twelfth Night,* we find the actual stage-orientation utilized, now by Jonson, Chapman, and Marston in their play oriented *Eastward Ho!* acted on the Blackfriars east–west stage in 1605 by the Children of the Queen's Revels:

Quicksilver. Look not westward to the fall of Don Phoebus
 but to the east—Eastward Ho!
   Where radiant beams of lusty Sol appear . . .

Nor is this all. Eleven years later, in the Prologue to *The Devil is an Ass,* Ben Jonson gives us a further and more vivid picture of the east–west Blackfriars stage, this time with the King's Men in action. Just as in the public theatres, the stool-sitting crowd of gentlemen-critics here fill the south or upper side of the high stage, facing across it to the body of the auditorium. The east or Heaven end with its music and windows above is to their right, and to their left the west end or Hell, where Satan and Pug will very soon be coming up through the scuttle.

But such numbers have made a habit of crowding on the stage—which is smaller than the Globe's platform— that the players are forced too close together, and thereby unavoidably obstruct the view. When the actors stand north, backs to the body of the house, playing to the stage-sitters and the head-galleries at the south, these have the best of it. But when to vary and distribute the effects they stand south and play to the rest of the house, the critics during that time get their backs. These arrogant and crowding critics however want it all their

side of the hall and under the east or Stage Right end of the stage: 'in paviamento per orientalem partem predicte Aule & in pavia- mento subter orientalem finem Cuiusdam Theatri anglice the Stage in Aula predicta.'—'The Children of the Chapel at Blackfriars', in *Nebraska University Studies* 8 (1908), 43*n.*

own way. They shove, nudge, or kick the players and tell them to turn. Jonson's Prologue begs them to be reasonable. Come, come, gentlemen. Crowd as you will, this is after all an amphitheatre, plays are acted in the round. Even critics must accept actors' backs at least *part* of the time:

Yet, Grandees . . .
Doe not . . . force us act
In compass of a cheese-trencher. This tract
Will ne'er admit our *vice* [fool], because of yours [your fault].
Anone, who, worse then you, the fault endures
That your selves make? when you will thrust and spurne,
And knocke us o' the elbowes, and bid, turne;
As if, when wee had spoke, wee must be gone,
Or, till wee speake, must all runne in, to one,
Like the young adders, at the old ones mouth?
Would wee could stand due *North*; or had no *South*,
If that offend: or were *Muscovy* glasse,
That you might looke our *Scenes* through as they passe.
We know not how to affect you. If youll come
To see new Playes, pray you affoord us roome.

One hardly needs to point out by the way that effective acting in the round, in contrast to the more limited movement imposed by the façade-stage, requires skilful 'turning'. To the stage-encircling Elizabethan audiences, this feature of the actor's art—which today must be re-learnt—was familiarity itself. During the civil wars a Parliament newsbook reported the killing of a leading actor in battle as follows:

Robinson the Fool slain, as he was turning and acting like a Player [1]

---

[1] *Perfect Occurrences*, 10–17 October 1645. This was William Robinson or Robins, famous in the title-role of Middleton and Rowley's highly popular play *The Changeling*.

—a description which would never occur to a theatre-goer educated to a façade-stage. Similar graceful turning round about is appropriately recommended for the actor playing the heavenly Coelum in Tomkis's *Lingua*:

> But I pray you who taught him speake and vse no action, me thinkes it had beene excellent to haue turn'd round about in his speech.

The expert player-in-the-round gives the impression of being *hic et ubique*, of holding the whole circle with his acting, like a skilled swordsman engaging a ring of assailants: such a man as the 'brave prince' attacked by the guard in Suckling's *Aglaura* 4.1:

> He's as active as he is valiant too. Didst mark him how he stood like all the points of the compass, and, as good pictures, had his eyes towards every man? [1]

To gather together and list some of the traditional meanings inherent in the scenic opposition and orientation of the Elizabethan amphitheatrical stage is to discover a wealth of dramatic significance:

---

[1] When the masters of fence hired the Rose, the Swan, or the Red Bull for their 'prizes', played on the stage in scarlet breeches and white laced shirts—the ancient military colours of England—the show was as fully 'in the round' as the plays or as a modern bout in the pugilists' prize-ring. As John Webster remarks of the Fencer (*Characters*, 1615)

> when he comes on the Stage, at his Prize, he makes a leg seven severall waies

—that is, seven bows round a circle, as though to all the seven gates in the City's circuit (Harben, *Dictionary of London*, 251)—quite like the German player-in-the-round: 'John Pansser . . . takes his hat off, bows to all four corners of the stage' (qu. J. Isaacs, 'Shakespeare as a Man of the Theatre' in *Shakespeare and the Theatre*, 1927).

277

<pre>
                    YARD OR PIT
NORTH and WEST   EAST and SOUTH
     LEFT   RIGHT
  HELL below   WORLD   HEAVEN above
  EVIL (devils)   MAN   GOOD (angels)
   DISCORD   HARMONY
    NIGHT   DAY
    BLACK   WHITE
                     THRONE
                   BEST SEATS
</pre>

It will be found that this unforgotten formalism of stage-topography will throw light not only on the numerous plays obviously fitted to it, but in most unexpected corners of others, once it is understood that the stage presented the Elizabethan world-picture.

To conclude with a view of Shakespeare employing his oriented stage charged with inherited meaning to enforce the significance of dramatic word and action, we may turn to the closing scenes of *Richard III*. In the supreme struggle on Bosworth Field, it will be Good against Evil until men can say with Richmond, 'The bloody dog is dead'.

The tents of the mighty opposites Richmond and Richard are pitched at the two ends of the stage, and every man, woman, and child in the audience knows where each of the two must stand. Hell end, Stage Left, at the north and west, the abode of evil and declining death, for Richard the murderer—whom Queen Elizabeth calls 'the devil', Queen Margaret, a 'hell-hound', and his own mother, a 'toad' who came on earth 'to make the earth my hell'.

> Earth gapes, hell burns, fiends roar, saints pray,
> To have him suddenly convey'd from hence.

Heaven end, Stage Right, at the east and south in the light of God's grace and glory, for the princely avenger Richmond, who in commending his soul to his Maker prays 'Make us thy ministers of chastisement'—while Richard opposite bodingly finds he has lost his wonted 'alacrity of spirit' and 'cheer of mind'.

When both are asleep in the night before the battle, out of the great central 'grave' trap between the two tents rise the ghosts of the murdered. In turn they bid the blood-guilty adversary at the hellish north and west 'Despair and die!' and, facing about to God's champion in the heavenly east and south,

> Virtuous and holy, be thou conqueror!
> Good angels guard thy battle! Live, and flourish!
> God and good angels fight on Richmond's side.

Then the black King Richard starts out of sleep in terror at the vision, knows he will despair, and in his tent 'the lights burn blue'.

In the morning Richmond, his heart 'very jocund in the remembrance of so sweet a dream', assures his army, who have the tactical advantage of the rising sun at their backs, that

> God and our good cause fight upon our side

—while 'God's enemy' Richard exhorts his men lined up at Hell Corner opposite to follow him, like another Satan,

> If not to heaven, then hand in hand to hell.

EPILOGUE

THIS present investigation into the form and the technique of the Elizabethan stage has not begun with the usual eighteenth-century assumption that a stage must be located at the end of a room. Hitherto, following Capell and Malone, all modern study has presupposed that Shakespeare's platform stage presented a unified façade: a wall showing scenic entrances from the 'back', with curtainable alcoves included below and above in the middle of it. And to suit this theory, it has been obliged to invent terms such as 'fore-stage' and 'inner stage'—expressions as utterly unknown to the Elizabethans as the uncouth conceptions they are coined to describe.

Such is the conjectural affair which handbooks of English literature and lecturers upon it do not scruple to represent as 'typical'. That no proof of its existence has ever been offered is less surprising when it is realized that there is none.

Such a one-side stage's admitted inability to accommodate many of the Elizabethan drama's scenes, the confusion and disagreement among its apologists, and its rejection after trial by expert producers, all suggest that the unsupported guess upon which it is based is a mistaken one. If we are to advance on a firm footing, a fresh approach is indicated: one moreover which adduces evidence, and does not ignore historical antecedents.

The theatre is a most conservative institution. Acting on the reasonable suspicion that the Elizabethan stage may therefore have had its beginnings not in the foreign

Renaissance stage with its unified scenic wall, but in the native methods which immediately went before—those of the pageant-stage, surviving from the Middle Ages—I have examined these. They prove to present the following facts:

1. Pageant-production was in the round, to an audience stationed on both sides, divided by an oblong stage.
2. The tiring-house or dressing-room was underneath, inside the hollow stage.
3. The scenic axis was *transverse*: the 'houses' stood facing each other from the stage-ends. Access to them was up through traps.

These principles governed Elizabethan companies on tour with their play-wagons or 'triumphs', performing in inn-yards and barns.

Search into contemporary evidence now reveals that the Elizabethan theatres retained every one of these peculiar features. One finds that their universal idea of a playhouse was an amphitheatre, with the stage in the middle; that their audience was called a 'round', a 'circle', an 'orb', even when the room itself was oblong: the select spectators facing down from the head of the chamber beyond the best side of the stage. In their customary built-up stages the Elizabethans' grave-like tiring-house was underneath, as contemporary references and the contracts for building the Fortune and the Hope both show. The actors accordingly had to climb up, in order to appear in or out of the end-houses on the stage—to *play above board*.

The scenic confrontation dictated by production in the

round maintained and objectified that essence of drama—contrast, antagonism, conflict. This *Gegenstand* gave their performances those bases for interplay, for attack and riposte, that visible vitality which vanished when the alien unified opera-scene superseded the native Elizabethan 'houses'. Exhibiting action and reaction between its ends diametrically opposed, Shakespeare's stage strikingly resembled a tennis court.

Its transverse axis differentiated it utterly both from our modern Italianate depth-stage and from the imaginary affair heretofore fancied as 'Elizabethan'. Since the production was in the round, the 'houses' or scenes at the stage-ends had to be of framework—kept open or 'transparent' except when briefly shrouded with drawn curtains or hangings to conceal an entrance or an exit, or to make a 'discovery'. This is the technique described for tragedies by Sir William Davenant:

> Houses . . . Two low Rooms upon a Floor:
> Whose *thorow lights* were so transparent made,
> That Expectation (which should be delai'd
> And kept awhile from being satisfi'd)
> Saw, on a sodain, all that *Art* should hide.

In addition to its form and technique, we discover Shakespeare's transverse stage also retaining the important medieval advantages of significant orientation, together with Heaven or 'the Walls' above at Stage Right with its music room, and Hell below at Stage Left, the post of the prompter. These basic features were so universally understood that the dramatists drew on them at will—as Shakespeare for appropriately allusive east–west placing of the houses in *Twelfth Night* and the tents setting

Heaven against Hell on Bosworth Field in the apparition scene in *Richard III*, and Middleton as late as 1624 with *A Game at Chess*.

So far from the inevitable confusion in which our attempts to present Elizabethan plays on Italianate stages result, the Elizabethan stage maintained the clarity of place, the true compass directions, the significant location of Heaven, the World, and Hell enjoyed by the Middle Ages. In so clear a frame of reference, meanings were never obscured or lost. Actor and spectator knew where they were, which is more than our enlightened age can say for itself. If we are to find out those meanings, and begin to know where we are in Shakespeare's plays, we must put those plays where they belong, on Shakespeare's stage.

And there is no need to raise millions to do it, either. Like the students at Tudor and Stuart Cambridge, any group with an unencumbered hall or gymnasium at its disposal is already equipped with an Elizabethan amphitheatre. The expense will be limited to procuring a removable or 'demountable' box-like stage-and-tiring-house, with curtainable end-houses,[1] to set before a general audience standing on the floor, with a timber grandstand or a gymnasium-gallery on its other side to seat the select audience.

Enacting Shakespeare in this amphitheatre, they will begin to understand the stirring experience of Olivier and Guthrie at Elsinore in 1937 in their performance— unrehearsed, even unpremeditated—of *Hamlet* in the

---

[1] So general is the interest in Shakespeare production, that should an enterprising firm design and put such a stage on the market, it might well prove a very profitable venture.

round. Like them they will discover that it is supremely on this stage that the play comes to life. Here at last, after centuries of exile on alien Italianate picture-stages, or more recently on 'artistic' compromises of bastard styles, Shakespeare is at home. And it was William Poel who first perceived the truth:

The plays were shaped to suit the theatre of the day and no other.

APPENDIX A
A HALL THRUST FULL

thither runne the people thicke and threefolde ... the
Theaters of the Players are as full as they can throng.
John Stockwood, *Sermon*, 1579.

This is the straine that chokes the theaters:
That makes them crack with full stuft audience.
John Marston, *What You Will*, 1601.

(As at a New-Play) all the Roomes
Did swarme with *Gentiles* mix'd with *Groomes*.
Pimlyco, or Runne Red-Cap, 1609.

you shall scarce have a roome
All is so pester'd.
Leonard Digges, on Shakespeare (1623), 1640.

ALL efforts to realize Shakespeare's stage have from the
start been bedevilled by the ineradicable habit of
ascribing modern notions to our ancestors. The same
fate has attended all attempts to determine the nature and
capacity of the spectator-accommodation at their plays.
We assume in the Elizabethan a length of thigh equal to
a modern upper-class average, and apply our up-to-date
ideas of the rights and privileges of spectators, as though
such matters undergo no change.

But the briefest reflection will remind us that the
modern theatre-designer's solicitude that every seat command a full view of the stage is of very recent date. From
many seats in theatres still standing one can see but a part
of the stage. In some, seats are sold directly behind
pillars, where one can *hear* the play, and that is all.

Over-anxiety about 'blocking of sight-lines' and nervous fear of turning the actors' backs to part of the house are very latter-day ailments of the impresario.

Further, a generation brought up lolling in the wide upholstered armchairs of the luxury-cinema is poorly equipped to realize how its ancestors sat, if indeed they could either find or afford a seat. When seats were neither reserved nor divided by arms, a crowding could (and did) result which would appal any tender theatre-goer of the present day. Yet as recently as 1910, at the Theatre Royal, Lincoln, 'We sat packed in that gallery, the feet of those in the row above resting on the seats of the row below.' [1]

This was sitting *on steps*, not even on benches set on the steps. You sat cribbed between A's right foot and B's left foot, with their respective knees knocking your shoulders. And that this step- or 'degree'-sitting was common in the two first London playhouses—the Theatre and the Curtain—is shown by Gosson:

at playes in London you shall see such heauing, and shoouing ... to sitte by the women; such care for their garments, that they bee not trode one [*by people scrambling over the steps, or by the adjacent feet of the As and Bs sitting behind*] ... such pillowes to ther backes, that they take no hurte [*from the knees of the same*]. [2]

We see the Cockney gallant bound for the playhouse providently tucking a pillow under his arm to earn the woman's favour.

The de Witt sketch of the side-galleries in the Swan shows no benches at all. Nothing but steps or 'degrees',

---

[1] Herbert Hodge, *It's Draughty in Front* (1938), 16.
[2] *The Schoole of Abuse* (1579), sig. C.

drawn exactly like the steps (labelled *ingressus*) to climb
from the yard into the first gallery. But if the penny galleries had none, we may probably assume that the two-
penny galleries on the best or stage-side of the house did
have benches: backless, no doubt, but the front rows of
them softened with bulrush-mats, if we are to believe
Thomas Platter on the Curtain in 1599. In the penny
galleries, he tells us, one could stand or sit; but in the two-
penny galleries (*sc.* on the best or stage-side of the house)
sit cushioned, and thence not only see everything very
well, but also be seen.[1]

There is plentiful evidence of a good deal of standing
in the galleries. While one cannot be sure of details, it
looks very much as though the penny galleries offered
three or more rising steps for first-comers to sit on. Behind these, the first row of standers, leaning their arms on
a breast-rail, were set high enough to see the stage over the
last row of sitters' heads. These in turn were backed by
further raised steps for more ranks of the rail-leaning
standers.

The depth of each seat-step is not given. Obviously
the shallower they were, the farther one's knees would jut
forward into or between the shoulders of those seated on
the step below. The only evidence I find on the point
comes from testimony about rebuilding the 'long north
gallery'—which was a *side* gallery—in the Whitechapel
Boar's Head inn-yard theatre, 1600:

yf the case were myne . . . I would pull downe this olde gallery to the ground and buylde yt foure foote forwarder toward
the stage into the yarde [*i.e., over the heads of the groundlings*]

---

[1] Qu. Chambers, *Eliz. Stage*, 2. 364–365.

. . . then would there be roome for three or foure seates more in a gallery and for many mo people, yet never the lesse roome in the yarde.[1]

This planner was thus allowing for each seat-step at most 16 inches of depth, or alternatively no more than a foot. A corrective useful to bear in mind when we set about trying to visualize Elizabethan conditions.

A similar corrective is needed for the audience at Court performances. These, one might romantically imagine, should present the opposite extreme of comfort. Surely those select gentlewomen and courtiers had comfortable chairs? (Miss St Clare Byrne estimates a farthingale as measuring more than two feet by three. Did they politely allow each gentlewoman six square feet of stand-ing-room, and even more of sitting-room?) No, no chairs. Well, if not chairs, surely these privileged court-iers were provided with benches? Unhappily, no. Not even benches. The Queen's object was not to bestow ease and comfort on an exclusive few, but to give all who had a right to be present the chance to crush themselves in thick and threefold, as tightly as they could.

Accordingly, what was regularly set up for the audi-ence at plays in the royal halls was an amphitheatre of 'degrees' enclosing the stage or playing-place: that is, tiers of *steps*, made of deal boards nailed on brackets, and set against all the four walls. Here the courtiers sat jammed, knees knocking shoulders, like the vulgar sort in the penny galleries of the Curtain and the Globe. Or

---

[1] P.R.O., *Samwel v. Woodliff*, C24/278/71. Cf. John Field on the collapse of the Paris Garden galleries, 1583: 'they . . . which stoode vnder the Galleries on the grounde, vpon whom both the waight of Timbre and people fell' qu. *Eliz. Stage*, 4. 221.

more precisely they sat if the hall was large enough to permit them to sit. In the smaller palace-rooms they could not sit: they *stood* on those steps, stood there throughout the performance. There it was a case of Standing Room Only, because with the sole exception of the Queen, nobody sat. Six square feet of standing-room each? A suffocating foot or foot-and-a-half, with the ruin of a farthingale, is nearer the truth.

Carpenters' bills from the Office of Works bring us back to the reality. For the Great Chamber, Richmond, Christmas 1590–91:

> Settinge up degrees Brackettes boordes & other necessaries for the plaies in the greate chamber & halpaces [platforms] for the people to stande on there . . .

Greenwich, 1585–86:

> making of Scaffoldes for the noble men and women to stande on . . .

Great Chamber, Hampton Court, 1592–93:

> makinge degrees for the Ladies of honor and people to stande on[1] . . .

And even in the more spacious Whitehall, on one occasion a crush of courtiers—so many hundreds that to sit was impossible—stood waiting in vain for Shakespeare's company to appear and perform:

> Much expectation was made of a stage play to be acted [16 February 1612/13] in the Great Hall by the King's players, where many hundred of people stood attending the same.[2]

---

[1] P.R.O., E351/3225, A.O.1/2413/15, E351/3227.
[2] *The Magnificent Marriage of . . . the Lady Elizabeth*, 1613.

Having exchanged romantic fancy for a dose of actuality, let us now consider modern efforts to approximate the spectator-capacity of the Elizabethan public playhouses. Typically, these employ modern measurements and standards as if they could safely be applied to the Elizabethans, which they cannot. For to begin with, those people were noticeably smaller than we are. One look at the surviving costumes and suits of armour is enough to remind us of that fact. At the Metropolitan Museum in New York, Bashford Dean could hardly find a man on the staff small enough to be fitted into the heaviest suit of Renaissance complete tilting-armour in the whole collection. The Elizabethan definition of the word *shaftment* shows the fact again:

the measure from the top of the thumb, being set upright, to the uppermost part of the palm [*i.e., the root of the little finger*] which is by a tall mans measure half a foot.

Now the length of the standard foot has altered only infinitesimally. My own hands are not abnormal for my size, and my thumb-palm 'shaftment' measures a good 6½ inches. Today my modest stature of 5 foot 6½ inches puts me below medium height; but by Elizabethan standards I should evidently be reckoned 'a tall man'.

Again, increase in stature takes place chiefly in thigh-length. And this measurement—from back to knee-cap when seated—is of course the essential one for calculating how close together rows of sitters can be placed. Ignoring the practical fact that these Elizabethans, being shorter in the shank, would require less leg-room, our historians confidently apply our modern standards to them. For the depth of each step or 'degree' at Whitehall, Miss St Clare Byrne is found 'allowing 32 in. for each seat-plus-gangway'.[1]

Modern fancy may grandly allow 32 inches. But it will be rudely recalled to reality by a glance at the plan of Inigo Jones's select little Palladian theatre built about 1630 in Whitehall, the Cockpit-in-Court.[2] Here in the lower or choice set, the degrees measure 27 inches each; but those above and behind are each no more than 15 inches deep—recalling the proposed 12- to 16-inch depth of the side-gallery seats at the Boar's Head. Even for small persons, to sit on 15-inch steps means sitting with knees crowding shoulders. But *did* they sit? In order to pack in more of the throng of courtiers eager to be with royalty at the play, they may have *stood* on those steps throughout the performance as they did at Richmond and at Hampton Court. But whether they sat or stood, to suggest a provision of individual *gangways* when each step is 15 inches deep is not even amusing.

In dealing with the capacity of the Globe, Dr J. C. Adams finds that

in modern theatres the usual space allowance for one person is 30 inches of depth and 18 inches of breadth in the gallery and 30 by 20 or 22 inches in the orchestra stalls.[3]

But since in open-air grandstands thicker clothing is the rule, a breadth of 22 inches per person is there allowed nowadays. Accordingly, Dr Adams lavishly allots each

---

[1] *Theatre Notebook*, January–March 1955, 50*n*.
[2] Frequently reproduced; *e.g.*, Chambers, *Eliz. Stage*, 4, frontispiece.
[3] *The Globe Playhouse* (1943), 86–87.

Elizabethan at the Globe 22 inches of breadth, and sets the rows 30 inches apart. Professor Alfred Harbage[1] had followed the far less prodigal allowance made by John Corbin in 1906[2] —that is, rows 30 inches apart, but each spectator granted no more than the 18 inches of width allowed in modern theatre galleries.

The unanimity of these historians in treating the Elizabethans by modern standards is complete, without so much as a glance at the records of theatre-practice in the interim. If we require 30 inches between rows, they must have done so too. If we exact a minimum of 18 inches hip-room, why, so did they. But the reader might willingly exchange such simplicity of reasoning for a little solid information on what our ancestors actually did.

Now in 1892 the architect-archaeologist Robert Weir Schultz asked some practical questions while engaged in a fascinating calculation of the capacity of the ancient theatre-auditorium at Megalopolis in Greece. Worked out, he says,

on an allowance, in the ordinary seats, of 13 inches [of width] for each person—the allowance indicated by the marks cut on the risers of the seats at Athens—and of 16 inches in the benches, [it] gives us a total of 19,700 persons. . . .

As this allowance of 13 inches per person seems at first so absurdly small, I have made enquiries with regard to the minimum space usually calculated for each person in a modern London Theatre. I am informed that although the minimum space per person recognized by the County Council is 18 inches, as a matter of practice theatre managers find that in the pit and gallery, where the seats have no dividing arms, people

---

[1] *Shakespeare's Audience* (1941), 22–23.
[2] *Op. cit.*, 369.

can be got to occupy as small a space as 14 inches per person, and that 16 inches is a good allowance.[1]

The thought of the small patrons of the Globe being allowed 18 to 22 inches, when their bulkier descendants in 1892 could be got to occupy no more than 14, comes from the realm of the pipe-dream.

Obviously what swells the width-allowance to 18 inches is the arm-rests, that very modern luxury. Even the most sumptuous seats in the 'lords' room' of the Elizabethan theatre were innocent of arm-rests. On reference to the experience of London theatre-managers near the turn of the present century, the sacred width of 18 inches in gallery-seats has here shrunk to a quite adequate 16 or even to a crowded 14; and we have gone back only to the Gay Nineties. What will happen to the august 30 inches of leg-room between rows if we go back farther still?

A backward leap of another century and a half, to John Rich's first Theatre Royal Covent Garden (opened 1733), lands us in a shocking state of affairs:

1 foot 9 inches [21] is the whole space here allowed for seat and void; though a moderate-sized person cannot conveniently sit in less space than that of 1 foot 10 inches [22] from back to front, nor comfortably in less than that of 2 feet.[2]

This Rich was notoriously a greedy rogue and a heartless. Even his moderately-sized eighteenth-century patrons sat inconveniently in those 21 inches from back

---

1 'Excavations at Megalopolis, 1890 1891', *Society for the Promotion of Hellenic Studies, Supplementary Papers*, I (1892), 41–42.
2 George Saunders, *A Treatise of Theatres* (1790), 83–84.

to front. The agony of the immoderately-sized can only be imagined. But the 30 inches of our day has already long disappeared, never to be found again.

Half a century earlier, in 1674, the more humane second Theatre Royal Drury Lane designed by Sir Christopher Wren had allowed 24 inches between rows in the galleries, and 25 in the more expensive pit. All these were backless benches, provided with no dividing arms. At about the same date Charles II's Office of Works, in putting up side-galleries for courtiers in the Hall Theatre, Whitehall, made them $4\frac{1}{2}$ foot wide, with 'two degrees for seates'.[1] This afforded each row a princely and almost unexampled 27 inches.

For a model of careful and realistic reconstruction of a seventeenth-century theatre of the oblong tennis-court style we must go to the Continent. Working from detailed documents she has discovered, Mme S. W. Deierkauf-Holsboer gives us a convincing picture of Paris's Théâtre du Marais, built 1644.[2] On turning the author's metric measurements into feet and inches, we find that the *amphithéâtre*, containing the most expensive seats—seven tiers at the end facing the stage—allowed $26\frac{1}{2}$ inches of depth each. The less costly *loges* along the sides of the room—two rows of 10-inch benches in a depth of 40 inches—allowed but 20 inches of depth each. This, when compared with the complaint against Rich for his in-

---

[1] Works 5/24, qu. E. Boswell, *The Restoration Court Stage* (1932), 253.
[2] *Le Théâtre du Marais*, 1951. The author wisely called in expert aid, acknowledging that of her father, M. W. J. Holsboer, architect and engineer at The Hague, of the late M. Henri de Magron, professeur honoraire à l'École Centrale, and of M. René Mazetier, architect at Meudon.

human 21 inches, seems to indicate that the eighteenth-century Londoner was noticeably longer than the Parisian of a hundred years earlier.

Before going back to England we should not omit to glance at the 'degrees' of Palladio's famous Teatro Olimpico, Vicenza (1584), still standing today. Each row of steps measures something over 21 inches deep. And in an unnoticed British Museum manuscript[1] I find the English plan of an early seventeenth-century theatre-auditorium in some (unnamed, possibly German) royal court.[2] This shows a floor sloping evenly forward towards the deep scenic stage (not in steps like the Teatro Olimpico and the Cockpit-in-Court), with two blocks of seats—the lower one in front ('D') more sumptuous, the one above to the rear ('G') less so. Both are composed of rows of backless benches, with foot-rests on the floor to support the feet against the slope. And here is a part of the written description:

The seats D [for Ladys & the Kings servants] are 8 ynches broade. They are two foote distante ech from other, so that 8 ynches therof serus for the seate, & the other 16 ynches for the Legs & knees. . . .

G. 13 other seats 18 ynches a sunder, wherof the seat conteyns 6 ynches.

I wonder how many historians of the theatre have ever sat for three hours on a board 6 inches wide? When compared with step-sitting, the difficulty with sitting upon a backless bench set on a sloping floor (with foot-rests

---

[1] MS. Addl. 15505, f. 21.

[2] Since its width is but 40 ft., it cannot represent one of the 50-ft. Whitehall Banqueting Houses; and its length of 115 ft. is too great for Hampton Court's Hall (105 ft.).

which keep the knees up) is that one's knees cannot pro-
trude beyond the edge of the somewhat lower bench in
front. If one is too long, one is inexorably shoved back
into the knees behind. Early in the seventeenth century
a seated length of 18 inches must consequently have been
thought average; and a brief experiment with a chair and
a tape measure will once again reveal how much smaller
than ourselves these people were who could sit in 18
inches from back to front. The short and long of it is
that where in practice they got in thirteen rows, our
modern 30-inch allowance would not get in eight. And
as for width, the number of persons to be accommodated
in these seats shows that 'Ladys & the Kings servants'
were granted 19 inches 'to sitt at ease', while the others
had 15·7, or less than 16 inches hip-room. Let us hope
we have heard the last of bulky farthingales requiring
6 square foot and more, and of widths of 18 to 22 inches
for common gallery-sitters at the Globe.

Bearing such actual dimensions in mind as points of
reference, we may once more consider my imagined reconstruction of the seating-arrangements in the Great
Chamber at Whitehall, when Shakespeare played before
Queen Elizabeth on St Stephen's Night, 1600. Since Miss
St Clare Byrne as a professed historian of the theatre has
voiced disbelief in it, let me reproduce it here:

Wooden 'degrees', or tiers of seats covered with green
baize, have been erected against all the four walls. Those
against the long sides of the Chamber . . . have three banks of
seats; but the one at the head of the room has seven, while that
against the lower end . . . towers ten tiers high. . . . On a car-
peted podium in front of the high stand at the head of the
chamber is set a rich canopied throne for the Queen, while on

the floor red velvet cushions are ready to seat selected ladies. Remaining open in the centre is an oblong about twenty feet wide and some twenty-five feet long. This is the floor for dancing; and . . . will serve as a stage for Burbage, Shakespeare, and their fellows to present the comedy.[1]

And here is Miss St Clare Byrne's criticism:

I cannot follow his reckoning of the size of the stage—or rather, acting-area—in the Great Chamber . . . According to the scale-plan, the room measured 60 ft. long by 30 ft. wide [*the actual dimensions were 62 by 29.—L.H.*]. He gives them a 'stage' 20 ft. wide by 25 ft. deep, with 3 tiers of seats each side, 10 tiers at one end and 7 at the other. Allowing 32 in. for each seat-plus-gangway, we are left with an acting area 14 ft. by 15 ft., and no room at all for the State.[2]

The answer to this is that my calculation allowed these Elizabethans degrees of 22 inches depth throughout: which is more than was allowed in the Teatro Olimpico, and far more than the 15-inch degrees of Whitehall's Cockpit-in-Court, not to mention the eighteenth-century Theatre Royal Covent Garden. Elementary arithmetic will show that 22-inch degrees, set in that room as I imagined them, leave a dancing or acting space 18 foot wide by 25 foot long, while allowing 6 foot of depth for the Queen's dais.

A critic acquainted with the conditions of Elizabethan court-performances would more reasonably have censured me for having allowed each person too much space, on the very plausible ground that many of the courtiers no doubt had to stand throughout the evening. At the court of Madrid in 1623 at performances in the *Salón de*

[1] *The First Night of 'Twelfth Night'* (1954), 86.
[2] *Loc. cit.*

Comedias (which were similarly amphitheatrical, 'in the round'), every one of the *grandes* was obliged to stand. And since only royalty had chairs, even the ladies permitted to sit had to sit on the floor: a floor cushioned only with a carpet.

As for the room required by each groundling in the yard of the public theatre, some modern estimates of the playhouses' capacity again appear far from realistic. Ignoring the unpleasing reports of 'being close pestered together' or 'pasted to the barmy jacket of a beer brewer' and of how the theatres 'smoakt euery after noone with stinkards . . . glewed together in crowdes', Professor Harbage considers that the groundling at the Fortune should have two and a quarter square feet, while at the Globe the even more liberal Dr Adams would allow him 3 square feet 'without undue crowding'. To the query, What under the sun could *prevent* undue crowding? the answer must be, Nothing but public lack of interest in the play. Who can imagine those doorkeepers turning away entrance-money so long as one more determined client could fight his way in? A dry comment on the fancy picture of an Elizabethan groundling granted three square feet of room to *stand* in is supplied by William Cobbett's testimony that in 1833 each Member of the House of Commons was obliged to *sit* in *half* that area: 'Why are 658 of us crammed into a space that allows to each of us no more than a foot and a half square?' [1]

Mme Deierkauf-Holsboer and her technical advisers present a refreshingly realistic contrast in their estimate of the standing-room capacity of the Théâtre du Marais. For its *parterre* containing $1519\frac{1}{2}$ square foot, they

---

[1] Qu. Maurice Hastings, *Parliament House* (1950), 115.

reckon a capacity of 1500: allowing each person a small fraction more than *one* square foot. Evidently they know the meaning of the term 'capacity', like the London managers of 1892, who packed their seated customers into 14 inches each.

At Cambridge under James I, the Vice-Chancellor and the authorities of Trinity College had also mastered the theatrical art of stowing the largest number of human beings into a limited space. The Hall of Trinity measures (inside) 40 foot wide by 90 foot long, or 100 foot including screen and entry (exactly the dimensions of Middle Temple Hall). In 1615 in this Hall at the amphitheatrical performance of Ruggle's *Ignoramus* were accommodated

(*a*) at the head, the King, the Prince, and their courtiers
(*b*) the transverse stage-and-tiring house, with its end-
scenes
(*c*) the Doctors, Regents, and Non-Regents
(*d*) strangers, upon the scaffolds
(*e*) others, standing on the floor.

Total spectators (including the many who stood for four mortal hours), more than 2000. Without bringing up the question of what constitutes 'undue crowding', we may ask, How many square feet each were the standers allotted?

To treat the Elizabethan theatre as a genteel architectural puzzle independent of sordid gate-receipts and noisome crowds is to deal in illusion from the start. But when we carry it to the point of fancying that occasionally part of the yard may have been 'cleared of groundlings' and used for acting, or that Mariana's barge in so highly popular a play as *Pericles* may have been 'brought in through the gate of the yard', it is really time to wake up. We may be jarred back to earth by J. M. Synge's record of a circus-performance at Dingle:

> The people . . . were seated all round on three or four rows of raised wooden seats, and many who were late were still crushing forward and standing in dense masses. . . . Here and there among the people I could see a little party of squireens and their daughters, . . . trying, not always successfully, to reach the shilling seats. The crowd was now so thick I could see little more than the heads of the performers, who had at last come into the ring, and many of the shorter women who were near me must have seen nothing the whole evening.[1]

An earlier poet, Edmund Spenser, had in London seen 'thronging theaters of people' similarly jammed, but often more dangerous in mood:

> All suddenly they heard a troublous noyes,
> That seemed some perilous tumult to desine,
> Confusd with womens cries, and shouts of boyes,
> Such as the troubled Theaters oftimes annoyes.[2]

And contemporaries corroborate Spenser:

> to the theatre to a play, where . . . I founde such concourse of unrulye people, that I thought it better solitary to walke in the fields, then to intermeddle myselfe amongst such a great presse.[3]

> And lette *Tarleton* intreate the yoong people of the Cittie, either to abstaine altogether from playes, or . . . to vse them-selues after a more quiet order . . . it is more than barbarously rude, to see the shamefull disorders and routes.[4]

---

[1] *In Wicklow, West Kerry and Connemara* (1919), 75–77.
[2] *F. Q.* (1590), 4.3.37.
[3] *Tarltons News out of Purgatory*, 1590.
[4] Chettle, *Kind-Harts Dreame*, 1592.

But this direct appeal went unheeded. Theatre-crowds continued to mean trouble. Twenty years later, Shakespeare notes little mitigation of gang-behaviour in his report of the formidable forty young club-swingers calling themselves 'the Hope o' the Strand':

These are the youths that thunder at a Playhouse, and fight for bitten Apples, that no Audience but the Tribulation of Tower Hill, or the Limbes of Limehouse, their deare Brothers, are able to endure.[1]

To subdue or throw out these lineal ancestors of the Teddy-boys there was no force of Metropolitan Police ready on call. The citizens, if they were to hear the play, had to do it themselves.

And in reconstructing a performance at Court we drift again into pure academic fantasy when we nonchalantly clear the lower end of the hall for the players' stage because of 'the obvious convenience for ingress and egress' of the main doors. Why pause to consider how 'obviously convenient' for the players those doors could be at Trinity, with more than 2000 people crushed into the Hall? Why trouble to recall that we have no evidence that those doors were ever so used? Or that in reality 'by reason of the tumultuous crowd at Court' at Christmas plays, detachments of giant Yeomen had to be posted there to defend them? Or that on Twelfth Night 1614/15 for *Mercury Vindicated* at the Banqueting House, we find platoons of the Guard set at the gates and doors, to hold back the force of the inrushing people?[2] Or that at a

---

[1] *Henry VIII*, 5.4.

[2] '*Postremus Saturnaliorum dies destinatus Spectaculo in Camerâ Convivali fuit*. Praetorianae Cohortes, ad fores Aditusque dispositae, ut Populi irruendis impetum cohiberet [*sic*].' Robert Johnston, *Historia Rerum Britannicarum* (1655), 501.

performance for Queen Elizabeth at Oxford the 'great presse of the multitude' up the steps to the door was enough to break down the stone guard-wall and to kill three men?

The Elizabethans and Jacobeans can do no more than tell us of crowding at Court so remorseless that 'some of the Ladies lie by it [*i.e.*, have taken to their beds]', and 'in the passages . . . were shutt up in several heapes betwixt dores and there stayed till all was ended'—and at the public playhouses of 'great multitudes . . . causing tumultes and outrages', and how 'the groundlings grow infinitely unruly'. If after such testimony from the eye-witnesses we can continue to suppose Whitehall a kind of overgrown doll's house with all its doors at our care-free disposal, and can go on fancying the Globe a sort of polite subsidized toy 'experimental theatre' in some university Drama Department, it is at all events not *their* fault.

When we find ourselves succumbing to academic hallucinations of audiences small, decorous, tractable, we may read what Mrs Sherard wrote to Sir Ralph Verney in 1657:

I hear by the by that Moll hath a great mind to see a play. If they be (as they have been this many years) tugged to pieces at them, I shall not like them.[1]

And should it be thought that surreptitious performances under the Commonwealth were hardly typical, we may skip nearly two centuries of progress and substitute Grill-parzer's attempt in 1836 to see Charles Kemble in *Julius Caesar*:

---

[1] Frances, Lady Verney, *Memoirs of the Verney Family* (1892), 3. 319. Spelling modernized.

Dr. B. insisted on going to the pit, but there was already a vast crowd of people all struggling like wild beasts as usual in England. As I more than once nearly had my ribs broken, I left my companion and took a seat in a box. . . . I should have liked to have seen the whole play, but as the half-prices are admitted at half-past eight, the theatre was literally stormed. Doors of boxes torn off. . . . They clambered out to the benches behind the backs of the people on the seats, . . . and there was some fighting. So in Act IV I said farewell to Shakespeare, tore my way through the crowd, and got to my lodgings feeling like a hunted stag.[1]

---

[1] From *Selbstbiographie*, tr. Francesca M. Wilson, in *Strange Island* (1955), 180–181.

APPENDIX B

SHAKESPEARE'S CURTAIN THEATRE IDENTIFIED

MANY people are familiar with the often-reproduced copy of Johannes de Witt's sketch of the interior of the Swan Playhouse. It is the modern world's only pictorial eye-witness evidence of the physical arrangements of the Elizabethan public stage. Antedating the first Globe by several years, the Swan was built about 1595 in Paris Garden, Bankside, by Francis Langley, a goldsmith and son of a former Lord Mayor of London. Direct Shakespearean interest was lent to this playhouse by my discovery (*Shakespeare versus Shallow*, 1931) of the poet's association in Surrey with Langley in 1597, indicating that it was his company of 'able players' which, 'lately afore' February 1597, were acting in Langley's recently-built, large, and sumptuous Swan.

That priceless drawing of the Swan Playhouse interior, together with de Witt's Latin description, was first made known in 1888 by K. T. Gaedertz from MS. Var. 355 in the library of the University of Utrecht. And, as though to show that Utrecht's treasures are inexhaustible, it is in an engraving found with another manuscript preserved in this same library (MS. 1198 Hist. 147) that we now discover our only known view of the *exterior* of one of the two first playhouses built in England. To the generosity of the library's director, Dr D. Grosheide, I owe the kind permission to reproduce part of it from a photograph

304

obtained some years ago at Utrecht by Mr Arthur M. Hind for the Print Room of the British Museum.[1]

This engraving (104 by 10·2 cm.), believed to be unique, bearing the legend *The View of the Cittye of London from the North towards the Sowth*, is found inserted in 'Englandts descriptie', the illustrated manuscript journal of Abram Booth, an agent of the Dutch East India Company, living in London from 1629 to 1636 (see A. Merens, *Een Dienaer der Oost-Indischen Compagnie te London in 1629*, 's-Gravenhage, 1942, with a reduced reproduction of *The View*). Presumably Mynheer Booth purchased his copy of the engraving in London. Though the print affords neither date nor name of artist or engraver, the original drawing must have been made about the year 1600, and certainly after 1598. It presents a skilfully executed panoramic view of London from an elevated point some distance north of the city.

We recognize such a view point as not only rare, since nearly all the known early views of London are taken from Southwark looking north, but also of immediate interest for Shakespeare. For it is common knowledge that his first playhouses were the two situated in the fields just north of the city, convenient to his dwelling in Bishopsgate, the earliest public playhouses built in England. First came the Theatre, erected by James Burbage in 1576. It was closely followed in 1577 by the neighbouring Curtain, under the control of Henry Lanman. The name 'Curtain'— no connection with a theatrical curtain—is from *curtina*, a walled piece of ground, a close: that is,

---

[1] About two-thirds of it were reproduced as an illustration to my article 'This Wooden O: Shakespeare's Curtain Theatre Identified' in *The Times* of 26 March 1954.

the former Curtain Close of Holywell Priory, upon which the playhouse was constructed.

As John Stow noted,

neare [Holywell, Shoreditch] are builded two publique houses for the acting and shewe of Comedies, Tragedies, and Histories, for recreation. Whereof the one is called the Courtein, the other the Theatre: both standing on the Southwest towards the field.

Their instant and tremendous popular following, especially at their Sunday performances, brought strong reprehension from the pulpits down upon these two 'sumptuous Theatre houses', these 'gorgeous playing places'. Preaching at Paul's Cross in the summer of 1578, John Stockwood declared, 'if you resorte to the Theatre, the Curtayne . . . you shall on the Lords day haue these places . . . so full, as possible [*sic*] they can throng'. Five years later Philip Stubbes styled them 'Venus pallaces', exclaiming, 'marke the flocking and running to Theaters & curtens, daylie and hourely, night and daye, tyme and tyde, to see Playes and Enterludes!'

The Burbage company, which Shakespeare joined, used both playhouses after 1585. But, at the end of 1598, after disputes with their ground landlord which involved closing the Theatre for more than a year, during which they played at the Curtain, the Burbages tore down the twenty-two-year-old Theatre, carted the timbers south to the Bankside, and employed them in constructing the first Globe, which must have been opened in the autumn of 1599. No view of the Theatre is known to exist.

After the beginning of 1599, then, only one of these first two still stood north of the city: the Curtain, described by the Privy Council in 1601 as 'the Curtaine in

Moorefeilds'. And I have found evidence that it stood there for the astonishing period of at least eighty-three years: a life far longer than that of any other Elizabethan theatre-building. In an unsavoury catalogue of 'Common Whores, Wanderers, Pick-pockets and Night-walkers', published in 1660, we read 'Mrs Mails by the Curtain Playhouse' (see my *Commonwealth and Restoration Stage*, page 92).

As well as knowledge of its location—in Shoreditch near the present-day Curtain Road, and south of Holy-well Row and Holywell Lane—we already had some clear contemporary evidence of this famous theatre's physical shape and appearance. A German merchant from Ulm, Samuel Kiechel, described the Theatre and the Curtain in 1585, before any others had been built, as 'peculiar houses'—*sonderbare heüser*—with 'three galleries above one another'—*drey genng ob ein ander*. About 1596 de Witt tacitly includes the Curtain in the four London *amphiteatra* or circus-theatres he saw. And the epilogue of the Day–Wilkins–Rowley *Travels of Three English Brothers* (1607) 'played at the Curtain' speaks of it as 'this round circumference'. Thus it must have been very similar in general appearance to the Swan of 1595 and to the Second Globe, built in 1613–1614, thirty-six years after the Curtain. And we should also expect to find, as we do in the case of the Swan, the First Globe, the Fortune, the Second Globe, and the Hope, that the Curtain was flanked by two enclosed staircases for access to its encircling galleries, built outside against its walls.

If, therefore, about the beginning of the seventeenth century, a draughtsman takes up a position north of the City facing south, pivots his eye like the lens of a pano-

ramic camera, and at his extreme left—in the open, on the
near side of the 'ribbon building' which extended north
to Shoreditch—sees and delineates an eminent peculiar
circular or octagonal edifice three stories high, with two
full-height structures against its walls, he is sketching the
Curtain in Moorfields. And this is in fact what we find in
this engraved *View of the Cittye of London from the North
towards the Sowth*—giving us our first and only sight of
the exterior of an early Elizabethan playhouse. Its round
or octagonal shape, its three stories, its two flanking
tower-like enclosed staircases to the galleries, all are
clearly shown.

But there is more. Emerging out of the ring of its roof
is the 'hut' over the stage, familiar to us from the drawings of the Swan and of the Second Globe. And sur-
mounting the hut's gabled roof stands the lofty flagpole
flying its flag—that welcome signal to the Londoners of
a playing-day. 'The maps regularly show flags on the
theatres', wrote the late Sir Edmund Chambers, quoting
lively contemporary references to them:

> Those flagges of defiance against God . . . as good as a flag
> upo'th'pole, at a common playhouse, to waft company. . . .
> Each playhouse advanceth his flag in the aire, whither quickly
> at the waving thereof are summoned whole troops of men,
> women, and children.

In spite of its rather small scale the engraving thus represents all the essential outward features of the Curtain
Playhouse, the theatre which in Chambers's opinion,
Shakespeare's company, the Lord Chamberlain's men,
used exclusively for nearly two years—from October
1597, until the beginning of September 1599, when the
Globe on the Bankside was ready: the theatre which

THE CURTAIN THEATRE

Identified in the only known copy of *The View of the Cittye of London from the North towards the South, ca.* 1600.

stood, though long disused, into the Restoration as the oldest surviving playhouse, built when Marlowe and Shakespeare were boys.

It was here at the Curtain that Robert Armin, Shakespeare's gifted comedian, for whom the poet later invented the brilliant rôles of Touchstone, Feste, and Lear's Fool, joined the company—advertising himself in his printed works as *Clonnico de Curtanio Snuffe*—Snuff, the Clown of the Curtain. And here the company performed Shakespearean tragedy and history. As we learn from Marston, *Romeo and Juliet* enjoyed great success here in 1598, winning 'Curtaine plaudeties'.

It was moreover 'on this unworthy scaffold' that Shakespeare first dared 'to bring forth So great an object' as *The Chronicle History of Henry the Fifth . . . Together with Ancient Pistol*. For his topical lines,

> Were now the general of our gracious Empress
> (As in good time he may) from Ireland coming,
> Bringing rebellion broachëd on his sword . . .

cannot have been delivered so late as the autumn of 1599, when the Globe first opened its doors. By that time Essex's Irish campaign had proved a manifest fiasco, and he deserted his post in September. It was therefore not the Globe, but the Curtain Theatre's 'round circumference' which first echoed to the thwacks of Fluellen's cudgel on Pistol's pate, and which Shakespeare employed in his stirring evocation of England's heroic theatre of war:

> Can this cockpit hold
> The vasty fields of France? Or may we cram
> Within this wooden O the very casques
> That did affright the air at Agincourt?

APPENDIX C

ALLEYN'S FORTUNE IN THE MAKING

So absorbing was this identification of Shakespeare's Holywell playhouse that until after I had published the foregoing report I neglected further study of this *View of the Cittye of London*. But already my eye had been caught by a remarkable large *square* building shown at the northern edge of the built-up area by Finsbury Fields, indeed the *only* square building anywhere in the drawing. Now Alleyn's famous Fortune Theatre, which was square, was erected in the first half of 1600, about the date of this unique *View*. I began to suspect that this square building seen by the artist was the Fortune, of which no drawing is known.

To find out first whether this construction was located in the picture where we know the Fortune stood—between Whitecross Street and Golden Lane, on the fringe of building outside the City limits north of Cripplegate—the preliminary step was to determine the artist's standpoint. This was done by taking a ruler to a plan of sixteenth-century London and drawing sight-lines on it, employing readily-recognized landmarks such as St Paul's, the Charterhouse, the steeples of Bow Church, of St Lawrence Pountney, and of St Dunstan-in-the-East, and the Tower of London, corresponding to the relative positions shown and the angles from which they are seen in the *View*.

I used the convenient plan in Kingsford's Stow, but found that the converging lines went off the north edge

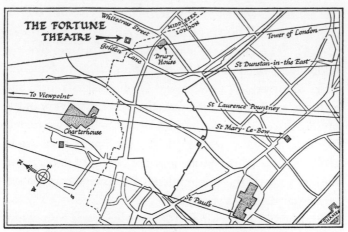

PLAN OF SIGHT-LINES IDENTIFYING THE
FORTUNE IN *THE VIEW OF THE
CITTYE OF LONDON*

of the plan before coming together. Transferred to John Rocque's 'London in 1741–5', their converging-point proved to be beyond Sadlers Wells, Islington, some yards west of the junction of St John's Street with the City Road (the crossroads familiar today as the 'Angel'), at a height significantly labelled 'Johnsons Prospect'.

On laying the ruler from this point to the Tower of London, one finds the site of the Fortune Theatre—'Playhouse Yard' between Whitecross Street and Golden Lane—appearing slightly to the east of its edge: precisely where the square building is seen in the *View*. Anyone repeating the experiment will be left in no doubt that the building represents the Fortune.

On inspection, three points make it equally clear that the theatre is shown unfinished, in the process of construction. First, the contract specifies three stories for the fabric, and two only are shown. Second, the main enclosing frame was to be covered with a tiled roof, and no roof is visible. Third, as Chambers remarked (*Eliz. Stage*, 2. 538), 'The contracts show that the Fortune, like the Globe, and the Hope, like the Swan, were to have external staircases.' (The Second Globe makes a fifth; and to these, as I have pointed out above, the discovery of the present *View* adds a sixth, the Curtain, whose two turret-like external staircases are plainly shown, as they are in Hollar's view of the Hope and the Second Globe.) But the drawing of the uncompleted Fortune shows no external staircases as yet erected.

Finished, the Fortune's three stories were to measure 12, 11, and 9 foot respectively, making a height of at least 32 foot, and with the addition of the foundation and the pitched roof of tiles probably more. Its width however was to be 80 foot, and completed it would thus be at least twice as wide as it was high. The present drawing obviously exaggerates the Fortune's height in proportion to its width, just as it does that of the Curtain, in the familiar manner of Visscher, Delaram, and Merian representing the Bankside playhouses (see J. Q. Adams, *Shakespearean Playhouses* (1917), 246, 248, 253, 256). Hollar's Long View is a notable exception to this practice.

At first sight I supposed the nearest gabled-and-chimneyed building behind (which might be taken to be *inside* the Fortune's frame) to represent the 'hut' over the stage. But the presence of a chimney, and the apparent position (if this *were* the 'hut'), which would place the stage with its boxes and lords' room at the northeast or worst side of the house, make this impossible—aside from the total unlikelihood that its 'hut' would be finished and tiled while the main frame was but two-thirds erected.

THE FORTUNE THEATRE

Identified in the same *View of the Cittye of London*.

The most remarkable feature of this unique drawing of the Fortune is the number and size of the windows—much larger than those shown either in the Curtain, the Hope, or the Second Globe.

Since the Fortune was contracted for on 8 January 1600 and finished in the late summer of 1600, the drawing must have been made in the first half of the year. With its representation of Shakespeare's Curtain and of Alleyn's Fortune—since the crude representation of the Bankside Rose in Norden's *Speculum Britanniæ* (1593) is little more than a cartographic symbol—it affords the only known Elizabethan external views of contemporary public playhouses.

INDEXES

1

INDEX OF PLAYS

INDEX OF PERSONS

INDEX OF SUBJECTS

'Theatre' meaning 'stage', 86–87, 93, 105

Théâtre du Marais, Paris, 294, 298–299

Theatre playhouse, Shoreditch, 125, 179, 265, 286, 305 *f*.

Theatre Royal, Lincoln, 286

Theatre Royal, London, *see* Gibbons's Tennis Court; Drury Lane; Covent Garden

Theatres, *see* Playhouses

Theobald's, 134

Théophiliens, French student-company, 103

'Threshold-scenes', hypothetical, 145

Throne, central, 226, 227, 232–234, 242, 245; lowered for *deus ex machina*, 30

'Throne'-side, inner long side of stage, 35, 37, 221, 229*n*., 232–233, 241, 244; *see* 'Front', 'Ground-front'

Tiring-house, dressing-room; under stage in pageants, 62–63, 68–69; in *carros*, 71–73, 76; and in playhouses, 83–89, 91–95, 153, 196; in *corrales*, 90, 113; in academic stages, 161, 163; windows to, 91–92; *and see* Cellar, Cellarage, *Vestuario*

Tormentor, a masking stage-drapery, 32, 256–257

Tormentors, red devils of stage Hell, 32, 49, 256

Transverse axis of stage, 31, 46, 76, 96, 98, 104–105, 116, 118, 124, 152, 154, 193, 196, 245, 281–282; *and see* Tennis court

Traps, stage-entrances, 'cuts', 'risings', 'descents': in pageants, 59; in public stages near corners, 33–34, 94, 153, 254*n*.; open on stage, 44, 93–95, 133,

209–211; enclosed in 'houses', 93, 95, 145–150; *see* Grave, Scuttle

Trinity College, Cambridge, hall of, 168–169, 189, 219*n*., 299, 301

'Triumphs', pageant - wagons, 67–69

Trumpets in playhouse, 35, 36–37, 38, 48, 252

Umhang, 102, 138, 141

'Understanders', *see* Groundlings

Universities, *see* Staging, academic

'Upper stage', imagined in 'scenic wall', 29, 57, 96, 100–102, 204, 225, 249–250; *see* 'Above'

Velaria, velarium, 138

Vels, 142*n*.

Vere Street, Theatre Royal, *see* Gibbons's Tennis Court

Vestuario, 72, 90, 113

Vitruvius on stage, 127

Vizards, black masks, 26–27

Vorhang, 102, 138, 141

Wagner Book (1594), 95*n*., 96, 135, 226*n*., 233, 239

Wagons, *see* Pageants

Walls, city-walls, 34, 69, 96, 97, 197–199, 203, 214–215; *see* Heaven

Wardrobe, upper, in public playhouse, 25

Watermen, 21–22

Westminster School plays, 'houses' for, 220–221

White Hall, Court of Requests, Westminster, 161, 258–259

Whitefriars playhouse, 179, 194, 195*n*.